A
NATURAL
HISTORY *of*
REVOLUTION

A
NATURAL
HISTORY *of*
REVOLUTION

*Violence and Nature in
the French Revolutionary
Imagination, 1789–1794*

Mary Ashburn Miller

Cornell University Press

ITHACA AND LONDON

First published 2011 by Cornell University Press

Printed in the United States of America

Library of Congress Cataloging-in-Publication Data

Miller, Mary Ashburn, 1979–
    A natural history of revolution : violence and nature in the French revolutionary imagination, 1789–1794 / Mary Ashburn Miller.
        p. cm.
    Includes bibliographical references and index.
    ISBN 978-0-8014-4942-0 (cloth : alk. paper)
    1. France—History—Revolution, 1789–1799.   2. Violence—Political aspects—France—History—18th century.   3. Natural disasters—Political aspects—France—History—18th century.
4. Rhetoric—Political aspects—France—History—18th century.   I. Title.
    DC158.8.M55 2011
    944.04'1—dc22   2010052643

Cornell University Press strives to use environmentally responsible suppliers and materials to the fullest extent possible in the publishing of its books. Such materials include vegetable-based, low-VOC inks and acid-free papers that are recycled, totally chlorine-free, or partly composed of nonwood fibers. For further information, visit our website at www.cornellpress.cornell.edu.

Cloth printing   10 9 8 7 6 5 4 3 2 1

For Scott

To nature then
Power had reverted: habit, custom, law,
Had left an interregnum's open space
For her to stir about in uncontrolled.
—WILLIAM WORDSWORTH, *The Prelude,*
    X.609–612 (1805)

CONTENTS

ILLUSTRATIONS

ACKNOWLEDGMENTS

This book was motivated by big questions: questions about how people respond to crisis, how language shapes action (or inaction), how the inexplicable gets explained. It was made possible by a number of institutions and individuals who supported my search for answers and who provided good company and good counsel along the way. Foremost among these is David Bell, my adviser at Johns Hopkins, who first encouraged me to ask difficult questions and to be meticulous in answering them. He has been an unflagging source of support: generous with his time, exacting in his expectations, and dedicated to his students long after they leave their dissertation defenses. He has been this book's most careful reader, and I hope that his influence is manifest within these pages.

It has been a true pleasure to write this book in environments that have been both collegial and challenging. While at Johns Hopkins I benefited from working closely with John Marshall, whose rigorous mentorship has made me a much better scholar. I am also grateful to Peter Jelavich, Richard Kagan, Mary Fissell, and Wilda Anderson. Their questions and comments first sparked this project's transformation into a book. At Hopkins I had the rare privilege to be among an extraordinary cohort of young historians of France, many of whom have become friends as well as colleagues; Eddie Kolla, Claire Cage, and Will Brown all provided insightful commentary and much-needed suggestions as the book neared completion.

Reed College, and Portland, have been my home as this project has grown into a book. Reed has not only provided generous research support through the Stillman Drake and Summer Research Funds, but also a community of friends who have been constant sources of support and levity, and of colleagues who have made me a better researcher as well as teacher. I owe particular thanks to Michael Breen, who read the manuscript in its entirety, and Sean McEnroe, who provided outstanding feedback and moral support throughout the process of revisions. I am grateful to my students, who constantly challenge me to expand the way I think about my research; the students in my "Crisis and Catastrophe in Europe" course deserve special mention, since they read, discussed, and offered suggestions on chapter 2.

The Fulbright Commission made possible a year of research in Paris, and I remain grateful to both Amy Tondu and Arnaud Roujou de Boubée for their confidence in this project when still in its earliest stages. While in Paris, I benefited from meeting Jean-Clément Martin, whose comments on my work have been particularly incisive and helpful. My work was facilitated by the staff at the Archives Nationales and the Bibliothèque Nationale de France, and particularly at the Département des Estampes. The Harry Frank Guggenheim Foundation has provided generous support for this research and its inquiry into the language of violence. A New Faculty Fellowship from the American Council of Learned Societies, supported by the Andrew W. Mellon Foundation, afforded me the time and resources to complete my revisions.

This work has benefited from being presented at conferences, including the Western Society for French History, the Society for French Historical Studies, and the Society for the Study of French History. The Project for American and French Research on the Treasury of the French Language (ARTFL) has been a wonderful resource; Mark Olsen has generously granted permission to include the images from the ARTFL *Encyclopédie* in these pages. An earlier version of chapter 5 and parts of the introduction appeared in *French Historical Studies* 32.4 (fall 2009), and I thank Duke University Press for permission to reprint it here.

I am grateful to the staff of Cornell University Press, and particularly to John Ackerman, for supporting this project and making the path to my first book far smoother than I ever thought possible. Dan Edelstein and Howard Brown, who started as anonymous reviewers, chose to identify themselves and have offered additional guidance since their initial reports. I am immensely grateful to both for their careful reading, their criticisms, and their generosity in offering their assistance to a young scholar.

At conferences, in classes, and in e-mail exchanges, conversations with scholars in French literature, art history, the history of science, and history have influenced my methodology as well as my conclusions; my thanks to Carolina Armenteros, Jeremy Caradonna, Pietro Corsi, Michael Fried, Jeff Horn, Eric Johnson, Antoine Lilti, Marisa Linton, Tom Luckett, Maximilian

Owre, Larry Principe, Elena Russo, Sophia Rosenfeld, Ronen Steinberg, Kenneth Taylor, Dror Wahrman, and Charles Walton. My first introduction to interdisciplinary approaches was as an undergraduate Political and Social Thought major at the University of Virginia, and I remain grateful to Michael Smith for his mentorship of that program. I owe special thanks to Michelle Miller, with whom I shared many a thought-provoking lunch at the BNF and who has always been willing to help with some of the nuances of French translation, and Kate Murphy, who has been both a dear friend and a mentor since my first days at Johns Hopkins.

My biggest debt of gratitude is no doubt to my family: to my sisters, Sarah and Emily; my mother, Barbara; my father, Timothy; and particularly to my husband, Scott, who makes every challenge easier and every day joyful. At its heart, this book is about the power of language to limit or to encourage action. The voices of my family have always been voices of support and affirmation. And to thank them for that—there are not enough words.

INTRODUCTION

A t daybreak on 10 August 1793, the people of Paris gathered at the ruins of the Bastille to take part in the Festival of Unity and Indivisibility. According to the festival organizer, Jacques-Louis David, the day and the festival were to begin together, so as to make clear the association between "France's regeneration" and "the rising of the day's star, which makes us tremble with the joy of nature."[1] At the Place de la Bastille, the crowd stood before a statue of Nature whose bosom gushed forth flowing waters; an inscription at its base reminded the assembled Parisians that they were all Nature's children.[2] The president of the National Convention, the legislative body of the French Republic, filled a cup with her waters and drank; several citizens of Paris then followed his example, each one raising the cup to his lips with a panegyric to the renewal it offered and the joy it brought. The official account of the festival approved by the National Convention recorded that an elderly man proclaimed to the crowd, "I am on the brink of my tomb, but in pressing this cup to my lips, I believe in being reborn with the human race that is being regenerated."[3]

From this dramatic beginning, the crowd processed through a series of monuments that had been erected throughout the city to commemorate the most significant events of the French Revolution. The national pilgrimage immortalized, first, the storming of the Bastille; the October Days of 1789, when a crowd marched to Versailles demanding bread and prompted the royal family's relocation to the Tuileries in central Paris; the fall of the monarchy on 10 August 1792; and, finally, the suppression of the federalist revolts in the early summer of 1793, when several cities throughout France had risen up against the Jacobins. To signify that the journey was still ongoing, and that additional monuments were yet to be built, the festival's procession ended at the Champ de Mars, where the citizens of Paris swore a patriotic oath to uphold the Constitution of 1793 before an altar of the Fatherland.[4]

In its recitation of the canonical events of the Revolution, the festival is familiar enough. Yet in its representation and interpretation of those events, the festival employed an unusual lexicon, namely, images and metaphors drawn from the natural world. The start of the procession, the statue at the Place de la Bastille, was not a memorial to the patriots who had died on 14 July 1789, but rather, an Egyptian-inspired icon of Nature.[5] The triumphal arch constructed on the Boulevard Poissonnière to honor the October Days bore an inscription lauding the people, who were described as a "torrent."[6] At les Invalides, a Herculean representation of the French people stood on the summit of a mountain and drowned a hydra, a symbol of federalist rebels, in a swamp.[7] The festival treated the Revolution as the work of nature, facilitated by "torrents"; the people, standing on their "sacred mountain," had become nature's agents, unstoppable forces of renewal. In Mona Ozouf's reading of the festival, it "celebrated a triumph, [and] had nothing to say about dangers.... [It] was silent on violence."[8] Yet each of the stations commemorated events that either were violent or carried undertones of violence. Far from silencing the violence of its most significant moments, the festival instead naturalized the events as mere steps in the "regeneration" sprung from Nature herself. David and his backers on the Committee of Public Safety were presenting the history of their Revolution to the Parisian public as a story of natural history.

As the events of the Revolution unfolded, those who witnessed, led, and participated in them were compelled to find ways of making sense of the rapid and often overwhelming transformations taking place around them. In their attempts to put into words events that defied description or imagination, revolutionary leaders, playwrights, journalists, and festival organizers like David often consulted the book of nature.[9] Floods, lightning bolts, volcanic eruptions, and earthquakes all found their way into festivals, plays, and political speeches as descriptors of revolutionary activity. The revolutionary calendar famously sought to align the temporal lives of republican citizens with the cycles of nature.[10] Even political factions bore the marks of the natural world: by 1792 the political Left in the national legislature was known as the Mountain; its moderate counterpart, the Swamp. Yet, as the Festival of Unity and Indivisibility suggests, moments of violence were often both integrated and concealed through allusions to the natural world. Joseph Fouché, a member of the National Convention sent to the rebellious city of Toulon in 1793, wrote to the

Committee of Public Safety proposing that they "exercise justice as per nature's example" as he called for the total destruction of the city: "Let us strike like lightning," he wrote, "so that even the ashes of our enemies disappear from the soil of liberty."[11]

The language used by revolutionaries and the metaphors with which they conceptualized the work they were undertaking helped to structure citizens' understandings of the Revolution. Keith Baker's seminal work has brought the importance of these imaginings to the fore. In defining political culture as a "set of discourses or symbolic practices," Baker proceeded from the view that political power is embedded in language.[12] Therefore a comprehensive understanding of the Revolution requires historians "to identify a field of political discourse, a set of linguistic patterns and relationships that defined possible actions and utterances and gave them meaning."[13] Understanding the language with which revolutionaries made claims—claims to authority, sovereignty, or responsibility—is essential to understanding the unfolding of the Revolution. For Baker, this is perhaps clearest in the notion of the term "revolution" itself. In the early days of the Revolution, earlier meanings of the multivalent term were merged and manipulated to create a vision of revolution that was experienced, willed, disruptive, progressive, and universally important. In Baker's words, "Revolution as historical fact was irrevocably translated...into revolution as political act, [a] decisive expression of the will of a nation reclaiming its history."[14] In transforming the meaning of the term "revolution," French men and women also transformed the possibilities created by it. A revolution was not something that was merely experienced; instead, it could be controlled, directed, and enacted.

Thus language was shaped by its historical moment—individuals drew on a variety of meanings of "revolution" crafted over the course of the eighteenth century—but, more important, it could shape political action. Well aware of its potential, revolutionary actors self-consciously engineered political language as well as symbolic representation; they were deeply attuned to the importance of symbols as marks of changing authority.[15] In this context the ubiquity of language drawn from the natural world in revolutionary speech, including public discourses, plays, and festivals, demands further analysis. Why did revolutionaries turn to the natural world as they sought their explanations and descriptions of revolutionary activity? And, above all, how did the frequent invocation of the natural world shape the political dynamic of the Revolution?

This book is an inquiry into the natural history of the Revolution crafted by revolutionaries, and into the ways in which they integrated the narrative of Revolution with the narrative of the natural world. Like Baker's work, this book seeks to situate revolutionary language in its political and cultural context to determine the meanings attached to it and the potentialities created by it. Yet even as this research is indebted to Baker in its methodology, it ultimately challenges his conclusions: in its analysis of the figurative as well as the literal meanings of revolutionary language, it reveals a notion of governance, sovereignty, and revolution that was surprisingly divorced from human will or individual agency. As the Festival of Unity and Indivisibility suggests, by 1793 the Revolution was often presented to the public not as the embodiment of the general will, but as nature's handiwork. Placing revolutionary public language in the context of contemporary scientific and popular conceptions of nature uncovers a clearer view not only of revolutionaries' ideas of the revolution itself, but also of their explanations of its violence; what is more, it offers a new way to understand the radicalization of 1793 and 1794. The idea that violence and disruption were sometimes necessary and constructive forces in the natural world was translated into an exoneration of political violence. By making violence a necessary and natural part of the Revolution, rhetorical conflations between natural and political processes provided an absolution, and a providential purpose, for revolutionary activity, and allowed for a justification, and sometimes a sacralization, of bloodshed.

On Natural History

The French Revolution took place in an era in which scientific knowledge had become newly accessible, and relatively popular, among the literate classes.[16] As the article on "natural history" in the *Encyclopédie* maintained, "In the present century, the science of natural history is more cultivated than ever before; not only do the majority of 'men of letters' make it an object of either study or amusement, but there is an ever-growing taste for this science spreading throughout the public."[17] Yet precisely what that "science" was, was very much in flux. As Emma Spary has demonstrated, the boundaries of "natural history" were both vast and permeable; naturalists "might include within the discipline the practices of classifying, collecting, writing, experimenting, cultivating, and preserving."[18] The field embraced what would now be understood as earth science and meteorology, as well as botany, zoology, and anthropology.[19] Attempts to explore, narrate, and interpret the natural world in its infinite manifestations became a leisure activity for elites and the foundation for a more widespread interest in the second half of the eighteenth century.[20]

Recent scholarship has demonstrated the important role that knowledge of the natural world had in the process known as "enlightenment."[21] The gathering of natural specimens became a kind of social networking, as did the collecting of natural history prints; crowds marveled at balloonists ascending above the city, and men and women of society frequented scientific lectures at the Jardin du Roi, the Musée du Monsieur, or the Palais Royale.[22] In 1785 the *Nouvelles de la république des lettres* reported on a "public occupied successively with physics, natural history, and chemistry," that "swarms into courses where they [the sciences] are taught,... rushes to read books about them, and... welcomes avidly everything that brings them to mind."[23] By the 1770s and 1780s at least thirty French-language journals were devoted to scientific questions; the leading newspapers of the day included summaries of recent scientific texts; and the century's best sellers included the comte de Buffon's *Histoire Naturelle*, the Abbé Pluche's *Spectacle de la Nature*, and Baron d'Holbach's *Système de la Nature*.[24] The naturalist and sentimental novelist Jacques-Henri Bernardin de Saint-Pierre, whose *Études de la Nature* went through four lavish editions between 1784 and 1791, received gushing letters from readers who praised the "excellent work" that brought them to tears over the beauty and harmony of nature.[25] These texts, though different in their methods and goals, richly convey not only the wonders of the natural world but also the reading public's fascination with studies of nature.

Academies and institutions cultivated this widespread intellectual interest. The 1770s and 1780s saw the growth of a host of newly prestigious scientific institutions. The Société Royale de médecine was created in 1775 and dubbed a formal academy in 1778; Paris's Société d'agriculture was reorganized in 1785.[26] Formal essay contests sponsored by local academies throughout France emphasized questions about the natural world, with the Académie Royale des Sciences asking participants to ruminate on such subjects as mineralogy, sea salts, cotton cultivation, sea walls, comets, and saltpeter production in the 1780s.[27] The Jardin du Roi transformed under the eye of Buffon and his successor, André Thouin, from a royal pleasure garden to a site of study that gathered together specimens and plants from around the world; professors taught courses on physics, chemistry, and natural history.[28] Public lectures on natural history were given to the Parisian public by some of the leading lights of the era, including Antoine François de Fourcroy, Pilâtre de Rozier, and Gaspard Monge.[29]

In addition to attending public lectures, reading natural histories or their reviews in newspapers, and cultivating personal collections, Parisian members of the "Republic of Science" were quite literally mesmerized by science and pseudoscience in the 1780s.[30] The Austrian Franz Mesmer arrived in Paris in 1778, positing that all of Nature was linked by a universal fluid, and promising a restoration of a natural equilibrium through his practices. Robert Darnton has suggested that mesmerism was one of the most popular and widely discussed topics of the 1780s; between 1783 and 1784 no topic was covered more thoroughly in the *Mémoires secrets* and the *Journal de Paris*.[31] Wide swathes of society attended his scientific spectacles; the interest in Mesmer transcended social class, and in fact reflected his worldview that linked natural harmony—that is, the physical balance of the "universal fluid"—with social and moral harmony. The social and the physical were inherently linked. In the words of Nicolas Bergasse, perhaps the foremost popularizer of Mesmer's ideas, "Any change, any alteration in our physical constitution thus produces infallibly a change, an alteration in our moral constitution. Therefore, it suffices to purify or corrupt the physical order of things in a nation in order to produce a revolution in its morals."[32]

As mesmerism suggests, the natural world could be seen not merely as a space separate from society, but rather as a source of information and possibly amelioration for civil society. The notion that the physical and moral, social, or political realms were connected was not only widespread; it also justified and glamorized studies of nature. If the physical and moral worlds operated according to the same laws, then understanding the natural world was ultimately a necessary step toward improving the lives of man. Man was, for naturalists in the second part of the eighteenth century, a part of nature rather than a creation separate from, or even necessarily in dominion over, the natural world. Buffon, like Linnaeus before him, grouped man among the animals—albeit as the "masterpiece" of the species.[33] D'Holbach argued, in the *Système de la Nature,* that "man is the work of nature, he exists in nature, he is subject to his laws and cannot escape them."[34] Rather than seeing nature either as a tool used by God to benefit or punish man, or as a reminder of man's fallen state, these naturalists saw man as being interconnected with the natural world and constrained by its laws. This restructured cosmology distinguished these studies of nature from many of their earlier counterparts; as Anne-Robert-Jacques Turgot—who would later embrace physiocratic thought and apply natural law to France's economic structures—wrote in 1750, describing previous generations: "When they were contemplating nature, it was as if they fixed their gaze on the surface of a deep sea instead of on the sea bed hidden by the waters, and saw there only their own reflection."[35] Once man was liberated from the blinders imposed by this reflection, and saw himself as a part of the natural world rather than as the purpose of all nature's operations, only then could he begin to apply those laws to the progress of mankind.

To treat natural history as a sphere separate from philosophy, theology, history, or even politics is something of an anachronism. To the eighteenth-century scholar, these pursuits were entwined; their language, goals, and even methodologies overlapped. As Rhoda Rappaport has made clear, eighteenth-century geologists—itself an anachronistic term, given the absence of professionalization—often imagined themselves as historians, studying the "monuments" and "archives" of the past.[36] Similarly, Pluche, Bernardin de Saint-Pierre, and Buffon alike integrated popular literary styles into their natural histories: Pluche adopted the form of dialogues, and Buffon prided himself on his literary stylings. Meanwhile, parts of Rousseau's *La Nouvelle Héloise* and *Emile* doubled as studies of nature, and Diderot dabbled in explicating nature in his *Interprétation de la Nature*, as did Delisle de Sales, who was otherwise known for his histories and theories of aesthetics but whose *Philosophie de la Nature* went through three editions between 1771 and 1777 despite scathing critical reviews.[37] Although these texts cannot appropriately be categorized as natural histories, they demonstrate both the significance of the natural world in Enlightenment thought and the fluidity of boundaries between disciplines. Just as Rousseau's *Social Contract* was deeply informed by his idea of the state of nature, so, too, could studies of nature reveal truths not only about the physical world of minerals, animals, and plants but also about the social world of human interactions and religious notions of divine intervention and human agency. Thus nature became a space of authority, and a basis for understanding human relationships as well as natural ones. In the words of Lorraine Daston, "What was genuinely new about the Enlightenment cult of nature was...that it elevated nature to supreme authority."[38] It was the source of truths and of laws that could be applied to moral and political spheres as well.

The men of France who would go on to be the public voice of the Revolution—its leaders, journalists, and chroniclers—were far from immune to this scientific fervor of the late eighteenth century. Jean-Paul Marat had been a *physicien* and had published several texts on electricity and fire. Committee of Public Safety members Lazare Carnot and Claude-Antoine Prieur-Duvernois (known as Prieur de la Côte d'Or) were trained engineers. The Marquis de Condorcet was both a *philosophe* and a mathematician, and Jean-Sylvain Bailly, the mayor of Paris from 1789 to 1791, was an astronomer. Hérault de Sechelles, later to serve on the Committee of Public Safety, idolized Buffon, visiting him at his home in Montbard; Condorcet wrote an elegy to the immortal naturalist.[39] Bertrand Barère, Maximilien Robespierre, and Dominique-Joseph Garat all took part in essay contests sponsored by the ubiquitous academies devoted to the arts and sciences throughout France, and the Girondins Etienne Clavière, Jean-Louis Carra, Antoine-Louis Gorsas, and Jacques-Pierre Brissot were involved in mesmerist circles.[40]

Despite decades of research into the scientific discourse of the Enlightenment, little work has yet been done on how revolutionaries' involvement in the eighteenth-century "Republic of Science" may have influenced their conceptions of political and social arrangements.[41] And yet a brief glance at revolutionary discourse suggests that physics, geology, and meteorology were all useful vocabularies for understanding and explaining the profound changes in the political terrain of the 1790s. In fact, the scientific knowledge of the late eighteenth century seems to have facilitated the development of new means of imagining and explaining the world that revolutionaries were attempting to create. Admittedly, not all revolutionaries were well versed in scientific knowledge; nor were all practitioners of natural history ardent patriots.[42] Yet there is no denying that if Rousseau and Voltaire, Jefferson and Locke, influenced the revolutionaries' view of the world around them, so, too, did their readings and experiences in natural history.

In eloquent speeches from the rostrum at the Convention, in raucous shouts from the theater *parterres,* and in newspaper surveys of public spirit throughout France, revolutionaries seized upon natural imagery to describe the force and justice of their political activity. From Brissot to Robespierre, from Carnot to Condorcet, revolutionary leaders demonstrated a familiarity with natural history that seeped into their political discourse and their political understandings. While individuals on all parts of the political spectrum used what I will call naturalized language, suggesting its widespread appeal, the period between the late summer of 1793 and 1794 gave rise to the highest incidence of this discourse, invoked primarily by Jacobins and their supporters. Yet the "revolutionary" language that is analyzed throughout this book should not be understood as only the property of the elite political class or of the journalists who commented on their maneuverings. Police records leave traces of crowds that left plays singing about life on the "mountain," the naturalized shorthand for the Jacobins, and Parisian *sociétés populaires* expressed their enthusiasm for "collecting lightning," referring to the process of culling saltpeter. Language drawn from the natural world also often moved from the provinces to the capital—a fact that is perhaps of little surprise, since provincial residents' lives were more likely to be marked by hailstorms or flooded swamps than Parisians'. The proceedings of the National Convention on 15 September 1793—a mere ten days after the entry of a delegation from the Paris Commune to the Convention floor, demanding that terror be put on the agenda—offer a stunning perspective on the varied and overwhelming usages of these images. In only a selection of examples from a single day's correspondence, volunteer officers from Dordogne described the "lightning bolt" launched at "traitors and intriguers"; the mayor of Ville-sur-Lumes proclaimed that the "mercenary hordes...will be...pulverized by the unstoppable lightning bolts, thrown...by the god of Nature"; the town of Creil expressed its excitement at hurling "revolutionary lightning" to crush federalist "reptiles"; and the Grenoble *société populaire* lauded the "pure republicanism and regenerating fire" flowing from the "crater" of the Jacobin volcano.[43]

In many respects, this is a recognizable rhetorical practice. One can find natural analogies for human behavior at all moments of history; indeed, it is not uncommon even in the twenty-first century to hear a scene of destruction described as resembling the path of a tornado. And eighteenth-century French men and women lived lives that were much more deeply embedded in the natural world. For most French citizens, the year was marked by cycles of tilling, planting, and harvesting; hailstorms and ice frequently destroyed harvests, as they did in the difficult winter of 1788–89, and rivers overran their banks to damage crops and property, as the Loire did in 1790–91.

Yet revolutionaries' invocations of the natural world broke with convention in several ways. First, they used natural imagery in ways that often reflected recent findings about the natural world, and that demonstrated a widely diffused, if rudimentary, scientific understanding. Members of the revolutionary generation reworked natural images, so common in classical and biblical sources, by refracting them through the lens of early modern studies of nature. Yet revolutionary analogies with the natural world differed from a modern observer commenting on the similarity between the destruction of war and the devastation caused by a tidal wave in another significant way, namely, their positive valence. The "torrent" described by the Festival of Unity and Indivisibility was an incontrovertible source of progress and renewal, not a way of condemning or describing destruction.

Natural tropes provided a way of integrating apparent *disorder* into a narrative of eventual order. If, as the naturalist and novelist Bernardin de Saint-Pierre claimed, "thunder refreshes the air... [and] without hurricanes in the tropics, ants and locusts would render the islands there uninhabitable," then moments of disorder and tragedy could be identified as important for maintaining, or even improving, the natural world.[44] If the same logic applied in the political sphere, then episodes of violence— even if they seemed unjust—could be claimed as necessary for reestablishing order or purifying the new France. The narrative linking nature and revolution allowed revolutionaries not only to explain violence but also, in some cases, to exonerate or even encourage it. The logic of the natural world offered revolutionaries a crucial means of explaining and justifying transformation and violence that, at first glance, seemed inexplicable.

On Violence

Violence has been an important part of nearly every history of the Revolution, beginning even with the Festival of Unity and Indivisibility. Within years of the Revolution's outbreak, the revolutionary generation witnessed regularly what Antoine de Baecque called the "unbearable spectacle" of mass execution.[45] By August 1793 the Parisian public that took part in the procession organized by David had not only confronted the events depicted in the festival, but they had also read about the gruesome Glacière Massacres in Avignon in 1791; they had witnessed the blood of the September Massacres staining their streets in 1792; they had heard stories of, or even had sons or brothers who had fought in, the devastating civil war in the Vendée.

From Alexis de Tocqueville's Frenchmen, habituated to violence and arbitrary justice by the Old Regime, to David Andress's Parisians, unfazed by bloodshed, some historians have conceived of violence as such a banal part of early modern existence that justifications and explanations were, to an extent, unnecessary.[46] Yet this dramatic violence took place at the close of a century that had grown cautiously optimistic about the possibilities for peace. In the eighteenth century Montesquieu, Fénelon, and their contemporaries preached the virtue of politeness and commerce as a means to cooperation among peoples. D'Holbach had argued that the natural state of man was a peaceful one; the *Encyclopédie* maintained that "war is a convulsive and violent sickness of the body politic; this body is only healthy—that is to say, in its natural state—when it is at peace."[47]

While violence had certainly not disappeared during the eighteenth century, it had begun to require explanation.

And the men and women of France were not mute bystanders to the violence of the Revolution. Indeed, Patrice Higonnet's assertion that the Revolution, and particularly the Terror, must be viewed as a traumatic event suggests that something within the logic or alleged banality of violence broke down.[48] In the wake of the September Massacres, the journalist Louis-Marie Prudhomme suggested that all Parisians had been deeply affected by the presence of gruesome violence.[49] The guillotine itself was a source of trauma; the machine, intended to be a humanitarian response to the need for capital punishment, horrified its witnesses with its immediacy.[50] What is more, the state-sanctioned violence of 1793 and 1794, as well as the September and Glacière Massacres, took place in moments when it was recognized that some innocent people were being killed alongside the guilty. The violence of the revolution not only merited but received justification in this context.

One of the foremost explanations of violence generated by revolutionaries, and studied by recent historians, was vengeance: according to scholars like Sophie Wahnich and Colin Lucas, revolutionaries portrayed violent events as just punishments for counterrevolutionary crimes. Thus Wahnich, who maintains that the Revolution must be understood as an emotional experience, argued in her 2003 *La Liberté ou la mort* that the fear and horror felt by the people of Paris in the wake of counterrevolutionary activity burst forth in moments of popular vengeance, such as the September Massacres, or was channeled through law, as in the Terror.[51] In both instances, violence was made legitimate by being portrayed as a punishment for unpunished crimes. Likewise, in Lucas's thoughtful analysis of the September Massacres, he has argued that in revolutionary justifications of violence, legitimate violence was violence carried out by the sovereign in retribution for past crimes.[52] Since the people, by 1792, were sovereign, and tyranny, aristocracy, and royalism were now crimes, then violence *by* the people, against adherents to the Old Regime, was legitimate. To prevent this violence from spiraling out of hand, however, the state claimed to be the mouthpiece of the people, and therefore the arm of the sovereign. The Terror "transferred revolutionary violence away from the real people and onto the revolutionary state presented as the reification of the People."[53]

Lucas's conclusion is an insightful one, revealing much about revolutionaries' understandings of the violence they were undertaking. And there is little question that revolutionary violence did escalate in response to counterrevolutionary activity. But the actual causes of violence are not always reflected in the public justifications of violence; vengeance was not the only logic available to, or used by, revolutionary leaders. Lucas's emphasis on retributive violence makes sense *only* if the violence itself is transparent: accusations of vengeance are tenable only if it is plausible that a crime has originally been committed. Yet both revolutionary leaders and witnesses recognized that some undeserving people were the victims of revolutionary violence. Police reports noted that bystanders questioned the guilt of some of those who were guillotined; on 7 Ventôse, Year II (25 February 1794), complaints arose regarding the execution of an elderly man whose death was undeserved: "What crime, many asked, could a man in this state of decrepitude have committed?"[54] A report on 3 Germinal (23 March 1794) recorded that citizens in a café were complaining that patriots were languishing in prisons: "There are patriots who are locked up—if that is the case, why aren't they set free?"[55] Marat, writing soon after the September Massacres, admitted, "In the number of enemies of liberty covered with civic masks that were denounced to me, it is possible that some equivocal men, even some innocents whose civism was poorly demonstrated, have been mixed in the crowd."[56] Likewise, on 30 Frimaire, Year II (20 December 1793), a group of women appeared before the Convention to lobby for the release of their loved ones, calling for "the freedom of all innocent detainees, and victims of error or human passions." In response, Robespierre acknowledged, "It is certain that some victims of aristocracy can be counted among the detainees; as a consequence of revolutionary measures necessitated by circumstances, some innocent people have been struck down."[57]

It was in these moments, when revolutionaries were faced with potentially innocent deaths, that references to the natural world proved to be particularly prevalent. The natural world was not the only means of explaining or legitimating violence used by the revolutionaries—indeed, the idea of just vengeance would be invoked repeatedly throughout the Terror—but it could be used at those crucial moments when other mechanisms fell short. Naturalized rhetoric shifted the temporality of just violence from the past to the future. "Just" violence takes place on two temporal levels: in an appeal to the past or a hope for the future. The first proclaims that crimes have been committed; we must now right them; this punishment is *deserved*. The other suggests that these sacrifices are necessary for the ultimate good of the nation; the blood shed will not be in vain. Appeals to the natural world removed the focus on retribution—victims of natural violence were not necessarily *deserving* of their punishment—and instead spotlighted the establishment of a future order.

In her work *On Violence,* Hannah Arendt clarified this temporal distinction as the fundamental difference between legitimacy and justification. "Legitimacy," she wrote, "when challenged, bases itself on an appeal to the past, while justification relates to an end that lies in the future. Violence can be justifiable, but it will never be legitimate."[58] Thus legitimacy can be claimed through an electoral mandate, a bloodline from the past, or a crime that requires retribution: all look temporally *backward.* Justification, however, looks forward. For Arendt, violence *requires* a "providential" mind-set, the belief that blood shed today will lead to a better tomorrow. Naturalized language facilitated this forward-looking justification of violence by imposing a providential worldview on revolutionary changes. In the words of Marat, "The political machine never rights itself except through violent convulsions [*secousses*], like the air is purified only by storms."[59] The "convulsions" were justified not by vilifying the guilty victims, but instead by focusing on the eventual, if distant, outcome of the acts.

Analyzing the justifications of violence cannot always contribute to our understanding of the causes of violence, but the two can sometimes be entwined. Whether the September Massacres were, in fact, attempts to avenge crimes that had gone unpunished, whether they were outbursts of fear and anger that had been too long suppressed, or whether they were orchestrated executions engineered by a group of political elites seeking to establish a firmer grip on the people of Paris, the fact that they were justified in language that evoked the natural world, as chapter 2 demonstrates, is significant. It is significant, first, because if justifications are accepted, then they can become precedents for future violence; each successful justification gets added to a repertoire of excuses and exonerations of bloodshed. As Donald Sutherland has pointed out, the tendency to excuse crowd violence and the failure to condemn or stop vigilante vengeance "made politics lethal."[60] The stories we craft about our pasts can shape our futures. But justifications can also influence responses *to* violence. If, according to Marat, political revolutions required violent convulsions, or if, as per David's festival, the Revolution itself was the necessary and inexorable work of Nature, then to fight against its progress was as ineffective as yelling at a tornado or standing defiantly in the path of a lava flow. As Joseph Fouché wrote, defending the people of Paris against accusations of being a violent horde: "One may as well accuse the waters of the sea for being stirred when they are battered by wind."[61]

Whereas numerous studies of revolutionary language have focused on the ability of language to create new opportunities and assert new sites of power, this analysis of the natural history of revolution demonstrates the *negative* power of language, its ability to *close* doors and *limit* action. In doing so, it reflects recent work in cognitive linguistics that affirms the importance of figurative language in explaining and understanding the world around us.[62] Raymond Gibbs, for example, has demonstrated that metaphors are particularly useful tools for creating a kind of mental shorthand for understanding and interpreting events; metaphor seems to facilitate understanding and retention of narratives more than non-figurative language does.[63] What is more, as George Lakoff and Mark Johnson have suggested, metaphors can help to shape and constrain action; they can become "self-fulfilling prophecies."[64] In their famous example, to conceive of an argument as war is to limit, or at least limit the potential for, certain choices: compromise becomes only a last resort; other ends, such as learning more about your "opponent," or considering alternative points of view, play a secondary role to the goal of defeat. Establishing a metaphorical relationship between revolutionary acts and uncontrollable phenomena of nature precluded the possibility of dissent; one may as well complain against God for causing the Lisbon earthquake, as Louis-Marie Prudhomme would write in the winter of 1792.

Revolutionary Like Nature

On 26 May 1794, or 7 Prairial according to the revolutionary calendar, Bertrand Barère mounted the podium of the National Convention on behalf of the Committee of Public Safety. After two years of war against most of the nations of Europe and five years of attempts to stabilize a new form of government, the French public he addressed was weary and shaken. In the previous four days both Maximilien Robespierre and Jean-Marie Collot d'Herbois, two of Barère's fellow members of the Committee, had been the purported targets of assassination attempts. Well aware of the need to harden the resolve of his audience, the former lawyer, essayist, and journalist attempted to raise the spirits of the French while also expressing the resoluteness of the Committee in these contentious times. Urging his countrymen to be stalwart in the face of adversity, he reminded them to sustain both their pride in the nation's accomplishments and their courage to fight to the death when necessary. "These are the sentiments of all the French," he proclaimed, "because they know that they belong to a nation that is revolutionary like nature, powerful like liberty, and ardent like the saltpeter that they have wrested from the depths of the earth." He then proposed that no English or Hanoverian prisoners henceforth be taken, a chilling proposition that was met with rousing applause.[65]

In Barère's proud depiction, France was not merely revolutionary, but "revolutionary like nature." And he used this telling phrase not to describe a reclamation of natural rights, or an extension of liberty, but alongside a call for merciless violence against France's enemies. In this moment of crisis, two weeks before the Festival of the Supreme Being and the passage of the Law of 22 Prairial (10 June 1794) that ushered in what has become known as the "Great Terror," the mouthpiece of the Committee of Public Safety invoked the natural world as a model for the French Revolution. Nor was he alone. The very same day, at the same rostrum, Robespierre lauded the efforts of the national legislature, which was "founding the first republic in the world" and, in so doing, was "returning...nature, which had been exiled, to mortals."[66] The Committee of Public Safety ordered the reproduction of two hundred thousand copies of each speech to be circulated throughout the Republic—one for roughly every 150 people in the nation.[67] The Revolution's unique relationship with nature was to be broadcast widely.

What might it mean to be revolutionary like nature, to have a constitution that resembled nature, as Committee of Public Safety Member Jacques-Nicolas Billaud-Varenne requested on 28 Brumaire (18 November 1793), or to enact justice like nature, as Joseph Fouché had demanded in December 1793? After the Jacobins fell from power in the summer of 1794, Joachim Vilate, a former judge on the revolutionary tribunal, offered his own interpretation of Barère's phrase for his readers: "Barère said, at the national podium, *the French are revolutionary like nature*...Forgetting its touching traits..., its slow and majestic march in the successive cycles of stars, of elements, of flux and reflux in the ocean, they [the Committee of Public Safety] only envisioned [nature] in its accidental convulsions, the eruptions of volcanoes, the earthquakes in Lisbon and Sicily."[68] Vilate had his own political motives for distancing himself from the rhetoric of the Committee of Public Safety, but his interpretation raises a fundamental question: How can we determine what aspects of "nature" the leaders of the Revolution between 1789 and 1794 were seeking to emulate?

To best illuminate the various meanings attached to phenomena from the natural world, this book moves thematically through a series of natural tropes that played important roles in the revolutionary imagination. As Vilate's testimony makes clear, analogies rely on a transparent understanding of the terms of comparison; someone with an understanding of "nature" as a pastoral space of respite would comprehend Barère's remark quite differently than someone to whom the term "nature" connoted the Lisbon earthquake. To understand metaphor, we must understand the cultural context that makes it possible. After an opening chapter exploring scientific and philosophical responses to natural disasters in the eighteenth century, the following chapters trace the rhetorical trajectories of a number of natural phenomena: "revolutions of the earth," a term used to describe terrestrial convulsions like floods or earthquakes; lightning; mountains and swamps; and volcanoes. As chapter 1 demonstrates, the host of new meanings and ideas associated with the natural world as a result of scientific inquiry over the course of the eighteenth century transformed their metaphorical power. Inherited classical, mythological, literary, and biblical meanings merged with new ideas about the powers of lightning, volcanic eruption, and terrestrial change.

Situating each trope in its philosophical and scientific context allows access to the variety of meanings that revolutionaries could have been seeking as they crafted their analogies; following their enunciations between 1789 and 1794 provides insight into the various reasons that revolutionaries opted to evoke these images as they depicted, explained, and justified revolutionary behavior. The natural world allowed them to make claims about the controllability of revolution and of its violence, about participation in revolutionary activity, and about nature itself. Of course, the metaphors were not fixed: as chapter 5 in particular demonstrates, changes in political dynamics facilitated the development of new meanings and connotations. The volcano came to connote different things—volatility, progress, or anarchy—at different moments of the Revolution. Thus metaphors were shaped by the political sphere, but were also shaping it.

In conducting this research, I have examined metaphors and similes alike; my interest has been in discerning what made these terms from the natural world such a useful vocabulary, and in establishing the relationship that was being posited between natural and social or political phenomena. Despite the linguistic engineering of many revolutionary leaders, words can often be flippantly or ill-chosen, so I have been careful to look for widespread patterns of use. I have tried in my research to distinguish between anomalous or ambiguous examples and enunciations within a broader pattern. This helps to explain some omissions: the terms "storm" and "torrent," for example, were used in such a panoply of ways over the course of the Revolution that it is difficult to situate them in a pattern, or to discern any clear changes in their use based either on scientific findings or political changes.

The book is organized thematically, but it also has a chronological argument. In correspondence to the Convention, festival programs, and addresses from the legislative floor, the sheer volume of references to natural phenomena increased dramatically between 1793 and 1794. The tenor of those references also changed in that period, as nature became an increasingly active force in revolutionary rhetoric. As nature was returned from its exile, it became not just a model for revolutionary activity but a participant in it: according to Bertrand Barère, Vesuvius erupted on behalf of the French Army in the summer of 1794, and Prieur de la Côte d'Or claimed that nature had specially placed "revolutionary lightning"—or saltpeter—in the soil of France in December 1793.

By 1794, if France was revolutionary like nature, as Barère claimed, then so, too, was nature itself revolutionary. Nature, rather than the people, became the force behind the Revolution. Given the coincidence of this shift in language with the radicalization of the Revolution, this chronology suggests that despite the timelessness of evocations of the natural world, there was something unique in the radical Jacobin Revolution that made such appeals more salient. As a result, this inquiry into the natural history of the Revolution urges a reconsideration of canonical interpretations of the Terror.

Among revolutionary scholars the foremost historiographical debate of the last thirty years has been about the origins of the Terror, between historians who argue that external circumstances created the conditions for the Terror and those who see the logic of the Terror as nascent in the ideology of the Revolution itself. For the first group, the emergence of a very real and very powerful counterrevolutionary movement served to polarize and radicalize the Revolution, creating a need for unexpected and unpredictable solutions.[69] For these historians the Terror was an act of human will, based on rational, though not always admirable, responses to escalating events. As Timothy Tackett has elegantly argued, "a whole series of unanticipated events…compell[ed] individuals both to confront problems they had never expected and to develop new solutions far more radical—and sometimes more violent—than those they had previously imagined."[70] Those "solutions," and the justifications crafted for them, often reflected preexisting social tensions but were not inherent in the Revolution itself. On the other hand, advocates of the idea that revolutionary violence was inevitable, such as François Furet and Patrice Gueniffey, maintain that there could have been no French Revolution without the Terror. In Furet's famous words: "The truth is that the Terror was an integral part of revolutionary ideology."[71] In its embrace of the Rousseauian idea of the general will, the Revolution's refusal to accept opposing, or even plural, voices forced its radicalization.

But in their allusions to the natural world, Jacobins diminished the role of the popular will. "The people" were, in Furet's words, "the Revolution's claim to legitimacy," and the Terror was the result of a competition to embody their will and eradicate any opposition to that collective voice.[72] And yet, as Dan Edelstein argues in *The Terror of Natural Right*, the general will seems not to have been the cornerstone of the Jacobin philosophy of governance, particularly in Year II.[73] As the role of the people and the general will diminished, the role of nature increased. And nature provided a way of exonerating or even encouraging revolutionary violence, of limiting opposition to "natural" acts, and of engaging the population in revolution even while removing them from sovereignty and legislation. It was nature, not the people, who were the impetus for the Revolution as immortalized by the Festival of Unity and Indivisibility; it was nature that was being returned to its rightful place by the Revolution, according to Robespierre's speech on 7 Prairial (26 May 1794). In many respects, nature became the new sovereign; the people were merely its providential instrument. The natural history of revolution suggests that the Terror was not a result of a radicalization in hopes of realizing the general will, but instead was understood to be, and was portrayed as, the rule of nature—agentless, inevitable, destructive in its preservation of order—put into effect.

In Brumaire of Year II (November 1793), Prudhomme's journal, *Révolutions de Paris,* assessed the "public spirit" of Paris in the wake of terror being made the "order of the day."[74] In revolution, he wrote, sometimes innocent lives would be lost, just as nature's transformations wrought both beneficent and malevolent consequences. Prudhomme explained, "It is thus that hail, which purifies the atmosphere, destroys... the good grain as well as the sterile hay or the poisonous vegetation. But these mistakes are inevitable, and for the Revolution to be complete, it is better for it to sweep away more than less in its whirlpool."[75] By positing, first, that hail was necessary to the purity of the atmosphere and, second, that revolutionary Terror was analogous to a hailstorm, Prudhomme not only made Terror an inevitable and natural act for the sanctity of the Republic, but he also transformed the death of a few "good grains" into necessary results of the natural revolution. The language of the natural world, which had gained currency over the course of the eighteenth century, became a way of explaining the inexplicable, of mediating the gap between the just death and the innocent execution; it allowed for a vision of revolution that was simultaneously sacred and agentless, inevitable and uncondemnable.

1

ORDERING A DISORDERED WORLD

On 16 September 1793, a writer for the *Feuille du Salut Public*, the official mouthpiece of the Committee of Public Safety, offered his vision of an ideal government by comparing politics to nature. "Everything moves, clashes, collides [*se froisse*] in nature; it is in this movement that life, equilibrium, harmony are born. The political world resembles the material world in this regard. It constantly needs action and reaction; from this shock emerges light from light, truth from truth, harmony and order without which nothing can endure, no matter how perfect the government."[1] In this account, harmony and order were not in spite of, but because of, activity and agitation, and the model for his political ideal was the natural world.

The incessant activity of the natural world could hardly be ignored by an observant eighteenth-century French man or woman. As Donald Geoffrey Charlton has noted, the second half of the century saw a marked rise in interest in images of nature that were not pastoral but, rather, destructive; patrons of the artist Claude-Joseph Vernet, for example, specifically requested scenes of tumultuous seas and shipwrecks.[2] Natural histories, which had grown increasingly popular over the course of the century, sought to make sense of destructive nature, and a broad public discussion about natural disasters followed both the Lisbon earthquake of 1755 and the Messina and Calabria earthquakes of 1783. Parisian elites could experiment with creating earthquakes from sulfur and water at dinner parties, read poetry commemorating Lisbon in the *Année Littéraire,* or enter essay contests about the causes of earthquakes or the prodigies of comets. Yet, as the *Feuille du Salut Public* suggests, these destructive and disruptive events often entered the public sphere not as signs of divine vengeance or as reminders of the randomness of the natural world; instead, naturalists and philosophers alike tended to integrate these moments of disorder into a narrative of a natural order that was either divinely organized or self-regulating.

From Buffon to Mesmer, from elite academies to public lectures, and from the 1755 Lisbon earthquake to the 1789 freeze that destroyed French farmland, conversations about nature and natural history entered the public sphere. In constructing an idea of nature as purposed and ordered, many natural histories imposed a kind of providentialism on the operations of the natural world that did not necessarily require an active or intervening deity. That providentialism was often affirmed by responses to natural disasters; although natural crises, most notably destructive earthquakes in Lisbon and in Messina in the second half of the century, problematized the idea of an ordered universe, they also fostered an optimism that asked observers to have faith in a future, if as-yet-unforeseen, good. As the *Feuille de Salut Public* revealed, it was in those moments of activity and violence that harmony and order could be reborn.

The poet Ponce-Denis Écouchard Le Brun, writing in the wake of the devastating 1755 Lisbon earthquake, evoked the simultaneous destruction and regeneration of the natural world.

> All things are born; all things die; all should be reborn;
> Everything loses the form of its being,
> Fragile creation of the elements:
> Nature, active and fertile,
> Re-creates the world constantly,
> Eternal in its changes.[3]

Natural histories and responses to natural disasters accustomed a broader public to naturalized language and analogies, and made more commonplace this vision of nature as an ordering and purposed, even if sometimes destructive, entity. The diffusion of natural knowledge, the establishment of the idea of a self-regulating and purposed natural world, and the theodicies emerging in the wake of natural disasters in the late eighteenth century, all fostered the development of a secular providentialism that would come to define the natural history of the French Revolution.

Natural Historians Confront Disorder

As both Le Brun's poem and the *Feuille du Salut Public*'s analogy suggest, disruption and agitation were impossible to ignore in observations of nature, and increasingly over the course of the eighteenth century, they were recognized as an integral part of the processes of the natural world. Indeed, this question of order, even in the midst of apparent disorder, may well have been the predominant concern in eighteenth-century studies of nature. In its diagram of human knowledge, the *Encyclopédie* divided natural history into three sections: the uniformity of nature, deviations of nature, and uses of nature. "Uniform nature" included celestial, meteorological, and terrestrial phenomena, as well as histories of minerals, plants, and animals.[4] However, many of the events and objects categorized as "deviations" of nature were explained, in specific entries, as understandable natural phenomena that were not anomalies but rather accessories to the natural operations of the earth. For example, the entry on "*prodige physique*" described two types of "prodigies": the first were supernatural miracles, "which do not merit any belief," and the second were "purely natural effects, but which take place less frequently and seem to be contrary to the ordinary course of nature," and so have been ascribed erroneously to supernatural causes.[5] Likewise, the entry on "*pluie prodigieuse*" explained these miraculous rainfalls in purely natural terms, attributing rains of fire to the ashfall of nearby volcanoes, and rains of blood, improbably enough, to butterflies dropping globules of red sap.[6] In Diderot's entry on "Imperfect," he wrote, "there is nothing imperfect in nature, not even monsters. All is linked [in nature], and a monster is an effect that is just as necessary as a perfect animal. The causes that converged for its production are related to an infinitude of other causes, just as those are linked to an infinitude of others, and so on, reaching until the eternity of things."[7]

This is not to claim that the anomalous and the apparently abnormal were entirely absent from scientific curiosity; a rich literature on monsters and miracles suggests otherwise.[8] However, many natural histories sought to marginalize such events; some naturalists, including Buffon, believed that natural aberrations could provide no education for the *savant*.[9] In Buffon's eyes, the monstrous and the anomalous had no place in natural histories. Indeed, it was the search for order that defined his methodology as a naturalist. It was only understanding and inquiry that revealed the apparently disorganized and confusing as ordered and interrelated. In his introductory remarks to the *Histoire Naturelle*, he explained, "When one...casts one's eyes for the first time on this storehouse [of nature] filled with diverse, new, and strange things, the first feeling which results is an astonishment mingled with admiration...Through familiarizing oneself with these same objects, through seeing them frequently, and, so to speak, without design, little by little they form durable impressions, which soon link themselves in our spirit by fixed and invariable relations, and from there we can lift ourselves to more general views."[10] He indicated that the orderless found an order through natural history. Though adamantly opposed to the *esprit de système* that attempted to impose a false order on the study of natural history, Buffon nevertheless believed in a kind of transparent ordering that would emerge from the study of sensory experience and detailed observation.

Perhaps because of the tastes of the eighteenth-century public, many of the century's popular natural histories gestured toward a teleological view of the world, aligning science with providentialism. Natural histories provided explanations for the origins and transformations of the world, often describing the particularities of diverse species in great detail. Yet, in many cases, these particularities were attributed to "final causes," positive ends intended by, and sometimes known by, God alone. Bernardin de Saint-Pierre's suggestion, in his *Etudes de la Nature,* that a melon is sectioned so it can easily be shared within large families is perhaps the most famous, and derided, of these propositions.[11] Jeff Loveland, in his cogent analysis of the rhetorical strategies used by natural historians, suggests that these "final causes" were so popular that they were often considered necessary for attracting readers. Situating his study in the context of a competitive and lucrative marketplace for natural histories, Loveland states, "Throughout the century the public had a huge appetite for final causes and providence."[12] Thus even Buffon, who criticized the idea of final causes, nevertheless employed them regularly in his histories.[13] After the publication of the first volume of *Spectacle de la Nature,* the abbé Pluche was pressured to increase his providential language, demonstrating a certain public taste for final causes.[14] In linking science with providence, many natural histories affirmed belief in a purposed existence for both man and the natural world.

Certainly d'Holbach the materialist had little patience for final causes, particularly as Bernardin de Saint-Pierre understood them. His argument against them ridiculed the notion that the natural world offered any proof of a divine creator. He granted the "power of nature" but not the "wisdom, goodness, [or] foresight" of any supreme being. Yet at the same time he embraced another kind of fatalism, a notion of a self-regulating nature that abided by its own laws: "everything that nature does is necessary and is but the consequence of its laws."[15] The strident atheist's position actually gave *more* authority to nature: while its activity may not have been clearly purposed, it was necessary. And while the activity of nature was not directed toward the benefit of man—a notion that d'Holbach found both ridiculous and hubristic—he did at times suggest that it was directed toward its own perpetuation. While his materialism stated, "Whatever is, is necessarily so," his texts could sometimes echo Alexander Pope's famous words: "Whatever is, is right." As Lorraine Daston and Fernando Vidal have noted, "The most inexorable authority is that of necessity, against which all human will strives in vain."[16]

Thus, in his description of earthquakes in the *Encyclopédie,* d'Holbach noted, "We see that the innards of the earth are perpetually ripped open by blazes that are constantly acting with more or less violence; causes so powerful cannot but produce effects that influence our entire globe. They should, in the long run, change its center of gravity, dry out some regions only to submerge others; in short, [they] contribute to making nature complete the cycle of its revolutions."[17] The idea of earthquakes "contribut[ing]" to the earth's cycle suggests that there was a natural path that the earth could not help but follow. Likewise, in his article on volcanoes, he maintained that they were necessary elements of the earth's terrain because of their ability to evacuate noxious gases from its interior; he went on, "We also see that providence has placed volcanoes in all the regions of the globe."[18] Materialism itself suggested a kind of secular providentialism; nature had its laws that could not be broken, and to which man must submit with the same servitude that Job manifested in abandoning his fate to a God beyond his comprehension. In the final chapter of *Système de la Nature,* d'Holbach spoke as the Voice of Nature, making moral demands and meting out punishments for those who dared to break nature's laws: "Consider the vengeances that I exact upon all those who resist my decrees. Look into the hearts of criminals, whose content faces hide a tattered soul."[19] He concluded, "May the sorrows that destiny forces the child of nature to undergo be comforted by the pleasures that wisdom allows him to taste; may he learn to submit to necessity."[20] He replaced divine justice with natural justice, and theology with a faith in the sustaining operations of the natural world.

Thus inquiries into the natural world not only portrayed what the world looked like and was comprised of, but they often also suggested the purpose of each creation, or its relationship to the broader mechanisms of the earth, imposing a teleology—and sometimes a theology—on natural history. In the words of Jessica Riskin, "The natural world, as sentimental empiricists described it, was imbued with agency, and that agency was more mundane than divine."[21] Although some physico-theologies, which sought to integrate theological and natural explanations of the world, explicitly linked final causes with a divine purpose, these teleologies could also be secularized, as Riskin suggests. The natural world was, in a sense, self-regulating: "Nature's parts, by acting according to their inclinations, tended to maintain their relations in a proper state of balance."[22]

Whether through d'Holbach's understanding of natural necessity, or Bernardin de Saint-Pierre's deployment of final causes, studies of nature brought to light an order that regulated and defined the material world. For Bernardin, that order was proof of God's existence; for d'Holbach, it was evidence that the natural world was self-sufficient. Lorraine Daston's work on discipline in eighteenth-century natural history likewise reveals a concern with explaining the apparently anomalous as a part of the natural order. By examining entomological studies, Daston has demonstrated that original research in natural history demanded rigorous observation of minute details and discipline of an almost monastic quality. The detailed methodology was remarkably similar to the approach taken by political economists describing the tools and implements in a modern workshop, in that both studies demonstrated "the habit of dissecting organisms and tools into component parts, the keen eye for optimal solutions to mechanical problems, [and] the penchant for copious and minute descriptions."[23] Just as precise and specialized tools denoted a well-organized workshop, so, too, did the diversity of natural creations signify an ordered—and divinely created—universe. Through their detailed observations, naturalists elevated the base and the insignificant to demonstrations of God's wisdom. In this sense, nature was a space in which the individual redeemed the whole, and vice versa. The tiny and strange only made sense as a part of the greater system, and the greater system was demonstrated by the existence of precisely crafted components.

The natural world even provided the foundation for a new theological vision. In Rousseau's educational treatise, *Emile,* the Savoyard curé who introduced the young tutor to religion needed only the natural world as his evidence of God, and as the source of his morality. Indeed, nature and sentiment were the *only possible* paths to religious understanding: "I closed all books. There is only one that is accessible to all eyes: the book of nature, and it is in this great and sublime book that I learned to serve and love its divine author."[24] Neither text nor inherited knowledge nor custom could provide a path to truth: only nature could provide a sense of the divine and the virtuous. In *Emile* nature itself was an authority: it was not a space of virtue because God made it so, but, rather, belief in God was possible because of the beauty and harmony of the natural world.

Likewise, deism's appeals to an argument from design meant that nature proved the existence of God: the precise interactions between the components of nature suggested a wise, and purportedly benevolent, creator. In taking nature rather than revelation as its evidence, deism posited that God's credibility and authority were based on the order of nature, rather than vice versa. Moreover, deism imposed a providentialism on the operations of the world: although a clockmaker-god may well be removed from the world, he nevertheless forged not only an order, but an end and a teleology for the universe. Machines are definitionally not only crafted but purposed, with each component playing a role from which it can not deviate. Like Rousseau's vicar, the eighteenth-century deist could find in nature proof of providence.

In their proclivity for final causes, and in a methodology that sought to make sense of, or ignore, apparent anomalies, eighteenth-century natural histories tended to impose an order on the natural world that suggested either a divine creator or a self-sustaining natural world. Yet, at the same time, eighteenth-century Europeans faced traumatic natural events that cast doubt on this ordered vision: volcanoes erupted, hailstorms destroyed crops, rivers flooded, earthquakes devastated Lisbon and Sicily. These moments provide a unique lens through which to analyze perceptions of order, disorder, and providence in the natural world, and to see the ways in which discourses from natural history informed, and were informed by, responses to these natural disasters. Natural crises in the second half of the eighteenth century, far from shaking scientists' and philosophers' belief in an ordered and purposed world, instead tended to affirm that faith, and asked observers to look for systems and patterns that would make sense of monstrous events. In these moments of crisis, in which the idea of a providential universe was most clearly tested, natural history provided a new form of theodicy, which justified individual tragedies by suggesting an eventually beneficial outcome in which earthquakes, volcanic eruptions, lightning strikes, and hailstorms ultimately restored and regenerated the natural world. As Bernardin de Saint-Pierre blithely explained,

> Hailstorms, which sometimes accompany thunderstorms, destroy many insects, and they are only frequent in seasons when they hatch and multiply: in summer and spring.... We have already discussed the necessity and utility of volcanoes, whose fires purify the waters of the sea, just like thunder purifies the air. Earthquakes come from the same cause.[25]

A History of Natural Violence: The Lisbon Earthquake of 1755 and the Messina and Calabria Earthquakes of 1783

In the spring of 1789, after seeing his flock of French men and women endure a difficult and often devastating winter, the archbishop of Paris issued a Lenten sermon that noted the unique coincidence of political and natural unrest. Nature's wrath had brought floods and hailstorms, bad harvest and illness, made even more troubling by the political "storms" also at hand. Never before, he asserted, had the present generation found itself in so critical a position, faced with *révolutions* both natural and political. Yet, in a theme appropriate for his Lenten sermon, he urged the faithful not to be shaken by these events, but instead to find opportunity in them for penance and forgiveness: "The 'wise men' of the century will see in natural revolutions, as well as in political ones, only the confluence of natural causes, only the games and caprice of chance. When the elements are unleashed against us, when the Earth is struck with sterility, the man of the world murmurs against the disorder of Nature, and is afflicted without consolation; but the man who is enlightened by the supernatural light of Faith, will discover in these events the operations of a sovereign wisdom that orders everything by means and ends that are well beyond the weak thoughts of man."[26] Despite appearances, the world operated with a logic that was God's, not man's, and that was impenetrable to the human mind.

The archbishop's sermon raised the essential question emerging in the wake of natural crises and disasters, which demanded a response from believers and nonbelievers alike: How are such tragedies possible in a world that has any reason or order to it? For believers, this is the fundamental question of theodicy: Why does evil exist in a world where God is supposed to be all-knowing, all-powerful, and at the same time all good? For nonbelievers, this question poses a confrontation with either chaos or order: Do natural disasters mean that there is no force governing the earth, and that all is merely chance, or that the laws of nature, imagined by many in the eighteenth century to regulate the mechanisms of the Earth, contain allowances for apparent disorder and destruction instead of order and conservation? Scientific, philosophic, and religious responses to natural crises and disasters throughout the second half of the eighteenth century affirmed the idea of an ordered and purposed world, even when faced with individual moments of apparent disorder and devastation.[27] Ultimately, not even the archbishop's maligned "wise men" saw disorder in nature; rather, many perceived an order that was not necessarily ordained by God, but instead was dictated by Nature itself.

In addition to the more quotidian ravages by storm and the occasional flood, the 1780s had seen dramatic hailstorms devastate the crops of many farmers throughout France. As the archbishop of Paris noted, the winters of 1787 and 1788 were particularly difficult, to the extent that the king established a fund to aid those whose land had been damaged.[28] Well into 1789 the National Assembly still struggled with how to handle the damages, suggesting a farmers' mutual assistance fund that August.[29] Indeed, these events brought the natural world into political discourse in a quite literal way: flooding in the Loire led to an inundation of indemnity requests in the National Assembly in 1790 and 1791.[30] In addition, the mountainous regions of France, and the Pyrénées in particular, became increasingly popular geographies to study, in part because of their propensity for floods and avalanches.[31] What is more, earthquakes in Messina, Italy, and the eruption of Mount Vesuvius in 1779 had made appearances in the French press and in Sunday sermons. Not only were French men and women reading about theories of nature in scientific texts or learning about the wonders of the natural world in public lectures and academy contests, they were also well aware of the potential destruction of nature through their lived experience with natural crises.

Without a doubt, the most philosophically significant natural crisis of the eighteenth century, though distant from the lives of most French subjects, was the Lisbon earthquake of 1 November 1755. The seismic event has been seen as a watershed moment in the theological and philosophical responses to natural crisis, largely as a result of Voltaire's famous rejection of providential explanations in his "Poem on the Lisbon Disaster" and his satirical novel *Candide*.[32] The earthquake, which destroyed the fourth-largest city in Europe and took the lives of some thirty thousand victims, was made all the more severe by a consequent tsunami and ensuing fire that ravaged the city. Images of the event—no doubt dramatized but nonetheless chilling—show a city wracked by chaos and convulsions from all sides.

It took several weeks for news of the tragedy to reach the French public, but once word arrived, emanating first from Madrid on November 22, the event captured the imagination of novelists, poets, playwrights, and philosophers, as well as naturalists.[33] The devastation of Lisbon required explanation from those who survived it, or who "observed" it in newspapers, sermons, and pamphlets throughout Europe. Lisbon was widely recognized as a cosmopolitan city, a thriving port of commerce. Its destruction

Fig. 1 *Lisbone Abysmée* (ca. 1760, artist unknown). Bibliothèque Nationale de France.

forced Europeans to question any previously held optimistic belief in un-hindered progress. Nor could they merely justify the earthquake in punishing language by blaming the devastation on the sinful and luxurious lifestyle of Lisbon's residents: the quake took place on All Saints Day, and those who were fulfilling their holy obligation of going to Mass died in the largest numbers, unable to flee overcrowded churches before the rafters collapsed on them. On the other hand, the royal family, living in opulence, was spared in its entirety.

Any providential explanation of the disaster, suggesting that God was punishing the hedonistic capital of Portugal, was passionately countered by the first emotional, and then sarcastic, Voltaire. In 1756 he published his "Poème sur le désastre de Lisbonne ou examen de cet axiome 'tout est bien.'" His moral revulsion and deep sorrow at the "all is for the best" explanation is immediately perceptible.

Come, ye philosophers, who cry, "All's well,"
And contemplate this ruin of a world.
Behold these shreds and cinders of your race,
This child and mother heaped in common wreck,
These scattered limbs beneath the marble shafts—
A hundred thousand whom the earth devours,
Who, torn and bloody, palpitating yet,
Entombed beneath their hospitable roofs,
In racking torment end their stricken lives.
To those expiring murmurs of distress,
To that appalling spectacle of woe,
Will ye reply: "You do but illustrate
The iron laws that chain the will of God"?
Say ye, o'er that yet quivering mass of flesh:
"God is avenged: the wage of sin is death"?[34]

Moved and horrified by the spectacle of suffering and destruction, Voltaire railed against the heartless explanations of Christian observers. How could anyone claim that the women and children buried under their own roofs *deserved* their cruel deaths? And how could men stand without anger at a "good and free God" who nevertheless made playthings of man? God, and His "mistaken philosophers," seemed to lack compassion in the face of disaster. Furthermore, they did little to change it: although Voltaire never discussed the practical reconstruction of Lisbon, in the reality of the earthquake's aftermath, those who spent their days praying were of little use to the rebuilding effort. The Marquis de Pombal, in charge of reconstruction, actually banished a beloved Jesuit priest in the quake's aftermath, in part for encouraging individuals to retreat, meditate, and pray instead of work on recovery efforts.[35] Voltaire, like Pombal, had little patience for such observers, standing in fear and awe where they should have been moved toward action and compassion.

Two years later, Voltaire's famous satire *Candide* would take on the same observers. In it, the philosopher Pangloss played the role of the Providentialist, proclaiming that all things had happened for a reason, even if it was for some unseen good. As a result, Pangloss became a passive spectator, unwilling to change anything about his world, for it was already, famously, the best of all possible. When Candide and his compatriots traveled to Lisbon, Candide's benefactor, Jacques the Anabaptist, fell overboard. "[Candide] wanted to throw himself into the sea after the Anabaptist, but the great philosopher, Pangloss, stopped him by proving that Lisbon harbour was made on purpose for this Anabaptist to drown there."[36] Belief in a future good reduced men's role to mere witnesses, forced to stand complacently by while Providence did its work. Eventually growing tired of Pangloss's silver lining, Candide ultimately chose close friends, a garden, and the work of human hands. As he demonstrated with biting wit in *Candide,* Voltaire, after seeing the devastation of Lisbon, in essence threw up his hands and said, If this is what God can do, I choose man.[37]

Taking Voltaire as her point of departure, philosopher Susan Neiman's masterful *Evil in Modern Thought* treats Lisbon as a moment of rupture in European metaphysics. Her analysis of conceptions of Providence, responsibility, and intention hinges on responses to "evil" events. For Neiman, "modernity" began in the wake of Lisbon, for the 1755 quake marked the last time that "evil" could refer to something natural and accidental, as well as manmade and intentional. Neiman explains: "Before Lisbon, evils were divided into matters of nature, metaphysics, or morality. After Lisbon, the word evil was restricted to what was once called moral evil....Post-Lisbon thinkers used intention as the concept that determined good and evil, turning what had once been natural evil into mere disaster, and evil into that which was somebody's fault."[38]

The rupture that Neiman discerns after Lisbon was not so clear as she claims here, however. First of all, Voltaire proved the exception, rather than the rule, in his grappling with the disaster; his pessimism in the wake of Lisbon met with much criticism.[39] No doubt, some witnesses to and commentators upon the earthquake continued to stress its importance as a divine retribution for Lisbon's sins, and as a moment of penance for the rest of Europe. Yet the Leibnizian idea, so satirized by Voltaire, that "all is for the best," operated according to a radically different logic from that retributive standpoint. For God (or Nature) to have wrought such tragedy in the world, the violence needed to be either deserved—divine punishment for illicit action—or part of a greater plan, one beyond human comprehension. Leibniz had encouraged faith in moments of adversity, suggesting that human knowledge could never deign to reach the celestial heights of God's plan. "You have known the world only since the day before yesterday," he wrote. "You see scarcely farther than your nose....Wait until you know more of the world...and you will find there a contrivance and a beauty transcending all imagination. Let us thence draw conclusions as to the wisdom and goodness of the author of things, even in the things that we know not."[40] While the penitential understanding of the earthquake as divine punishment looked *backward,* and saw Lisbon as a moment of particular providentialism that was directed at a specific population that ultimately deserved its fate, the Leibnizian one looked *forward*, to an unforeseeable but no doubt positive end. It was therefore part of a universal providence, a part of the normal and inevitable operations of terrestrial life.[41]

Despite Voltaire's protestations, it was this second, forward-looking providentialism that largely emerged from philosophical, political, and scientific commentary alike. If there was a rupture after Lisbon, it seems to be in the rejection of a backward-looking retributive justification in favor of a forward-looking providential one. Very few observers would claim that the residents of Lisbon deserved their punishment. Instead, disaster was better explained by looking forward to a mysterious, but certainly good, end. Although some, particularly conservative, French men and women would continue to see disaster as divine punishment, most individuals, even in religious circles, found this explanation wanting. And even a smaller number embraced the chaotic and, in Rousseau's words, "hopeless" world that Voltaire imagined in its place.

In fact, Rousseau was one of the first and most vocal opponents of Voltaire's disdain for a destroyer-God. In a letter to Voltaire of 18 August 1756, published three years later as the "Lettre sur la providence," Rousseau raged against Voltaire's pessimism, arguing that we can not vilify God for such disasters; if anything, we could blame the Lisbon residents who chose to live in overcrowded sectors in poorly built houses.[42] He wrote to Voltaire, "A more exact proposition, instead of *tout est bien*, it may be better to say, *Le tout est bien*, or *Tout est bien pour le tout*." He continued by asserting the inscrutability of God's designs: "It is evident that no man can give direct proofs for or against [this proposition], for these proofs depend on a perfect understanding of the constitution of the world and of the goals of its author, and this understanding is incontestably beyond the intelligence of man."[43] In 1762, Rousseau would again reiterate his continuing faith in Providence in *Emile*'s "Profession of Faith of a Savoyard Vicar."[44] He chose hope in a future outcome that he could not yet see.

While Rousseau refused to see in Lisbon a disruption of the natural order ordained by Providence, political pamphleteer Ange Goudar saw in the earthquake an opportunity for rebirth and reconstruction. His 1756 *Discours politique sur les avantages que les Portugais pourroient retirer de leur malheur* argued that the devastation caused by the Lisbon earthquake could, in fact, work for the benefit of the Portuguese people. Goudar, a publicist for the foreign ministry who had recently lived in Portugal, could claim some authority on the city of Lisbon, and his *Discours* went through four French editions in 1756 alone.[45] On the one hand, Goudar argued that the earthquake would break the Portuguese dependence on England, with whom Portugal, and the port city of Lisbon in particular, had maintained a very close commercial and political relationship. It also would force the city to rebuild, to strengthen its ties, and to regain its sense of community, which had been weakened by a constant influx of foreigners throughout the first half of the century. Goudar explained the greater good caused by a moment of devastation, saying, "Just as floods are sometimes necessary to make rivers return to their natural course...there can be cases where, to reestablish a State, it is necessary for it to be partly destroyed, and to be destroyed by some extraordinary event."[46] For Portugal to return to its path to greatness, from which it had been diverted owing to infiltration by the English and the detrimental influence of luxury and leisure, it needed an earthquake to clear its slate and start anew. Goudar's invocation of the natural world, and the exigencies and destruction that were sometimes required to sustain the "natural course," gestures toward the authority that the natural world could have in describing the political realm, and also indicates that the idea that nature necessarily required some damages for its ultimate sustenance already held some currency in 1756.

The flood of scientific texts generated in the wake of the disaster tended to embrace a similar, if secularized, providentialism. While philosophical and theological responses to the disaster have garnered considerable attention in the historiography of the Lisbon earthquake, of equal importance was the deluge of scientific inquiries into the causes of both this specific earthquake and earthquakes more generally. These debates revolved not only around the question of *why* these events happened, but also around *how*, physically, the paroxysms took place. Given the importance of firsthand sensory experience in eighteenth-century science, reports generated in the wake of these earthquakes provided a unique opportunity for studying and understanding the earth's convulsions. Of particular interest was the fact that earthquakes had been felt throughout Europe in the past several years, suggesting an interconnectedness and a simultaneity that intrigued the scientific mind.[47] Subterranean fires, electrical activity, compressed air, and sulfurous exhalations all were proposed as likely causes. Exemplifying the rise of popular science, these debates played out in the *Mercure de France*, where a February 1756 letter from the Abbé Moreilhan sparked that newspaper's discussion of earthquakes, and in the *Journal des Savants*, which printed précis of several scientific inquiries for audiences that may not have had the time or money to read the texts themselves.[48] The Académie de Rouen sponsored an essay contest in 1757 on the causes of earthquakes; of the ten entries that are still extant, none proffered the same cause for the seismic activity.[49] Their prize-winning entry, by a relative of the future Girondin Honoré Maximin Isnard, was published in 1758 and was summarized—albeit uncharitably—in the *Journal des Savants*.[50] Grégory Quenet has called the discussions following Lisbon "one of the first popular scientific debates" because of the broad interest in, and thorough coverage of, the discussion of the physical causes and purpose of the earthquake.[51]

Indeed, some literary evocations of the disaster referred to this whirling scientific debate. In his "Ode sur la ruine de Lisbonne," the young poet Ponce-Denis Écouchard Le Brun lyrically evoked a number of theories about earthquakes' physical causes.

> Sulfur, the nutrient of thunder;
> Its black whirlpools swirl [in the innards of the earth].
> Salts, niter, tar:
> The mixture catches fire, rumbling,
> Their struggles heightened by winds;
> And their collision, signal of tempests,
> Makes the heavens thunder above our heads
> And Hell howl beneath our feet.[52]

The earth's convulsions were caused by sulfur, salts, niter, and bituminous elements. Had Le Brun added electricity and exhalations, he would have summarized, in verse, the debate played out in the *Journal des Savants* and in the Rouen essay contest.

As Le Brun's mention of Heaven and Hell suggests, many of these scientific accounts did not necessarily exclude God from their explanations; instead, they reduced the divine role to a secondary one. Just as Rousseau did not see the tragedy of the Lisbon earthquake as a result of God's intervention but rather as a consequence of the path of nature, so, too, did several naturalists invoke a creator-God who had brought about the earthquake through secondary causes alone. Elie Bertrand, a Swiss pastor and naturalist with a particular interest in geological phenomena, explained the tension between the desire to explain earthquakes scientifically and theologically, saying, "To be a *physicien*, one can't say that God is the immediate cause of earthquakes without recourse to second causes...But to be a philosopher, one can't explain these terrifying phenomena as if they were independent of Providence, to whom everything is subordinate."[53] Thus he, like many of his contemporaries, sought an explanation of these secondary causes. In Bertrand's opinion, the culprit was gaseous air trapped in subterranean passages; he noted that the places most likely to have earthquakes were those that have a cavernous terrain, contain nitrous and sulphurous materials, and enclose pockets of steaming water. Earthquakes decidedly did not take place in areas that were more sinful than others, but in regions that had physical differences that made them more prone to gaseous exhalations.

Bertrand, whose *Mémoires historiques et physiques sur les tremblements de terre* was praised in the *Journal des Savants,* also argued for the physical utility of earthquakes.[54] He compared them to fevers in humans, which were painful and arduous but also necessary for overcoming disease. "Let us not doubt," he wrote, "that these agitations of the earth have a physical use as well as a moral one.... I don't know how they could be imagined not to be useful for the conservation of the Mechanism of the Earth." He suggested that earthquakes likely increased fertility, or maintained the saltiness of seawater, or even prevented the corruption of the earth's waters by "giving rise to their mixing and circulation."[55] They therefore played an important role in the preservation of the earth's balance.

Even accounts of the earthquakes that did not give God an explicit role—as primary cause or otherwise—sometimes suggested that certain benefits could be gained from convulsions; for example, the opportunity to discern broader truths about the natural world was a possible result of the tragedy. The geologist Nicolas Desmarest's *Conjectures physico-méchaniques,* published in March 1756, argued that fiery explosions were the cause of earthquakes. The *Journal des Savants* noted that Desmarest's goal in describing and reflecting on the earthquakes was precisely what Lorraine Daston has suggested was the goal in entomology: using observation of individual circumstance to illuminate a broader truth or, in his words, "to provide attentive observers with individual and local circumstances, which can allow us to determine with precision the march of nature."[56] The apparent anomaly of the earthquake could, in fact, reveal the operations of nature and allow naturalists to discern patterns where previously none had been seen to exist.

The Lisbon earthquake clearly uncovered a fertile soil for the discussion of providence and purpose in the natural world. Whether as a providential event that had been dictated by God, or as an inevitable result of the earth's operations, the 1755 earthquake could be aligned with the idea of an ordered universe, against which Voltaire had argued so eloquently. The idea that the Lisbon earthquake was a sign of divine vengeance, and a moment of particular providence—a cessation in the natural order of the world based on an immediate intervention by God—was largely superseded by notions that the earthquake was a part of the natural order, necessary for the conservation of the earth.

This view of earthquakes was reinforced thirty years later, when a less-known but equally devastating earthquake hit the region of Calabria in Italy. Beginning on 5 February 1783, a series of tremors struck the area near Mount Etna, killing, in William Hamilton's estimation, forty thousand residents.[57] Perhaps even more than the Lisbon earthquake, the Calabria tremors gave rise to a groundswell of activity in the scientific public sphere. One contemporary source noted that "nearly all the parts of the inhabited world are resounding with the news of the disaster...most of the public papers are more or less frightening accounts of this unfortunate catastrophe," and reminded the reader of the moral and scientific impact of the event: "[It] should rivet the attention of observers of revolutions of the globe, at the same time that it drains the tears of sensibility for so many deplorable victims of nature's destructive scourges."[58]

Like the Lisbon earthquake, these tremors provoked a series of scientific texts assessing their causes and damages. Between April and June the *Journal de Paris* and *Gazette de France* noted the publication of a *Nouveaux détails historiques et météorologiques des tremblemens de terre arrivés à Messine depuis le 5 fevrier dernier et dans la Calabre;* the abbé de S.*L.*'s *Précis historique sur les principaux tremblemens de terre de la Sicile,* a collection of engravings titled *Voyage en Sicile, à l'isle de Malthe et à celles de Lipari,* a *Voyage pittoresque de Naples et de Sicile,* and Déodat de Dolomieu's *Voyages aux îles de Lipari fait en 1781.* Dolomieu followed up that text a year later with *Mémoire sur les tremblemens de terre de la Calabre pendant l'année 1783.* In addition, 1783 saw the appearance of the *Description historique et géographique de la ville de Messine,...et détails historiques et météorologiques du désastre que cette ville vient d'éprouver (le 5 fevrier 1783) par le tremblement de terre...,* a *Précis historique de la Ville de Messine, de la Sicile, etc,* and a translation of William Hamilton's *Détails historiques des tremblemens de terre arrivés en Italie, depuis le 5 février jusqu'en mai 1783.* The newspapers also suggested further reading, including d'Holbach's entry on earthquakes in the *Encyclopédie*—which, notably, gave a providential reading of earthquakes as helping nature go through the "cycle of its revolutions"—and a text titled *Histoire des anciennes révolutions du globe terrestre.*[59] The newspapers and naturalists alike believed there was an audience hungry for more information on these destructive convulsions.

Many responses to the Messina and Calabria earthquakes demonstrated their debt to, and the opportunities for, studies of natural history. The abbé Jean-Louis Giraud Soulavie, a priest with an interest in geology, took the opportunity of the earthquakes to inquire in the *Journal de Paris* about the possibilities of a geological expedition to the Pyrénées, Provence, and the Italian mountains. In his request for fellow travelers, he reminded his readers that "the disaster that has taken place in Calabria and Messina should enliven, encourage, and even reassure any *Savant* who would like to make useful discoveries...a true Observer of Nature will discover new truths in the very disorder of nature, if I may use that senseless term;...for what seems to our eyes to be a physical disorder is but a simple phenomenon that only an erroneous imagination could consider to be a disorder."[60] Clearly Soulavie was interested in refuting the notion of disorder in nature, but as a naturalist as well as a priest.

Literary responses to the quake also suggested an appreciation of recent scientific studies, echoing Le Brun's 1756 ode. A poem on the disaster dedicated to the Comte d'Artois linked the destruction of Messina with the "restoration of the human race," comparing it to the bloodshed of war. The poet wrote that it was felicitous to give the poem to "a young Hero who seeks to familiarize himself with all the horrors of the destructive art which nevertheless assures the greatness and tranquility of Empires."[61] The author's footnotes to the poem are particularly revealing: one, following a stanza reading, "This God repairs Nature, when you believe that he destroys it," noted that philosophers and naturalists, from Aristotle to the modern day, "believed that the surface of the earth, exhausted by too much consumption, needed to be repaired, and that this renewal took place through floods and fires."[62] The author also cited Buffon and studies of the fertility of Herculaneum's soil, before finally pitching a work that he himself was working on: *Observations et de[s] Conjecture[s] pour servir à la Théorie de la Terre*, in which he hoped to "indicate the causes of a terrible phenomenon that destroys so many thousands of creatures in order to preserve new posterities."[63] Even more clearly than the texts written in the wake of Lisbon, these responses emphasized the injustice and tragedy of innocent deaths alongside the promise of preservation and even regeneration.

This optimism was echoed by the 1783 *Description historique et géographique de la ville de Messine, etc. etc., et détails historiques et météorologiques du désastre que cette ville vient d'éprouver (le 5 février 1783) par le tremblement de terre,* which described the findings of a Scottish traveler, Patrick Brydone, during his voyages to the area. Quoting Brydone, the French author wrote:

> It is strange...that Nature uses the same Agent to create and to destroy, and that the same power, which is only seen as destructive in inhabited nations, is actually that which produces them. Sicily seems to have already experienced the sentence pronounced against all the world, but, like the Phoenix,

we have seen it reborn from its own ashes more beautiful and brilliant than ever before. We still glimpse, everywhere, the traces of these terrible revolutions; despite their violence, their effects have been beneficial.[64]

This providential, but not retributive, language treated earthquakes—even earthquakes as damaging as the one that had ravaged Calabria—as a source of rebirth and creation.

Even those witnesses who did attempt to impose a logic of a punishing God on the earthquakes did so in direct response to the deistic and naturalized explanations that seemed to prevail. One cleric, writing in April, defined his stance as a rejection of naturalists' theories.

When a violent earthquake manages to open abysses with a sudden explosion, swallow up large towns, disturb entire provinces, and in a single instant put to death more people than ten bloody battles, the vain and blind Naturalist will pompously describe for you the terrible furnaces that nature has buried in the entrails of the earth; he will tell you with ostentation that this same nature amasses little by little, in its laboratories that are inaccessible to our explorations and our eyes, sulfur, *bitume,* oils, salts, carbon, and earth; that these materials that remain cold and numb while they are isolated, acquire by their union and mixing...an awesome activity.[65]

Yet, he asked, who put those materials there? Who put them into motion? In describing the naturalist as prideful, as "pompous" and "ostentat[ious]," the writer suggested that there were truths beyond the scientist's gaze, and went on to explain that it was God who had made these "furnaces" and the mixing of their materials possible. In responding to the ubiquitous naturalist theories, the conservative writer did not deny their possible veracity. Nor did he treat the earthquake as something anomalous. Rather, he sought to integrate the natural theories with his own notions of divine creation of the earth and divine punishment for sinners.[66] Again, the natural world was not a place of disorder and purposelessness, but a teleological space in which all that was, was for the best, and even apparent tragedies and injustices had a salutary role.

At the heart of the discussions after both Lisbon and Calabria was the question of order in the midst of apparent disorder. Earthquakes were something aberrant, even monstrous, in their infrequency and unpredictability. Yet, as Grégory Quenet has made clear in his thorough study of eighteenth-century earthquakes, in the decades between Lisbon and Calabria, earthquakes became normalized to a certain extent: while they remained terrifying, they were nonetheless recognized as events with a long history.[67] Part of this shift took place as a result of the scientific vogue for collecting data on earthquakes and demonstrating their ubiquity; the 1752 *Histoire des anciennes révolutions du globe terrestre* included a long list of earthquakes from the death of Jesus until the present day.[68] Likewise, the *Collection académique*, an encyclopedic journal that translated significant texts into French, published in 1761 a "Liste chronologique des éruptions des volcans, des tremblements de terre, de quelques faits météorologiques les plus remarquables, des comètes, des maladies pestilentielles, etc., jusqu'en 1760," which was no less than 189 pages long. The entry for 1755 alone comprised fourteen pages.[69] These collections imposed a regularity on earthquakes and, particularly in the case of the *Collection académique*, attempted to find discernible patterns; in the words of Jeff Loveland, "Behind [this] work lay the hope that, from a viewpoint encompassing several millennia, earthquakes would turn out to be regular, not accidental."[70] By demonstrating the frequency and ubiquity of earthquakes, scholars hoped to establish them as a normal part of the earth's operations.[71]

Matthew Mulcahy has recognized a similar transformation in responses to hurricanes in the British Caribbean. Hurricanes were, by the end of the seventeenth century, more often "portrayed...as part of the larger natural order rather than as wondrous and unusual deviations from it" and were seen less as punishment for particular sins than as inherent parts of the divinely ordained natural order.[72] Not only were they necessary, but they were also potentially beneficial; as Pierre de Charlevoix, a French traveler and Jesuit missionary in North America, noted, "Providence...often gain[s its] ends by means that seem most contrary to [it]...[hurricanes are] as necessary to the well-being of things as calm and sunshine."[73] Charles Bonnet, author of the popular *Contemplation de la Nature,* likewise saw the benefits of hurricanes, explaining that when air's equilibrium was disrupted, "it causes tempests and hurricanes; but even this impetuosity has its utility: the air thereby sheds its damaging vapors, and the waters...are protected from a fatal corruption."[74] As chapters 3 and 5 describe in more detail, the same beneficent characteristics were also attributed to lightning bolts, which were seen as necessary to maintaining a natural equilibrium in the atmosphere, and volcanic eruptions, which came to be seen as potentially creative and restorative.

Significantly it was this story, of an ordered world and a beneficial outcome to disaster, that was repeated and emphasized in the years leading up to the French Revolution. By and large, witnesses of natural disasters throughout France would not, or could not, see them as entirely arbitrary

and meaningless. Tragic? Of course. Terrifying? No doubt. But surely—
surely—they had some purpose. In this sense, Voltaire, and his refusal to
accept a God or a Providence that could look with such dispassion or even
malice on its own creation, was a unique exception. Some writers agreed
with him—Delisle de Sales's *Philosophie de la Nature* refused to see the benefits of earthquakes, and several naturalists did not impose any kind of
beneficial or providential reading—but, strikingly, the story that was told
in the wake of these eighteenth-century disasters was one of order and
balance. Lisbon, by the 1780s, had not become evidence either of God's
destructive power or of His absence from the world, but rather could be
evoked as an example of regeneration and integrated into a narrative
about a purposed and restorative Nature.

The long-term philosophical lessons of Lisbon were not, as Voltaire
hoped and Neiman asserted, a rejection of providential understandings
of disaster but, instead, a normalization of disorder within a teleological
narrative of regeneration and order. By 1784 Bernardin de Saint-Pierre
would discuss Lisbon in his *Etudes de la Nature* not as an example of a
punishing God, or as an indication of an anomalous natural event, but
in his description of the feelings of the divine aroused by ruins. Ruins,
Bernardin maintained, not only gave rise to ideas of the sublime and of
human transience, as Denis Diderot had suggested they did in his critiques of ruins in salon paintings; they also elevated man to the divine
by causing detachment from "worldly" things.[75] Bernardin wrote, "When
Lisbon was overturned by an earthquake, its inhabitants, in escaping from
their houses, embraced one another, the great and the small, friends and
enemies, inquisitors and Jews, known and unknown; each one shared his
clothes and his supplies with those who had nothing."[76] The disaster was
actually a moment of sentimental unity and harmony. Nature, he insisted,
made everything, even ruins of disaster, more beautiful: "As [Nature] always edifies even while it destroys, it allows, emerging from the very cracks
of our monuments,... [flowers, fruits, and grasses], all the rock-dwelling
[*saxatiles*] plants that create, with their blossoms and their placement, the
most beautiful contrasts with the rocks."[77] Even the most destructive impulses of nature gave rise to beautiful harmonies.

Significantly, Bernardin de Saint-Pierre did not suggest that Lisbon had
been a divine punishment, or that the deaths caused by the earthquake
had been deserved, but instead indicated that it led to more beneficent
outcomes: harmony among peoples and beauty amid ruins.[78] The tragedy of the moment was not so much justified as it was silenced. And the
sentiment aroused by the disaster was pity, but pity fused with a sense of

the sublime. Indeed, accounts of Lisbon and Calabria alike had emphasized the awe provoked by the spectacle of natural destruction. In the
words of one observer in Messina, "The black color, the burning of everything around, an odor of sulfur, the continual trembling: all this was
made by nature to inspire terror. At times, we could only contemplate it,
as if stupefied, but much more in admiration than in fear."[79] The detritus
of natural disaster evoked faith rather than Voltaire's doubt, awe rather
than penitence.

Although he did not evoke the sublimity of disaster, the popular journalist Louis-Sébastien Mercier reminded his readers of the benefits of
the Lisbon earthquake in an article in his *Tableau de Paris* in the 1780s.
Echoing the argument that Goudar had laid out in the immediate aftermath of the quake, Mercier imagined the possible destruction of Paris, re-
calling some of the natural disasters that resonated with the French public
at the time. Not only did he describe Herculaneum and Pompeii, and the
remnants they left behind for future centuries, he also appealed to the
legacy of Lisbon, as both a warning and, in a sense, a reassurance:

> We have seen in the blink of an eye a capital buried beneath its ruins; forty-
> five thousand people struck dead; the fortunes of two hundred thousand
> subjects destroyed...what a tableau of the vicissitudes of human affairs! This
> terrible phenomenon happened on the first of November 1755. And yet,
> this lightning bolt that destroyed everything saved Portugal from a political
> standpoint; it was conquered until this disaster, which gave rise to its ref-
> ormation, equalized individual fortunes, reunited hearts and minds, and
> diverted the revolutions that were menacing it.[80]

To Mercier, this tragedy was, in fact, Lisbon's salvation. Indeed, looking
back thirty years later, Lisbon had become a well-planned and beautiful,
"Enlightened," city, the envy of many European communities. And to
Mercier, the admitted tragedy of the earthquake was what prevented far
worse and more "menacing" revolutions from taking place.

Politically, as in Goudar's and Mercier's accounts; spiritually, as in Bernardin de Saint-Pierre's; or physically, as the French translator of Patrick
Brydone suggested, earthquakes could regenerate the very ground they
destroyed. In part because of scientific inquiry, earthquakes, like hurricanes, were integrated into a narrative that normalized them and that
treated violence as a necessary component of the natural world rather than
an anomaly. The natural world was therefore a space of justice and order
for many eighteenth-century savants. The story of natural violence that
was passed down in the 1780s was not, ultimately, Voltaire's but, rather, was

a tale that mixed the sublime with the sentimental, the secular with the providential. In this sense Bernardin de Saint-Pierre's *Paul et Virginie* may well be the true novel of eighteenth-century catastrophe: the two young characters in the title lived amid nature's bounty on Mauritius, exemplifying a virtuous and uncorrupted life. Yet nature, source of their joy and their virtue, was also the source of their greatest sorrow: Virginie died in a terrible storm—a hurricane, a phenomenon that Bernardin, in volume 1 of his *Etudes,* had suggested was produced by Nature to purify the waters of the sea.[81] Devastated by grief, Paul was consoled by an old friend, the narrator of the tale, who told him, "Virginie still lives. My son, see that everything changes on the earth, and that nothing is lost."[82] Nature was a space of fecundity and virtue, but also a space of constant change and yet endless self-perpetuation.

Responses to the Lisbon and Messina earthquakes exemplify the public's interest in, and perception of, the natural world. The discussions in various venues—including novels, poetry, natural histories, and newspapers—about the disasters reveal a public that was deeply engaged in the workings of the natural world. They suggest the overlap between the philosophical, literary, and scientific realms, as poetry drew on recent scientific inquiries; as aesthetics, theology, and natural catastrophe collided in Bernardin de Saint-Pierre; and as Voltaire chose a novel as his vehicle for his philosophical response to optimism. Responses to these natural crises introduce a French readership that was interested not only in nature that could be categorized in natural history *cabinets* or pinned down in private collections, or in a pastoral vision of nature like that evoked by Rousseau, but also in nature as an active, creative, and sometimes destructive force.

And the lesson presented by a number of these discussions, Voltaire's skepticism notwithstanding, was one of faith: not necessarily faith in divine intervention in human affairs, or in a punishing God who used earthquakes or hurricanes to punish sinners—although that explanation for destructive events can still be found even today—but faith in the natural world to sustain itself, to be working toward an equilibrium or establishing a more ordered universe. Thus the discourses emerging in the wake of natural disasters provided a means of ordering a world that sometimes appeared to be in disarray and often affirmed a providential understanding of the natural world, justified not by past sins but by future outcomes. The providence understood by late-eighteenth-century French men and women was not necessarily retributive, but instead relied on faith in an as-yet-unforeseen future. What is more, the idea that nature and society, or nature and politics, could follow the same laws, as suggested by groups like the mesmerists and the physiocrats, made naturalized language a discourse that was applicable to the political sphere. Unwittingly, natural historians and students of the natural world provided members of the revolutionary generation with a means of conceptualizing political change, and with an authorization of activity that was providential without being explicitly religious.

In 1793, B. E. Manuel, a naturalist who proposed using natural history as the basis of a republican education, submitted his outline for a revolutionary education program in a text titled *L'Etude de la Nature*. In its introduction he asked a pertinent question for a France in crisis: "Will liberty triumph?" The answer he provided, however, reflected a providentialism inherited from studies of nature and inflected with the notion of physical necessity:

> Yes, but it is less true less because of the will of man, and more by the force of principles and the necessary course of things....The time has come when, in the political order of nations as in the physical order of worlds, the small masses should obey the great ones, and that these great masses, after more or less violent crises, more or less tumultuous eruptions, and more or less salutary purifications [*dépurations*], should finally find within themselves the eternal relationships that constitute the organization of Nature. The book of Destiny is open. The march of events is outlined, and no human force can stop its course.[83]

Manuel, a member of Paris's Society for Natural History, applied the lessons he had drawn from natural history to the political world; the reign of liberty was inevitable not because of, but in spite of, human will. The path of the Revolution was determined by physical necessity, and the difficulties—the crises, eruptions, and purges—that man had endured on the path were but steps toward the ultimate realization of the Revolution's end. The Revolution took place in a unique moment, in a time when the natural world could be dissociated from the divine but was still imbued with agency and providential purpose; when the language of the natural world was widespread and compelling; and when the laws of the natural world were seen as capable of shaping political and social operations. These factors did not make the revolutionaries' use of natural language inevitable, but they did make that discourse "thinkable" as a means of conceptualizing political change, and particularly violent political change. It is to that political discourse that we now turn.

2

TERRIBLE LIKE AN EARTHQUAKE

Violence as a "Revolution of the Earth"

On 1 December 1792, Louis-Marie Prudhomme's *Révolutions de Paris* assessed Parisian theater in the wake of the revolution of 10 August 1792. The fall of the monarchy on that day had brought an end to several counterrevolutionary productions and a burst of new patriotic ones, and yet it was a play performed under the guise of patriotism that was lambasted in the republican Prudhomme's journal: *L'Apothéose de Beaurepaire,* playing at the Theater of the Nation. The newspaper charged that *L'Apothéose,* despite having been written in honor of the recent martyr of the Revolution Nicolas-Joseph de Beaurepaire, in fact was spreading destructive, divisive, and counterrevolutionary propaganda.

Beaurepaire, the defeated general at the Battle of Verdun, became a symbol of revolutionary bravery when he chose to commit suicide rather than surrender to the enemy. The play attempted to commemorate the transportation of his ashes to the Pantheon, and the reviewer, likely Prudhomme himself, had anticipated a beautiful retelling of his heroic actions.[1] "Everyone already knows [the story]," he wrote, "but it would have been a pleasure to hear it adorned with all the charms of poetry."[2] But he was disappointed; instead of re-creating the glorious pantheonization, the play's characters instead began to complain about the people of Paris, culminating in a "violent jeremiad" against the events of September 2 and 3, 1792—days marked by the events known as the September Massacres. The reviewer accused the playwright of attempting to raise old divisions among a population that had finally grown peaceful. Vilifying, or even blaming, the people for the massacres showed a disrespect for the project of the Revolution. Indeed, it was the same as blaspheming the decisions of God. Prudhomme wrote:

> You ['*petits intrigants*'] are forever reproaching Paris for the popular judgments of September 2 and 3; they were terrible like the earthquake that

struck Lisbon. Did pious souls accuse Providence of a crime? Nothing happens on the earth, they said, without the order and permission of God. *Voilà,*
100,000 victims crushed beneath the ruins of an entire city that had been
overturned in the blink of an eye. Apparently it is God who chastises man;
one must adore and fall silent.

Fall silent, then, too, you petty schemers, and do not use newspapers, our
city walls, or the theater to slander the people over the slightest thing, and
to continually reproach them for a moment of inevitable severity, an act of
justice and even of vengeance.[3]

Prudhomme did not attempt to deny the atrocity of the massacres; indeed, the very edition in which the review of the *Apotheosis* appeared
opened with two gruesome engravings: one of a massacre of refractory
priests, the other of the prisoners of the Prison de la Force. These images
portrayed beheadings both in progress and completed, with bloodied
heads lying alongside revolutionary "judges." Prudhomme was certainly
not involved in an attempt to cloak the violence of the bloody days in
September. Instead, he wanted to silence opposition to it by drawing analogy to an event that had terrified and troubled all of Europe forty years
earlier: the Lisbon earthquake. Like the theodicies that emerged in the
earthquake's wake, Prudhomme's justifications did not rely explicitly on
the necessary guilt of those that died, but instead on the inevitability of
the act. Doubt was unproductive, even disrespectful; if the sorrows caused
by Lisbon could be excused, so, too, could the sorrows caused by a new
providence: the people.

Prudhomme's use of the Lisbon earthquake to describe the massacres
was rare, if not exceptional, even among his fellow supporters of the *septembriseurs'* actions. Yet the issues that he raised about the inevitability of
the events, and their relationship with the natural world, were certainly
not extraordinary; nor was his ultimate argument that they represented
steps toward a future good. The rhetoric emerging from debates about
the September Massacres indicates that a kind of secular providentialism
was enunciated by several supporters of the Revolution, in which the people became an unstoppable, omniscient, and ultimately benevolent force
that nevertheless wrought necessary destruction.

Many of these same arguments had already been developed in the wake
of another set of gruesome, if lesser-known, prison massacres. On the evening of 16 October 1791, the city of Avignon, newly annexed from the
papacy, had erupted in shocking violence. Sixty prisoners, both men and
women, held at the Palais des Papes had been executed by a throng of
pro-revolutionary patriots, their bodies thrown into the Glacière Tower.[4]

Within days the events became notorious as reports began to spread not only back to Paris, where legislators faced the question of how to handle their newly adopted territory, but also abroad, where opponents of the Revolution saw the massacres as evidence of the bloodthirsty character of the impassioned revolutionaries. Despite widespread horror in the wake of the events, the Legislative Assembly, in March of 1792, voted to extend an amnesty to the perpetrators of the "Glacière Massacres." The amnesty was based on two important ideas: first, that a revolution necessarily entailed violence and that people could not be held accountable for their actions as a result and, second, that the Revolution was over, and that any of its attendant consequences could now be forgotten. All crimes committed since the start of the Revolution that had the Revolution as their basis could be forgiven and forgotten. An analysis of the amnesty and the debates in the assembly reveals the foundations of a justification of violence as an inseparable component of revolution: revolutions, according to this logic, returned polities to a state in which violence was not only inevitable but unpunishable.

Two massacres, less than one year apart: both ostensibly in favor of the Revolution, although both sullying its very name with their horrifying violence. The debates about these events crystallized understandings of revolutionary violence—violence that was destructive, graphic, even terrifying, and that required explanation and justification. The notoriety of the murders demanded that the violent acts could not be ignored. In the legislative bodies of revolutionary France, these two moments marked times when the relationship between revolution and violence was thrown into question. Ultimately these debates reveal a logic that emphasized the inevitability and the necessity of the crimes, based on a justification that privileged a future good over a past misstep, or *égarement,* a term that was often used in describing the violence. According to this logic, it was *revolution itself* that made such violence necessary. And it was revolutions of the natural world, not the political one, that provided the grounds for this reasoning: a natural "revolution" signaled a series of events, some destructive, that were nevertheless necessary results of terrestrial convulsions.

These debates portrayed a revolution not of willed actors, but one of *necessity,* in which certain unpleasant events were merely inevitable by-products of the revolutionary dynamic. They demonstrate the Revolution's intellectual debt to the subject of natural history, and provide insight into the justifications of violence that would emerge under the Republic and the Terror. But there is also a difference between them: the debates over the Glacière Massacres took place in a moment in which it was believed that the Revolution had ended; the September Massacres, in a moment in which the Revolution seemed to stretch forward into an indefinite future. In the latter case, the justifications of violence likewise shifted toward the future, treating violence not only as an inevitable component of revolution, but as essential to its completion. Like the damages from revolutions in nature, no blame could be assessed for the damage wrought by these necessary consequences of revolution.

The Glacière Massacres: Avignon, 1791

In March of 1792, when the Legislative Assembly of France turned its attention from the gathering storms of war on their borders and fixed their eyes on the town of Avignon, they confronted a city mired in conflict. A papal territory for five hundred years, it was annexed by revolutionary France on 14 September 1791. Papal adherents and nascent revolutionaries clashed repeatedly in the town and its surrounding region; the tensions between the religious authority of the Pope and the political authority of France had already been strained by the 1790 Civil Constitution of the Clergy, which had prompted a papal condemnation. Their troubles came to a head on 16 October 1791. On that day broadsheets titled "Avis aux bons patriotes" began to appear throughout Avignon, excoriating the recent actions of the town's patriots, who had begun removing the city's church bells for use as scrap metal.[5] Augmenting the effect of these *affiches* was a quickly spreading rumor that the statue of the Virgin Mary in the Church of the Cordeliers was shedding tears of sorrow and anger at this defacement. A later investigation would reveal that the Virgin's face had been streaked with varnish and cinnabar to resemble tears.[6] To avenge her sorrow, a group of devout Catholics allegedly dragged Nicolas Jean-Baptiste Lescuyer, a prominent patriot, to the church, stabbing him and leaving him for dead. One witness saw him at the foot of the altar, "covered in wounds and blood," being struck by small children and adults alike.[7]

Lescuyer's fellow patriots, including the infamous Mathieu Jourdan, who claimed to have played a role in the storming of the Bastille and had acquired the sobriquet "Coupe-Tête," did not take the news of Lescuyer's death lightly.[8] They swore an oath to avenge his death and then arrested fifty or sixty citizens, locking them in the prisons of the Palais des Papes.[9] There, in the words of the secretary of the National Assembly, "all were slaughtered," their bodies thrown into a tower most commonly used as a latrine and covered with quicklime.[10] As one commentator on the events, L. S. Boisdesir, stated, "Men, women, the elderly, children, none was spared; it was necessary that anyone who was supposed to be an enemy of these brigands should die."[11] The events defied description; Boisdesir went on to write, "O spectacle of horror!...My pen refuses to describe it."[12] As Michelet poetically wrote in his *Histoire de la Révolution*, the event "entered the memory by the most secure path: fear. And it could not be erased."[13]

That same horrified ineffability marked the exposition of the events in the Legislative Assembly. On 17 November 1791, Pierre Edouard Lemontey, the secretary of the Assembly, read a letter detailing the massacres from the commissioners sent by the state to the troubled city. Though they had hoped to find the reports of massacre exaggerated, they reported, they found the truth to have been much worse than the rumors. In reading their description of the massacres, Lemontey's reading was interrupted several times by "movements of horror" in the audience, and he himself broke down in tears, eventually forced to abandon his reading.[14] Despite the horror that Boisdesir and Lemontey struggled to express, and despite the indelible mark that Michelet alleged was left on the French memory by the Glacière Massacres, the Legislative Assembly adopted a policy of *forgetfulness* toward the events: they granted an amnesty to their perpetrators, calling their crimes "relative to the revolution."

The question that faced the Legislative Assembly in March 1792—a full five months after the killings had taken place—was whether an amnesty, passed in the waning days of the Constituent Assembly, and aimed at providing a clean slate for the start of the new constitutional monarchy, would be extended to the crimes committed in Avignon in October 1791. Based on the language of the amnesty, only crimes that were related to the progress of the Revolution were eligible for governmental mercy. As a result, in their March debates, the members of the Legislative Assembly revealed their own understanding of "revolution" and of the role of violence in that revolution. By arguing that the Glacière Massacres were inherent in the processes of revolution, several members of the Legislative Assembly suggested that both the Revolution and its violence were outside human control and, instead, were subject to laws and a logic much more akin to the processes of the natural world.

The original amnesty had, by one of history's coincidences, been passed into law on the very day that Avignon gained entry into the French nation: 14 September 1791. On that day the question of Avignon's integration into France was decided upon in the National Assembly. Deputies on the right, including the comte de Clermont-Tonnerre, had argued for days against accepting the turbulent region before the establishment of peace within the territory.[15] However, in an impassioned and ultimately convincing speech, Baron de Menou proffered that the integration would be beneficial to both France and the Comtat, that the citizens of Avignon definitively had chosen to become a part of France, and, finally, that "humanity and national honor" required the Assembly to heed that wish.[16] In response to claims about the violence of the region, Menou offered an explanation that would prove eerily resonant several months later: "All the passions that stir men have unfurled there with that violence that is *inseparable* from a time of revolution.... These are, Messieurs, the physical and moral causes of the movements that are taking place in the two regions [*pays*] whose destinies are subjected to your deliberations."[17] The violence in the area was nascent in revolution itself; its causes were both physical and moral. From its debut onto the French stage, Avignon was seen as embroiled in violence wrought by the conditions of revolution.

The Assembly voted for the integration of Avignon and immediately turned its attention to a decree proposed by M. Bon-Albert Briois de Beaumetz in the name of the committees of the Constitution and criminal jurisprudence. The previous day, the king had raised the idea of an amnesty in a rather transparent attempt at clearing the names of those who had helped him during his failed flight from France in June. Louis XVI promised to accept the Constitution over which the National Assembly had been toiling; as a mark of the new nation created by their labors, he suggested that the past be forgotten and all "accusations and proceedings that have only the events of the Revolution as a cause [*pour principe*]" be put to rest.[18] This was important, he explained, "to soften the damages that a great Revolution always entails."[19] The king, like the radical Menou, pointed out that "a revolution" necessarily created troubles and damages; his proclaimed goal was to alleviate the pains wrought by the experience. In response, Briois de Beaumetz offered his proposed amnesty on the 14th, which was passed as a means of ending the Revolution and establishing solidarity and peace:

> The National Assembly, considering that the object of the French Revolution was to give the Empire a Constitution, and therefore that the Revolution should end at the moment when the Constitution is completed and accepted by the king; Considering that it will henceforth be illegal [*coupable*] to resist the constituted authorities and the laws, and that it is fit for the French nation to forget the marks of opposition against the national will before it had been generally recognized..., and that the time has come

to extinguish all dissension in favor of a common sentiment of patriotism, fraternity, and affection for the monarch...[decrees that] all legal investigations into facts relative to the Revolution, whatever their object, and all judgments rendered in similar instances, are irrevocably abolished.[20]

In the coming weeks, the amnesty would be extended to include deserters from the military and the mutinous soldiers of Chateauvieux, all for "crimes that are due to the Revolution."[21]

In many ways the king's proposed amnesty did not differ dramatically from amnesties that had been applied under the Ancien Régime: the *Encyclopédie* defined a *lettre d'amnistie* as "a general pardon, accorded by the king to people who have enacted acts of hostility or have revolted."[22] The *Dictionnaire universel des sciences morale, économique, politique, et diplomatique* described amnesty as "a forgetting, and a general pardon of all past offenses...a pardon that a Sovereign accords to his subjects, after a revolt or an uprising."[23] Yet the amnesty of 1791 suggested a slightly different approach to legislative "forgetting": under the Old Regime, amnesty was an act of munificence that established peace, not an exoneration of the initial act. The 1791 amnesty suggested that the original crime was itself irreproachable for two reasons: first, because law emerged from the general will, and therefore before that will was "generally recognized" no law could be applied, and second, particularly in the language of the king's request, because revolution and violence were inseparable, such that violence was "entailed" by revolution. The king's 1791 request for amnesty sought to demonstrate justice and to create the foundations of peace, but based on the notion that the crimes themselves were, in a sense, blameless: they were not the acts of vengeful individuals, but were acts that arose naturally out of the dynamic of revolution itself.

The question facing the Legislative Assembly in March of 1792, then, was whether this amnesty of September 1791 could be applied to the events in Avignon on October 16 and 17. The notion of applying the amnesty to the crimes of Avignon was first raised by a Moselle deputy, Jean-Pierre Couturier, on 16 March 1792.[24] Noting the coincidence of the amnesty law and the admission of Avignon to the French body, he maintained that "the crimes committed in Avignon...should also be remitted by this law"; the crimes, he argued, were the result of "*l'égarement*" and of a population divided by the machinations of "seditious priests."[25] He therefore proposed his decree:

> The law of amnesty of 14 September 1791 will take effect and will be extended to the Avignonnais...; by which all proceedings begun for crimes commit-

ted previously amid such circumstances and troubles and insurrections will cease the day that the present decree is accepted.[26]

In the three days of debate that followed Couturier's proposal, it was not the facts of the Glacière Massacres that were at issue but, rather, the question of what was in fact "relative to revolution."[27] On 19 March the debates were concluded, and the Assembly voted by acclamation for the extension of the amnesty. The final wording of the decree that ultimately satisfied both sides of the assembly offered amnesty to any "crime relatif à la Révolution" committed in Avignon until 8 November 1791, without explicitly noting whether that definition applied to the massacres.[28] The job of discerning that fact was, on 26 March, given to a tribunal in Avignon, who in August 1792 finally ordered the release of all prisoners held in the wake of the Glacière Massacres, in a document echoing many of the defenses that had been offered by the amnesty's supporters in the legislature.[29]

The debates in the Legislative Assembly over the extension of the amnesty were deeply polarized; almost all the individuals who spoke on behalf of the amnesty would soon be affiliated with either the Girondins or the Mountain, including Pierre Vergniaud, Elie Guadet, Marc-David Lasource, Jean-Antoine Grangeneuve, and Claude Basire.[30] Indeed, these political divisions were so clear that when an emissary from Avignon came to protest the application of the amnesty, he unwittingly chose a seat on the left side of the assembly hall following his speech, and Basire pointedly told him there was no place for him on that side.[31] Given that the perpetrators of the Glacière Massacres were among Avignon's most ardent patriots, this constellation of political affiliations was not surprising. What *was* surprising, however, was the *argument* with which these deputies, and their supporters in Avignon, defended the amnesty. Emerging from the debates is not only a fascinating vision of revolution held by the more leftist members of the Legislative Assembly, but also a justification of revolutionary violence that would find echoes in justifications of both the September Massacres and the Terror.

First, in the minds of the speakers on both sides of the Legislative Assembly, the Revolution was over. They portrayed themselves as having weathered the Revolution: they were surveying the damages of a past event, not continuing to legislate in a revolutionary moment. And it was the wisdom of hindsight that allowed them to grant the amnesty. In the words of Lasource: "If the decree of amnesty accorded at the end of the French Revolution erased all the crimes relative to that revolution, then the decree of amnesty should also be pronounced at the end of the

Avignon revolution, and should erase all the crimes relative to [it]."[32] It was only with the virtue of hindsight, and with the prospect of peace and solidity, that the deputies could efface the transgressions of the previous period. In this respect the amnesty was very much in line with Old Regime ideas of amnesty: Emerich de Vattel, in his work on natural law in international circles, had noted that "Amnesty is a perfect forgetting of the past, and since a Peace [between nations] is destined to nullify all the causes of discord, this should be the first article of a treaty."[33] The conflict had to be over, and its consequences determined, before an amnesty could be offered.

Yet, in looking back on the Revolution, legislators found that the past was not merely riddled with crimes that were best forgotten, but that it was woven with misdeeds that were inherent in revolution itself. These past crimes were not merely forgivable; they were *not punishable*. Advocates of the amnesty's extension professed a vision of revolution indicating that the Revolution had returned the city of Avignon to a state of nature, and therefore that the crimes committed there could not be punished by the laws of society. Jean-Baptiste Mailhe stated in his discourse of March 16 that "Law no longer had any power [in Avignon before their union with France]; they were in true anarchy; they were…like men wandering in the forests, before the institution of societies."[34] A judge assigned to the case made this point even more clearly, saying that this state of nature was a necessary result of the Revolution itself. Great revolutions, he alleged, *remade* men and completely transformed the bonds of society—which made law itself a tenuous concept in a revolutionary moment. Revolution made a social contract and therefore the rule of law impossible. "What good is Law amid this complete disorganization?" he asked. "Born from the very unison of society, produced by the general will, sustained by public force which is itself only the force of the social pact, [Law] remains in inertia while this society is divided."[35] If society was a collective body that created and enforced law, revolution had cast men, for a brief time, *out of society*, and therefore out of law.

Not only did revolution transform the rule of law, but it also transformed justice by removing the efficacy of exemplary punishment. This was an aspect of the argument put forth by Pierre Vergniaud. In his speech of 19 March, after declaring that certain crimes were inevitable in "great revolutions," he stated: "Such great revolutions are not annual, but rare." By emphasizing the exceptionality of the event, Vergniaud argued that punishment would not be able to accomplish its purpose, namely, to serve as an example to prevent the same crime from being committed again. "Do you believe that the memory of your scaffolds could prevent the fermentation of passions?"[36] The transparency of crime and punishment was ruptured by the very infrequency of the event. Revolutionary crimes were of an altogether different species than ordinary crimes, and to punish crimes of a great revolution would serve no future purpose. Indeed, in these debates, it was the *future*, not the past, that the legislature was urged to consider: Basire emphasized that it would be impolitic to keep focused on the past; rather, "it is with the future that the legislative body...should primarily occupy itself; it is to [the future] that it must sacrifice everything."[37] Given the extraordinary nature of the Revolution itself, and the fact that no future good could be served, prosecuting the Glacièristes was a waste of time and a violation of the principles of punishment.

Legislators also distinguished between public and private crimes, arguing that private crimes, which were based on personal vengeance, were punishable by law, while public crimes were "relative to revolution" and therefore should be amnestied. Randon, the judge called upon to explain the application of the law in Avignon, stated, "I call [a crime relative to revolution] any crime that is born in the revolution and that is committed by one party acting against another party.... When the individual acts alone, one can believe that he is acting out of private interest. But when it is a *body* that acts, one should believe that its only goal is the public interest."[38] Although the distinction between public and private crimes was as old as Roman law, the debates over the Glacière Massacres tied the idea of a public crime to the process of revolution itself. Filled with love of his country, and motivated by the public good, the patriotic Avignonnais "saw as an enemy all those who drove away public happiness, and thus, acting on behalf of...[the public good], he sacrificed to it all those who wanted to overthrow it."[39] Thus the prisoners held in the Avignon case had believed that they were acting in a "revolutionary" way, that is, in a way that sought to promote the elusive public good at any cost.

By making public crimes "relative to revolution," the rhetoric of the supporters of amnesty linked the transgressions of the Avignon patriots with the good of the Revolution as a whole. Far from being individuals seeking revenge for the death of a friend, the Glacière participants were motivated *by* revolution and *for* revolution. Not only did revolution, in these justifications, transform the very status of law by returning man to a state of nature and by removing the efficacy of punishment, it made violence *necessary* by fusing the public good with acts of violence. Public crimes—crimes eligible for amnesty—were, according to the Avignon tribunal, "born in the *effervescence* of spirits and the shock of passions."[40]

In fact, the words *effervescence, agitation,* and *secousses* appeared in almost every speech in favor of the amnesty. Significantly, the language legislators used to talk about the crimes was one of *physical necessity:* "effervescence" was a term drawn from physical science, used to describe the reaction produced by the merging of two substances; *secousse* was used primarily to describe medical or natural crises.[41] Though these words had other uses by the end of the eighteenth century, their prevalence in these speeches suggests a view of revolution in which disruptions were inherent, similar to inevitable disruptions in the natural world. According to this logic, revolutions necessarily caused upheaval, disruptions, and agitations that could neither be controlled nor stopped. Indeed, this language and logic had been used soon after the passage of the original 1791 amnesty; Adrien Duport addressed the Assembly on 16 November and presented a letter he had circulated to courts throughout France that encouraged as broad an application of the amnesty as possible. It read:

> A Revolution as widespread [*générale*] as that which has just been carried out [*vient de s'opérer*] in the French government,…could not but be felt in the constant and inalterable order that constitutes social harmony. The brusque passage from the old state to the state of liberty was necessarily accompanied by violent convulsions [*secousses*], and consequently by great disorders.[42]

Duport's language here is revealing: he used a reflexive verb, *s'opérer,* to describe the action of revolution; the revolution itself had a momentum and a power of its own. It had *necessary consequences,* in the form of *secousses* and disorder. Given Duport's background as a member of Mesmer's coterie, a group that attempted to cure medical disorders by provoking a crisis, he may well have envisioned this "brusque passage" in quite physical terms.[43] Vergniaud used this very idea to defend the extension of the pardon when he took to the podium in March. He stated: "We are not talking about ordinary crimes; we are talking about crimes committed in the effervescence that always accompanies great revolutions."[44] Like Duport, Vergniaud employed the language of natural science to describe the necessary effects of revolution.

Moreover, the crimes of Avignon not only represented the necessary consequences of revolution—consequences as inherent in the process of revolution as "effervescence" was to the combination of two chemicals—they also were portrayed as necessary to the outcome *of* the revolution. In other words, without the Revolution, the crimes would not have been committed; without the crimes, the Revolution would not have been completed. As early as 20 October, a mere three days after the massacres, a group of Avignon patriots had defended the crimes in those very terms: "If the Patriots had succumbed to so many attacks, Avignon…would have returned to papal dominion; these beautiful regions would have become the seat of the counterrevolution in France."[45] The ends in this case justified the means, which were themselves already justified by their inevitability. In the words of Brissot, writing in his newspaper *Le Patriote Français:* "Is it just to punish, with all the rigor of the laws, crimes committed during the silence of law, during a revolution and for that revolution?"[46] The Assembly, and the tribunal in Avignon, ultimately decided that it was not: the revolution created extraordinary circumstances that made punishment both unjust and impossible.

Many of the arguments that emerged in the March debates had been raised in a February letter published in Brissot's *Le Patriote Français*. Signed G. Boisguyon—presumably Gabriel Boisguyon, a member of the Paris Jacobin Club—the letter detailed the very issues that would be at the heart of the Legislative Assembly's discussions of Avignon. Like Vergniaud, he emphasized that punishment would be ineffective, since "the crimes of revolution can only be repeated in another revolution…of which examples are rare." Like the Avignon tribunal, he argued that "crimes that are inseparable from a revolution have…a public interest." And, above all, he argued that there were no willing or rational participants in revolutionary activities; instead, they were driven by a momentum beyond their control. "Whatever the atrocity of the crimes," he concluded, "they should be seen less as the act of those who guide [*conseillent*] them or execute them than as the effect of a public passion, in which each individual is only the involuntary and passive instrument of a violent agitation of the spirits, which leaves no freedom to reflect, to deliberate."[47] A revolution, far from creating opportunities for willed action and rational thought, instead forged a space of involuntary and even mechanistic activity. Crimes that were "relative to revolution" were agentless, collective, and ultimately blameless.

From these debates emerges a vision of revolution as something extraordinary, as something that returns man to a presocietal state, as something that carries with it inherent violence, and yet as something that simultaneously is concerned with the public good. Where did this idea of a revolution, as unstoppable and destructive, yet simultaneously benevolent and necessary, come from? What kind of revolution had "impetuous movements" and caused effervescence and tremors? Keith Baker, who traced the multivalent and changing meanings of "revolution" throughout the eighteenth century in his seminal essay "Inventing the French Revolution," posited that in the early days of the Revolution, these varied meanings came together to provide a vision of revolution that was willed and that opened a space for individual action; revolution, for Baker, became a "political act" and an "expression of the will of a nation."[48]

Yet the "revolution" in these 1792 debates bears far more resemblance to the ideas of revolution that Baker sees in the earlier part of the century, as "something that had already occurred, usually abruptly and without the conscious choice of human actors."[49] I am proposing an alternate intellectual source for this vision of revolution that was both destructive and constructive, and that was the product not of human will but of "effervescence" and agitation: understandings of the natural world and the revolutions in nature, not in the political realm.[50] As Baker has pointed out, the term "revolution" often signified moments of disorder and violence in the prerevolutionary period, and particularly in the popular genre of historical texts on nations' revolutions.[51] It also could connote progress and the development of a new order.[52] But only rarely were these two concepts—destruction alongside progress—explicitly linked in political writings.[53] Studies of the natural world, however, often offered uses of the term "revolution" that mirrored the vision put forth in the 1792 debates over the Glacière Massacres.

The *Encyclopédie* included numerous entries under the word "revolution," only a few of which are noted by Baker.[54] Yet one of the secondary definitions may well be the most important here: the idea of a "revolution of the earth." As the *Encyclopédie* noted, "*Révolutions de la terre* are...what naturalists call natural events, by which the face of our globe has been, and is continually, altered in its different parts by fire, air, and water."[55] Significantly the entry cross-referenced the entries on "Flood" and "Earthquakes"—subjects that emphasized the dual destruction and reconstruction of the natural world. As the previous chapter suggested, "revolution" was a term frequently applied to these terrestrial convulsions: Messina's tremors were a subject that would concern "observers of revolutions," according to the *Précis historique de la ville de Messine;* Kruger listed all the world's known earthquakes and floods in a work titled *The History of Ancient Revolutions of the Terrestrial Globe.* The French writer who quoted Patrick Brydone's description of the terrain around Messina chose to translate Brydone's reference to "terrible conflagrations" as "*révolutions terribles.*"[56] These "revolutions" of the earth were both destructive and creative. "Nature is occupied with destroying, on the one hand, to produce new bodies on the other," explained the *Encyclopédie* entry on "*Terre, révolutions de.*"[57]

In addition, natural histories of the eighteenth century emphasized the *exceptionality* of such revolutions. Indeed, their very infrequency made them almost impossible to study and to understand. Buffon, in his 1749 *Histoire Naturelle,* explained that extraordinary revolutions lay outside the normal equations of cause and effect; repeatedly he referred to earthquakes as "accidents"—necessary and natural, but outside the bounds of normal activity.[58] These were revolutions in which the normal rules simply did not apply—and Buffon described them in language that closely paralleled Vergniaud's statement that "great revolutions" like the French one were not "annual, but rare," and paralleled his conclusion that no rules could be drawn from them. "Causes whose effects are rare, violent, and sudden, should not concern us," Buffon wrote, explaining that it was only possible to discern transparent rules in operations that were constantly repeating and renewing.[59]

Charles Bonnet, a Swiss naturalist, in fact saw these "general revolutions" as the means of the earth's evolution. In his work, *La Palingénésie philosophique,* he explained, "Just as ordered [*organisés*] bodies have their phases or their particular revolutions, worlds also have theirs... Our earth has therefore also had its revolutions. I am not talking about those more or less gradual revolutions, which take place over centuries... Those types of revolutions are never more than local or partial.... I am talking about those *general* revolutions of the world that change the face of the globe entirely, and that give it a new being."[60] Likewise Dolomieu was reminded of these "general revolutions" in his studies on Messina and Calabria after the 1783 earthquakes; he wondered, "How many general revolutions has the earth that we inhabit undergone? How many times has it changed its form? We see everywhere the vestiges of its revolutions and of its catastrophes." We may never know, he insisted, how many times the earth's civilizations have been buried only to start anew.[61]

The uses of the term "revolution" were manifold in the eighteenth century, even within the natural sciences. Rhoda Rappaport has urged against an overly teleological reading of the word "revolution": in geological texts alone, "revolution" could refer to cyclical, successive, or "unidirectional changes."[62] The same writer might use it in all three ways. Geological revolutions could be "slow and tranquil," or disruptive and immediate.[63] Yet the terminology of a nascent earth science does provide a basis for the development of an idea of a revolution that was simultaneously disruptive and progressive. In the words of Alain Rey, "the changes, accidents, and revolutions of the Earth paved the way for what would be called *evolution.* Through [the idea of] a sudden upheaval, compatible with the brutalities of divine mandates passed down by the Bible,...the word *revolution* binds natural history with human history."[64] Violence, providentialism, and progress could be linked in the word "revolution," thanks largely to studies of natural history in the eighteenth century.[65]

The vision of revolution forged in the debates about the Glacière Massacres, perhaps unwittingly, replicated the vision of general revolution forged in natural histories. It is likely that many of the speakers had themselves read Buffon or another of the popular naturalist texts written over the course of the century; it is known that several of them, including Adrien Duport, had in mesmerist circles considered the role of momentary disruption in restoring order. There was a logic of revolution available in the natural realm, upon which defenders of violence in a political revolution could, and sometimes did, draw. Sometimes that model was made explicit. For instance, the great naturalist and Legislative Assembly member Bernard Germain Étienne Lacépède, in his 1790 proposal for a republican educational program, made an explicit cognitive link between natural and political revolutions. His plan for instruction featured exclusively natural history in its first year. He explained that, having started their education with the natural world, schoolchildren would better understand the vicissitudes of the political one: "Won't it appeal to [the student] even more to study moral revolutions, the birth and fall of Empires, and all the effects of genius, virtue, and passion on this earth whose physical revolutions he will have [already] studied, and on which he will have already noted the impact of the powerful force that constantly reworks, organizes, and molds the debris of all things that have been struck and destroyed by time?"[66] The revolutions of the earth could be a way of understanding the revolutions of the political realm.

What emerges from the debates over the Glacière Massacres is a justification of violence based on collective action, gesturing toward the natural world—though not yet explicitly invoking it—as a model for understanding the movements and the effervescence of revolution. What is more, the debates reveal a commonly held belief that revolution itself carried with it necessary and unstoppable turbulence; they manifested a vision of revolution that was not under human control but instead was subject to vicissitudes that could not be restrained or tamed. Yet the debates also took place in a moment in which the government believed that the Revolution had passed and that its ends had, for the most part, been met.

The very moment the Revolution ceased to be seen as over, this logic became a profoundly dangerous tool for justifying violence. What the defenders of the amnesty in Avignon saw, *in retrospect,* as an inherent part of revolution and therefore as blameless, became necessary steps toward a future and unknowable good once the "second revolution" of 10 August was under way. The overthrow of the monarchy on that date meant the start of a *new* new regime: the new governing body, the National Convention, took office on 20 September 1792 and instantiated the Republic. With the apparent continuation of revolution, the rhetoric of what was "relative to revolution" changed: violence enacted on behalf of the revolution was not only necessarily a product of that revolution and unable to be stopped; it also was necessary for the outcome of that revolution and therefore *should* not be stopped. The debates over the Glacière Massacres saw the introduction of the idea of a law of necessity, of revolutions necessarily causing disruptions and violence, and of disruption and apparent disorder as necessary to the outcome of revolution. As the members of the Legislative Assembly established peace and restored order in the troubled city of Avignon, they also laid the foundations for justifying chaos and violence as mere facts that were "relative to revolution."

The September Massacres: Paris, 1792

In the context of the Glacière debates, and the vision of revolution emerging from them, Prudhomme's comparison of the September Massacres to a historic "revolution of the earth," the Lisbon earthquake, fits into a broader discussion about the role of violence in revolution. Following the September Massacres, the vision of revolution put forth by Jacobins implied that a revolution was often uncontrollable and inherently violent but simultaneously purposed and constructive. Several of the same themes from the Avignon debates were reprised in Jacobin defenses of the uprising: they took place in an extraordinary time, and they were necessary *égarements* that were both the result of the revolutionary dynamic and necessary to a positive outcome. As Robespierre memorably asked in the wake of the massacres, "Do you want a revolution without a revolution?" implying that a revolution necessarily entailed a certain amount of disruption and violence.[67] However, although discussions of the Glacière Massacres led to a broad consensus on the Left about the inextricable relationship between the massacres and revolution, the September Massacres created a rift between Jacobins and "Brissotins" on this very issue. In fact, in *opposing* the Massacres, the Girondins reiterated a similar notion of revolution, nature, and controllability to the one they had posited during the Avignon debates, but they simultaneously refused to accept that the

September events were, in a sense, "relative to revolution." In other words, the Girondin argument rested on the idea that *if* the massacres had been spontaneous, agentless, and a product of the revolutionary dynamic, then they could not be condemned; they sought to prove, however, that the killings were the result of machinations from individuals in positions of power. Thus both the Girondins and Jacobins shared a common view of the innocence of nature and the people—natural movements and popular movements alike could not be erroneous—but ultimately took opposite stances on whether the massacres themselves were condemnable.

In addition, because the Jacobin defense of the massacres relied on a vision of revolution that was ongoing and not yet complete, a new element entered the debates that had not been prevalent in the Avignon discussion, namely, faith. As Prudhomme suggested in his discussion of the massacres, a providential justice underlay the popular uprising. Several Jacobins, and the official letter of the Paris Jacobin Club to its subsidiaries, appealed to this same vision of revolutionary violence, and particularly crowd violence; not only was it necessary, a product of revolutionary momentum, but it was also formative of a new order that could only be understood and judged after the Revolution itself was over.

On the morning of 2 September 1792, revolutionary France, having toppled its monarchy a mere three weeks prior, was under attack from enemies both internal and external: while France was in the midst of holding elections for its new governing body, the Prussian Army held the city of Verdun under siege, with its collapse imminent, and rumors of a counterrevolutionary plot brewing in the prisons of Paris circulated throughout the city streets. Over the next three days the city's prisons were raided, their prisoners dragged out into the streets and put before immediate tribunals of the people that decreed either death or freedom for suspected traitors. By the evening of 6 September, more than a thousand people had been killed, many in allegedly gruesome and spectacular ways, and Paris and France were reeling in shock and disbelief at their own citizenry's ability to commit such atrocities.[68]

While David Andress maintains that "bloodshed held no terrors for the Parisians," many eyewitnesses noted the horror and trauma of the events.[69] In November, the question of whether prisoners freed during the massacres should be retried was raised in the Convention. Dominique Joseph Garat, the minister of justice, maintained that they had already endured the death penalty, having already undergone the trauma of anticipating death: "But what does the death penalty consist of? Is it in the blow that delivers death? No, it is in the apparatus that prepares it, that announces it, that shows it, that brings it nearer to the living being. All the pain of death is therefore in its horrors, and all its horrors precede it; everything disappears once the mortal blow is struck."[70] The apparatus of the massacres—not just the penalty meted out by them—was itself terrifying. In response, Prudhomme noted the shared trauma of all who witnessed the events, not just of those who awaited punishment: "We all shared in it, we who were not even suspects. Who among Parisians was not a witness to these bloody executions? Who did not see the earth stained by these frightening marks? Who did not see cadavers obstructing streets and loaded in piles onto carts?"[71] Although it is true that the tribunals acted with some degree of justice and mercy—more than half the Abbaye's prisoners were freed, and a mere thirty-five women were executed at La Salpêtrière—they also acted with a ruthlessness and a bloodthirstiness that alarmed and horrified both legislators and a broader public.[72] Like the Glacière Massacres, their very *publicness* demanded either punishment or justification by the authorities.

In the immediate aftermath of the events, both Girondins and Jacobins expressed a certain amount of horror over the events but also shared in the attempt to justify "the people's" actions. Whereas later debates about the massacres would pit the Girondins, or "Brissotins" as they were primarily known at the time, against the Jacobins, the first few weeks of reporting and legislative discussion reveal more consensus than division. Marcel Dorigny has concluded that, between 3 and 13 September, "it seems clear that three of the principal Girondin newspapers [Gorsas's *Le Courrier des 83 départements*, Mercier's *Les Annales patriotiques et littéraires*, and Condorcet's *La Chronique de Paris*] approved of the massacres of the prisoners, did their utmost to justify them, and saw them above all as a means of defending the Revolution."[73]

The idea that the people acted out of necessity, in response to specific threats, was initially shared by authorities on both sides of the Legislative Assembly.[74] Marat, on 3 September 1792, emphasized the need for people to take justice in their own hands, stating that "the Commune of Paris hastens to inform its brothers in every department, that a portion of the ferocious conspirators held in prison have been put to death by the people, in acts of justice that seemed, to them, to be essential for restraining the legions of traitors hidden within its walls..., at the moment when they were about to march upon the enemy."[75] His language was not all that different from Condorcet's *Chronique de Paris*, where an article on 4 September proclaimed, "[It was an] unfortunate and terrible situation, in which the character of a naturally good and generous people was forced to carry out such acts of vengeance."[76] Both Condorcet and Marat emphasized the *justice* of the event in avenging traitors, as well as the necessity of their vengeance: to Marat the massacres were "essential," and to Condorcet they were "forced." And nearly all maintained that the events had been a day of shame, over which it was necessary to "throw a veil." The Jacobin Michel Azéma called the massacres "humiliating," "days of mourning and nights of darkness."[77] Jean-Marie Roland declared on 3 September, "Yesterday was a day over whose events we must perhaps leave a veil."[78] The *Chronique de Paris* asked that the Assembly "draw a curtain" over the day.[79] The consensus seemed to be that the events were just, they were necessary, and they were best forgotten—not unlike the Jacobin/Girondin stance on the Glacière Massacres.

Yet over the course of the next three months the September Massacres became a lodestar around which political constellations aligned. Dorigny sees the French victory at the battle of Valmy as the turning point from a consensus on the events toward a division; the 20 September 1792 battle reduced the imminence of the threat of overthrow by invading armies, rendering violence less urgent or necessary. After that, the Girondin account of the massacres tended to focus on the alleged machinations of radical organizers of the bloodbaths. And the veil—invoked by numerous "Brissotins" in the immediate wake of the events—became a rallying point for the Jacobins, a means of affiliating the massacres with a great, if unforeseen, future.

Amid these debates the language of nature was recurrent, powerful, and illustrative, particularly in describing collective action. On 3 September Roland, the minister of the interior, published a letter rich in natural metaphors that was read aloud to the National Assembly. Roland's invocations of the natural world revealed his shifting thoughts about the controllability of the massacres themselves. He wrote: "The anger of the people and the movement of the insurrection are comparable to the action of a torrent that overturns obstacles that no other power would have destroyed, but whose flooding will bring ravages and devastation if it is not quickly returned to its riverbed."[80] Roland's struggle with the *journée* is immediately clear. He saw the events as understandable, even natural—rivers overrun their banks, "seas, stirred by storms, continue to roar long after the tempest"—but also as mournful and alarming.[81] Above all he treated the people, and the insurrection, as natural forces, but he simultaneously believed that the events were ultimately controllable, and he insisted on the establishment of boundaries by the governing body. In Roland's metaphor, nature can and should be reined in, even if it could not always be controlled entirely.

Roland's letter also reveals a profoundly conservative view of the relationship between the people and the governing body. Rather than the people dictating their interests to the legislators, it was the legislator's job to "enlighten" the people as to their proper interests.[82] Roland retained a faith in the ability of the enlightened man to restrain, illuminate, and control the forces of nature—or, in this case, of man in his natural state. When the river runs over, it is the job of the legislator to build levies, and if he does not, then nature will continue to run its wild course. "Everything has its limits," he declared. Equilibrium could not be restored by natural forces alone. (Indeed, this letter was written on a day, 3 September, when seawalls and canals were being debated in the Legislative Assembly: the nation of France was also questioning nature's controllability in its policy decisions.)

Nearly two months later Roland would make similar points in a *rapport* delivered to the National Convention. On 29 October he admitted that "it would be absurd to claim, unjust to insist, that the *bouleversement* of a revolution did not carry with it some individual sorrows, some irregular operations; it is the fall or the loss of trees and plants near an overflowed river, whose rapid course causes damages in overcoming great obstacles."[83] Like in the Avignon debates, revolution was a natural force, entailing certain "sorrows." Yet Roland insisted on the necessity of controlling whatever could be controlled: "But we must carefully distinguish between that which belongs to the nature of things, and that which can result from the passions or premeditated plans of a few individuals; for we should endure with courage and tolerate with patience…that which comes from necessity, while we must oversee with attention, contain with force, and restrain with severity all that results from the extravagance of ambition or the machinations [*entreprises*] of wickedness."[84] In distinguishing between the uncontrollable and the contrived, he admitted that some events—namely, natural events—simply *cannot* be controlled, only endured and tolerated. But he warned against the tactic of treating the September Massacres, which Roland explicitly denounced later in the discourse, as a natural and inevitable event, urging his listeners to look with scrutiny on such attributions. Human behavior and decisions can be controlled and punished, although natural "overflows" cannot.

In Roland's discussions, that which was collective and agentless was akin to the natural world; he continued to appeal to a law of necessity linked explicitly with the world of nature. *Revolution itself* was comparable to the uncontrollable operations of nature. Yet he simultaneously sought to divorce the massacres from the logic of nature—*and of revolution*—by positing that they had been planned, and that they were the product of "ambition" and "wickedness," not collective and spontaneous action. As Roland makes clear, the questions of nature, collectivity, and controllability were at the heart of the debates about the September Massacres.

Whereas in discussions of the Avignon massacres, natural language became a means of exonerating violence, the debates over the September Massacres made appeals to human responsibility in order to condemn them. Indeed, one of the key ways of objecting to the massacres among Brissotins was finding agency within them—that is, removing them from the realm of uncontrollable nature and giving them actors, conspirators; in short, criminal parties. Brissot's means of countering the Jacobin defense was to argue *for* agency and for planning, and against necessity, providence, and nature. On 24 October, after his expulsion from the Jacobin Club, Brissot wrote, "I will prove that this atrocious scene [of the massacres] was not the effect of chance, of a spontaneous sentiment of the people; that instead it was premeditated and prepared behind closed doors [*dans le cabinet*]."[85] Brissot removed responsibility from the people of Paris themselves, attempting to demonstrate that the massacres were not collective but were engineered by a small group of conspirators. To place *individual reflection and action* at their basis was to remove the massacres from the realm of the necessary and the natural and, indeed, of the revolutionary.

Similarly, Vergniaud, who had argued so passionately for the uncontrollability and "effervescence" of the Glacière Massacres, offered one of the first and most strident condemnations of the carnage of early September. On 17 September he declared, "If we only had the people to fear, I would say that we had everything to hope for, for the people are just and abhor crime."[86] "The people" were inherently innocent and just. But the massacre was *not* merely the people at work, but instead was the project of a series of conspirators, including "the satellites of Coblenz" and "detestable scoundrels." As a result, he called on the legislators to punish the *septembriseurs*, saying, "May the National Assembly and its memory perish, if it spares a crime that would leave such a stain on the French name."

Thus while Vergniaud had appealed to the language of nature and the collective to exonerate the Glaciéristes, he sought to identify private individuals with particular interests behind the September Massacres. Just as the Avignon debates had distinguished between private and public crimes, with public crimes being "relative to revolution," Vergniaud, Brissot, and their Girondin compatriots distinguished between the work of private individuals and a revolutionary public. The uniting of the collective, the revolutionary, and the natural is significant here: the people could be a natural force, one that not only eliminated responsibility but, in a sense, sacralized action. In the debates about the September Massacres, this relationship was questioned by neither the Jacobins nor the Girondins; the distinction between their arguments lay, first, in whether the "natural" force of the people should be restrained, as Roland suggested on 3 September, and second, in whether the people or a group of private citizens were the motors of the massacres.

Indeed, Prudhomme's assessment of the massacres as a natural event relied on the relationship between "the people" and nature, and also between "the people" and God. He correlated "the people" with God in their omniscience, omnipresence, and omnipotence; it was the "popular judgments" that were like an earthquake, and "the people" who executed the act of justice. Prudhomme had already compared the people to God in the immediate aftermath of the massacres: in an article titled "The People's Justice," he wrote: "The people who, like God, see everything, are present everywhere, and without whose permission nothing takes place here below, hardly were aware of this infernal conspiracy, when they took the extreme path...to prevent the horrors that [the conspirators] were preparing for them, and to show themselves without mercy to those who would not have shown mercy to them."[87] Their acts could not be judged, as they were inevitable; their bloodshed had been with a future end in sight—namely, the "prevent[ion of]...horrors." Unlike Roland, who called for a tempering of such collective force, Prudhomme saw the very collectivity of the massacres as evidence of their justice and necessity. Prudhomme's assessment illuminates Antoine De Baecque's conclusions in his *Glory and Terror,* in which he noted that the horrifying spectacle of mass death was valorized not only by the sheer quantity of its victims but by the mass consensus of the crowd inflicting the violence. Witnesses described the massacres as both unbearable and important, even necessary. "The 'unbearable spectacle' of massacred corpses seems to be thinkable only through the abstraction of 'the mass,' that is to say, the rhetorical justification of the acts of the crowd. The collective is thought of as an active being, an agent of History, embodiment of a national destiny whose most unbearable details can be forgotten."[88] Yet, as Prudhomme illustrates, the collective was not just a *national* destiny in these debates; it was a *natural* one. "The People" operated as a force of nature, with all the unquestionable justice and inevitability of an earthquake.

Thus the Jacobin defense of the massacres relied on *removing* agency and situating the event in the context of a revolutionary moment—namely, to identify the massacres as being "relative to revolution," in the terms of the Avignon debate. Most of these justifications emerged in a series of debates in October and November, as the legislators sought to determine whether criminals that had been released over the course of early September should be arrested or retried. Among Jacobins, a few significant strands of thought emerged: first, the massacres, like revolution, took place in an extraordinary time when traditional rules did not apply; and, second, they had been necessary and inevitable consequences of the effervescence that made the revolution of 10 August possible. In this way they turned opponents of the massacres—particularly the Girondins or "Brissotins"—into opponents of 10 August, as one was the necessary cause of the other. Finally, because the Revolution was not yet over, they were actions that would be justified and legitimized far in the future. For the moment Prudhomme put it best: *Il faut adorer et se taire.*

Like the "revolutions of the earth" evoked by the debates in March 1792, the events of the September Massacres took place in a revolutionary moment that rendered ordinary laws inapplicable. Even the Girondin Roland, in his letter of 3 September, wrote: "I know that revolutions do not work themselves out [*se calculent*] by ordinary rules."[89] Azéma, the Jacobin deputy from the Aude, emphasized the exceptionality of revolutionary days: "This is a case of the exception to the rule, invariable in all other cases, that the same causes should necessarily produce the same effects; for, in the insurrections of 10 August and of 2 and 3 September, the same cause produced entirely different effects."[90] The natural link between cause and effect had been ruptured in these extraordinary times of revolution. Similarly Jean-Lambert Tallien, an apologist for the massacres from their outset and the author of a circular that encouraged the provinces to partake in similar acts of "justice," maintained in his *La Verité sur les événemens du 2 septembre* that, although there were specific causes to the massacres, their effects were as yet unknowable. "[The events of 2 September were] terrible without a doubt, which, in a time of calm, would have provoked the vengeance of the laws, but over which, in a time of revolution and agitation, we must pull a veil, and leave to historians the care of consecrating and assessing this era of the revolution, which was much more useful than we think."[91] Tallien emphasized the *exceptionality* of revolutionary time, a time when laws and rules no longer applied, and a period when the immediate present and past could not yet be understood. Only with virtue of hindsight would the events be properly recognized as an almost-sacred event, worthy of "consecrat[ion]."

In fact, the Revolution took on a logic and a movement all its own, following laws beyond the control or the grasp of man. In Azéma's words: "For the revolution of 10 August to take place, great movements were necessary;...it is almost impossible to stop such violent and prompt agitations, and to restrain the effects sooner rather than later."[92] The Revolution had taken on a momentum that was *unstoppable*, and whose motions had been necessary to overthrow the king. These "agitations" would have both good and bad effects—but both were necessary for the Revolution itself to continue: "It is nearly impossible, in the *impetuous movements* of a revolution,...to separate what is salutary to an entire society from what can be terrible for a few of its members....The great good and the small evil...cannot but walk side by side in great popular and tumultuous movements."[93] Azéma's language reiterates the vision of revolution put forth in the debates about the Avignon amnesty: it necessarily had a momentum beyond human control, which gave rise to "small evils" as its consequences. Yet he, more than any of the defenders of amnesty in the Avignon case, saw these inescapable evils not merely as by-products of the revolutionary dynamic but as minor sufferings that needed to be endured to achieve the "great good."

Moreover, Azéma repeatedly invoked the imagery of nature in describing the necessary violence of 2–5 September. The exceptionality of the moment was itself akin to a natural event: "These partial and isolated misfortunes, in a time of insurrection and popular justice, are inevitable,...like the damages that take place near a flooded river."[94] He continued, "How would we uncover all the individual sins, committed in the whirlwind of these days of storm, of tempest, which cover everything with an impenetrable veil?"[95] Drawing on the same language of "fermentation" and "agitation" that had been so prevalent in the Avignon debates, he explained that after the arrests of 10 August, "Mistrust...redoubled the agitation, [and] stirred up those fermentations that, like the harbingers of storms and tempests, preceded 2 and 3 September—the unfortunate result of the revolution of 10 August."[96] Finally, he linked these "fermentations" explicitly with the revolution of 10 August, which was itself compared to a purifying storm: "The tempest that purified the atmosphere of France on 10 August ignited all the human passions that inevitably produced extraordinary commotions that could not be calmed in the short period of three weeks. When thunder roars, its noise echoes again and makes itself heard, even after the lightning bolt has erupted and has brought death; often it causes more devastation after it strikes than it does while it is striking."[97]

This language explicitly linked the 10th of August with the 2nd and 3rd of September, uniting them in a single and naturalized event that had unfortunate but inevitable consequences, and that *together* were necessary for the success of the Revolution. The agitations of September were but the inevitable by-products created by the effervescence of 10 August. Collot d'Herbois, speaking at the Jacobin Club, echoed the difficulty of separating the individual misfortune from the overall good, and emphasized the necessity of the September events not only as inevitable results of 10 August but also as imperative for the outcome of the Revolution: "We bemoan the *individual evils [maux particulières]* that [the *journée* of 2 September] produced, but realize that, without this same day, the Revolution never would have been accomplished.... Without 2 September there would be no liberty, there would be no National Convention."[98] Collot d'Herbois emphasized the necessity of the *journée* and the long-term benefits that far outweighed the "particular" infelicities of the massacres.

Likewise, on 4 November, Claude Basire, vice president of the Committee of Surveillance in the National Convention, addressed the Société des Amis de la Liberté et de l'Egalité. He urged his listeners not to get caught up in the ugly details of the revolutionary experience: "A revolution is always hideous in its details." Instead, they should take a broader perspective, which would make sense out of all the tiny tragedies. "It is in its entirety, and in its consequences for the regeneration of the empire, that the statesman should envision [the revolution], and if he finds himself sorrowfully affected by the troubling spectacle of a few *individual* sufferings, he should be sufficiently compensated by the indescribable joy that the sentiment of universal benevolence provides."[99] Basire is one of the few legislators who also spoke about the Avignon amnesty, and there is a certain continuity between his two speeches. On 16 March he had argued against prosecuting the Glacière crimes, saying that the legislature "must sacrifice everything" to the future rather than focus on the past.[100] Although he did not defend the crimes themselves by this logic, he did emphasize that a future good should outweigh the crimes of the past. By September, he used this logic to justify the massacres themselves; the "hideous details" were but necessary by-products of the revolutionary momentum.

Thus the Jacobin rhetoric surrounding the September Massacres replicated the vision of revolution illustrated during the Avignon debates; it reveals a vision of *political* revolution that closely parallels a *natural* revolution: it is largely unforeseen (and hence agentless); it is unstoppable (and hence blameless); it has unexpected consequences, and yet its over-all good—the regeneration it makes possible—outweighs the "particular" evils that may be its unintended results. Yet by asking French men and women to withhold judgment at the time and accept the events as neces-sary to an as yet unrealized future, the debates also imposed a theodicy on the events, linking natural forces, "the people," and a providential worldview which demanded not reason, but faith in an unforeseen end. In the hands of the Jacobins, the "veil" that Roland had suggested as a means of covering France's shame became a cloak of faith in the final outcomes of the Revolution. One day after Basire's speech, in language that echoed the Book of Job, Bertrand Barère condemned the overzeal-ous scrutiny of the September Massacres, saying that "we must not put the Revolution on trial."[101] Similarly Tallien had asked that the task of inter-preting the massacres be left to the "historian," who would be able to see the utility in the events that seemed, at first glance, tragic.[102]

In this context Prudhomme's invocation of the Lisbon earthquake be-comes both chilling, in its exoneration of collective violence as inevitable and sanctified, and emblematic, in its embrace of a providential logic of revolution based on natural revolutions. It also illuminates the devel-opment of a justification of violence that would prove resonant during the Terror. Both Colin Lucas and Pierre Caron have proposed that the violence of the September Massacres was legitimated by being portrayed as an act of sovereign justice, carried out by a new ruler (the people) against a new criminal (traitors and royalists). In the words of Pierre Caron, "We find here...the simple transfer from the king to the people, his heirs, the theory of...*justice retenue.*"[103] *Justice retenue,* or "retained justice," allowed the king to execute justice without heeding forms of judicial process. Yet in Prudhomme's analogy to the Lisbon earthquake, "the people" were *not* the new king; they were the new *providence.* In re-lating the massacres to the Lisbon earthquake, he also gestured toward a punishment that looked not back, at the guilt of a criminal, but for-ward, at the necessary steps taken to ensure a particular end. In Azéma's words: "Justice is not vengeance; justice punishes not [against] crimes that have been committed but to prevent crimes that will be committed in the future through severe examples."[104] Justice was not retributive, but exemplary. Just as apologists after the Lisbon earthquake had invoked an unknowable order, a far-off future, in which the "individual sorrows" of the fatal day would be understood, so, too, did the Jacobins call upon a future goal and good that would justify the misfortunes of revolutionary effervescence.

By 30 November, the Jacobin society had solidified its position on the massacres. In a circular to affiliate societies throughout France, the Jacobins of Paris, presided over by Louis Michel LePeletier, made a three-point exposition of their stance on the controversial *journées*. First, they linked 10 August with 2 September, treating the latter as the necessary and inevitable consequence of the first. The point was made clearer through comparison with 5–6 October 1789, which, according to the society, solidified the victories of 14 July. Like a fulfilled prophecy, the pattern was repeated in 1792, with the success of 10 August only being truly confirmed after the massacres of September. What is more, advocating this stance made excoriating the Brissotins all the easier: it turned enemies of 2–5 September into enemies of 10 August, and hence of the Republic. Second, the circular emphasized the justice and mercy of the Parisian populace, giving anecdotal evidence of individuals who were spared by the crowds on 2 September, and highlighting the importance of ridding the city of internal enemies who had escaped proper justice before Parisians took up arms in the war against the outside powers.

Finally, and most significantly, the circular manipulated the language of the Brissotins, asking that its fellow societies draw a veil over the events. Not just *any* veil could be thrown, however, but a "religious" one: one that was not permanent, but temporarily drawn until future generations could judge the events: "Let us draw…a religious veil over all these events, produced by one of these great revolutions formed in the womb of eternity [*conçues dans le sein de l'éternité*], and that can be judged only by a liberated posterity, not by we who have been shaped by the prejudices of slavery."[105] The events of a "great revolution" could not be understood by flawed humans who were corrupted by their own histories; their adjudication had to be postponed until the revolution was complete. The revolutionaries were not accountable to the current generation, but to a posterity that could, with hindsight, discern the order out of the apparent disorder of revolution. In the Jacobin circular, Roland's veil of shame became a veil of faith.

If we are looking for the roots of this future-oriented justification, Prudhomme leads us there himself. Natural violence, in the form of earthquake, hurricane, volcanic eruption, or plague, was one of the few ways outside of war that eighteenth-century Europeans had come face to face with mass destruction, of which Lisbon's devastating earthquake of 1755 is doubtless the most significant example. Experiences with the natural world, and the violence and tragedy wrought by it, provided a language with which to understand the political world. This language of inevitability, rooted in the natural world, was not itself a necessary product of the Revolution. Rather, it emerged in response to specific violent events. The rhetoric of terroristic violence was already extant in 1792, as debates in the wake of the Glacière Massacres reveal; however, it developed in the wake of violent events that were simultaneously shocking in their magnitude, somewhat opaque in their choice of victims, and yet also adamantly on the side of the Revolution. In the coming years the natural world could be invoked to fuse a sense of sacrality and inevitability with revolutionary violence.

In 1794 *Barra, ou la mère républicaine,* a play commemorating the heroic death of Joseph Barra (or Bara), premiered in Dijon. Barra, at a mere thirteen years of age, had been killed by counterrevolutionary forces in the Vendée, and the play, written by a Mme Nicole-Mathieu Villiers, honored not only him, but his "republican mother" who was willing to sacrifice her son for the good of the Revolution. In the play Brigitte, a hesitant patriot, asked Mme Barra about some of the misfortunes wrought by the Revolution, saying, "I admit that the revolution was inevitable and that its goal is admirable, that it promises infinite benefits to us; but don't you recognize that a mass of abuses have crept in that make any sensitive heart tremble?" Her wise friend, and the "republican mother" of the play's title, replied, "The abuses are inseparable from the work of humanity, and especially from a change as prodigious as that which is taking place [*s'opère*] among us."[106] Dorothée Barra went on:

> The revolutions of governments, like great crises in nature, topple everything, in order to regenerate everything. Sorrow, no doubt, for those who are struck by the explosions of one or the other volcano! But, while children and fools hit the wall that they blindly collided with, wise men submit with grace to the imperious law of necessity. Happy! For from the midst of chaos we are plunged into, one can see...the emergence of order and perfection.[107]

Those who could not submit to this truth, and abandon themselves and their private interest for the greater good, were not, in Mme Barra's eyes, true republicans.

Mme Villiers, like Prudhomme, made explicit the relationship between natural revolutions and political ones: both entailed violence and sorrow, but these were necessary steps toward regeneration and order. Out of the apparent disorder of an earthquake or a massacre came the order of a providential universe or a new political regime. The massacres in Avignon and in Paris in 1791 and 1792 laid the foundations for the "law of necessity" that underpinned this ominous vision of revolution: agentless, inevitable, and modeled after crises in nature. This vision required faith, but, even more, it required adoration. Faced with the natural and providential course of revolution, it was useless, even foolish, to attempt to resist; rather, a true patriot should submit to necessity. He should "adore, and fall silent."

3

LIGHTNING STRIKES

In his famous speech of 5 February 1794 (17 Pluviôse, Year II) on the principles of political morality under a revolutionary government, Maximilien Robespierre asserted the necessity of both terror and virtue during the Revolution. Under the "stormy" circumstances France was now enduring, he maintained that extraordinary measures needed to be taken, and he attempted to silence criticism of recent policies pursued by the Committee of Public Safety: "It has been said that terror was the mainspring of despotic government. Does your government therefore resemble a despotism? Yes, like the blade that shimmers in the hands of a hero of liberty resembles that with which the agents of tyranny were armed." The weapons of the old regime remained, but they were transformed in the fight for liberty. He continued: "And is it not to strike the heads of the prideful that lightning is destined?"[1] The lightning bolt—symbol of tyranny and arbitrariness in the Ancien Régime—became an agent of revolution. By using images and words associated with despotism and asserting their transformations from instruments of tyranny to instruments of revolution, Robespierre attempted to justify the use of drastic measures to solidify the Revolution. Though the *tools* might look the same, both the authority wielding them and their targets had changed.

While the French Revolution and particularly the declaration of the Republic carried with it a host of new symbols, including tricolor cockades and Herculean representations of "the people," revolutionaries also retained certain images of authority and sovereignty from the Old Regime. As Mona Ozouf demonstrated when she noted a "transfer of sacrality" in the revolutionary festival, revolutionaries did not so much demolish all the symbolic rituals of the past as they did borrow and reinterpret them. Lightning, long understood as a signifier of sovereignty, was no different.

Yet the trope of lightning combined older connotations with recent scientific discoveries; over the course of the eighteenth century new findings about the powers of lightning as an agent of electricity generated new understandings of *la foudre* as a potentially beneficial and empowering force. These new discoveries, carried across the Atlantic by Benjamin Franklin but also debated by individuals including the Abbé Nollet and Jean-Paul Marat, raised the question of the controllability of lightning. Whereas there was little hope of controlling earthquakes manifested in the literature emerging from Lisbon or Messina, the development of lightning rods suggested that lightning could be directed toward useful purposes or, at the very least, be diverted from a path of arbitrary destruction.

In fact, on 18 Floréal, Year II (7 May 1794), when he laid out his program for festivals that would be the heart of a republican national education, Robespierre referred to this newfound faith in the ability to control lightning. Specifically, he called upon the French to replicate the revolutions in man's relationship with the natural world in their political revolution:

> The world has changed, it should change again...Man has conquered lightning and diverted [*conjuré*] lightning from heaven....Everything has changed in the physical order; everything should change in the moral and political order. Half the world's revolution is already complete; the other half should be accomplished.[2]

Man, over the course of the Enlightenment, had managed to tame lightning; Franklin had, in Turgot's famous words, "seized lightning from the heavens." The secrets of nature were being unveiled to man; he nevertheless, according to Robespierre, remained in ignorance about moral and political revolution. It was that second, more important, revolution, that the Incorruptible encouraged his countrymen to undertake. At the conclusion of his speech, Robespierre exhorted: "Thunder over the heads of the guilty and hurl lightning at all your enemies...Command to victory but, above all, plunge vice into nothingness."[3] If properly enlightened individuals could control *natural* lightning, and direct it toward the proper targets, then so, too, could properly enlightened citizens seize the metaphorical lightning bolt of sovereignty, and use it to punish the guilty and restore equilibrium to the political atmosphere. After learning to direct lightning in the natural sphere, man could deploy its power in the political one.

With the potential to control lightning, however, came the question of who could direct its power, and what targets it should be diverted toward.

As a result, rhetoric about who could wield lightning—whether the king in 1789, the "people" in 1792, or the Convention in 1793–94—provides insight into changing ideas about sovereignty in revolutionary France. But so, too, did the potential targets of that directed lightning change over the course of the Revolution: Robespierre exhorted patriots to take aim at the "guilty" and the "prideful," but ultimately the victims of lightning were individuals who had demonstrated their inability to be redeemed or revolutionized. While prerevolutionary writings often used lightning to signify the arbitrary power and thus injustice of kings, Jacobin descriptions of revolutionary violence invoked *la foudre* to signify moments of targeted and just destruction, necessary for the salvation of the Republic.

The imagery of lightning also sheds light on notions of civic responsibility in revolutionary France. *La foudre* was used as a synonym for gunpowder as well, and therefore came to play an important role in the mobilization of French men and women in the war effort. The people of France were asked to take part in the production of "revolutionary lightning" by mining saltpeter in a national campaign begun on 14 Frimaire, Year II (4 December 1793). In manufacturing lightning, the people's civic contribution was sacralized, as they became not the wielders, but the producers, of thunderbolts. The trope of lightning demonstrates the attempt of revolutionaries to align their work with the forces of nature, but it also provides a useful case study into the ways in which old symbols and metaphors were reworked and themselves regenerated. In the electrically charged atmosphere of revolutionary France, the lightning bolt allowed for justice and regeneration, wielded by the nation itself.

Lightning in the Atmosphere

In literary and political sources, *la foudre* seems to have been primarily used in four main ways in the decade prior to the outbreak of revolution.[4] The first two are of less interest to this book: a literal lightning bolt, and the metaphorical *coup de foudre*, referring to something instantaneous or, more idiomatic, love at first sight. The second two uses have interesting political implications, particularly as we trace their continued enunciation throughout the revolutionary period. *La foudre* could be used to refer to weaponry or specifically cannon fire, as in the Abbé Raynal's description of young America's military force: "Its *foudre* will forever fall on coasts that can be taken by surprise, on waters that are too poorly guarded by distant forces."[5] Finally, it was an emblem of tyrannical punishment, wielded

Fig. 2 Philippe-Jacques de Loutherbourg (1740–1812), *Voyageurs surpris par un orage.* Musée des Beaux-Arts, Rennes, France. Reunion des Musées Nationaux / Art Resource, N.Y.

either by despotic kings or vengeful gods. Thus Delisle de Sales regretted that the Romans put "lightning" in the hands of their "emperors who oppressed them"; l'Abbé Barruel reminded readers of *Les Helviennes* that "*la foudre* still thunders over [the tombs of Epicurius, Lucretius, Spinoza] . . . , and announces the God that survives them."[6] Louis-Sébastien Mercier went so far as to describe *lettres de cachet* as "that lightning bolt of absolute kings" in his *Tableau de Paris,* a sentiment echoed in the parish of Jouars-Pont-Chartrain's 1789 *cahier de doléance.*[7] Neither of these uses was new to Louis XVI's reign. Indeed, Antoine Furetière included both definitions in his 1690 dictionary: "*Foudre,* figuratively, the anger of God, or kings . . . One says, also, that cannons vomit their *foudre* against a place, when they strike it vigorously."[8]

Yet even as these older, figurative uses of the term *foudre* persisted, scientific inquiry was beginning to map new meanings onto the term, derived from advances in understanding of the processes of natural lightning. Lightning bolts continued to awe and even mystify the eighteenth-century observer; reports abounded of lightning burning skin with tree-shaped scars, leaving its victims naked, or reducing them to powder. And the most common means of warding off lightning remained ringing church bells. In his 1761 *Dictionnaire de physique,* the Jesuit priest and Avignon physics professor Aimé-Henri Paulian answered the question, "Is the sound of bells capable of diverting the cloud that contains lightning?" with the reply, "Is the cloud still far away? The sound of the bells will move the air and prevent it from approaching the area . . . but if it is found, unfortunately, either above the bell tower or near it? Then the agitation of the air will serve only to encourage the electrical cloud to open, and the lightning will fall on the head of the bell ringer."[9] In their *cahier de doléance,* the members of the parish of Herblay requested the right to ring their church bells freely, since they believed that the sound of the bells could divert storms.[10] Several *philosophes* and scientists understandably tried to end this practice, as it actually put individuals in more danger, as bell ringers climbed tall towers to ring iron bells. Jaucourt, in the *Encyclopédie,* noted numerous superstitions surrounding lightning, most notably that it was perceived to strike "scoundrels and the impious." He went on to excoriate the fact that these ancient beliefs still abounded. "Even though it is more enlightened on the nature and formation of lightning, the human race is still not healed of all these vain superstitions."[11]

Similarly Jean Lanteires, a Lausanne professor of *belles lettres* and the founder of the *Journal de Lausanne,* expressed his frustration about the continued superstitions of "the people" toward lightning as late as 1789.[12]

According to Lanteires, the sites of lightning strikes were often considered either sacred or cursed and their victims portrayed as deserving of divine anger. At the same time, he noted a certain confusion arising from the facts of lightning strikes: on the one hand, people tended to believe that lightning struck those who were guilty, but they also could easily observe that some victims seemed innocent, or that cities such as London, supposedly full of vice and crime, had a miniscule number of lightning deaths.[13] As a result, the average European simply *could not figure lightning out:* they did not know if they should be afraid of lightning or thankful for it. Yet Lanteires himself proved unable to explain sufficiently either the behavior or the motives of lightning; he was particularly troubled by an instance in the neighboring village of Grand-Mont, where a young woman was found, "in the middle of the path, dead, absolutely naked and with her face turned toward the heavens. All her clothes had been torn and were dispersed in the area."[14] Despite a valiant effort, Lanteires could not scientifically explain the devastation wrought on her body—nor the heavenward glance, eternally fixed on the point of her destruction. In an essay that exemplifies the ambiguity surrounding natural events, Lanteires tried to show the world its naiveté in upholding superstition about lightning, yet he himself could not adequately interpret either its action or its purpose.

Simultaneously, however, scientific study was beginning to understand lightning, appreciate its natural benefits, and even domesticate it. In 1782 Marat, then an aspiring scientist, attempted to demystify the force of electricity in his *Recherches physiques sur l'électricité.* Marat noted that there was no more important, nor more fascinating, branch of physics than electricity: "There is no other phenomenon, seen as a whole, that offers a spectacle at once more singular, more imposing, more terrible."[15] It was the "glory" of his generation to have the opportunity to shed light on the mystery of electricity. Indeed, Marat's research demonstrated that electricity was a life-giving force, related to the heat of the earth—in fact, it was necessary to plant, animal, and human existence. Although it had previously been seen as a "fearsome scourge," Marat maintained that "this fluid...has its place among the springs of the mechanism of the world: What am I saying? It works for the preservation of our days."[16] Thus Marat had come to believe, and to assert based on his scientific research, that lightning, as a manifestation of electricity in the air, was a necessary force whose purpose was not to destroy the sinner but, instead, to maintain an equilibrium in the atmosphere.

Likewise, in his later work, Buffon expressed a belief that electricity was one of the earth's fundamental powers, a materialization of Earth's natural heat source. As a result, it flowed through the earth and was capable of causing both internal and external disruptions. A subterranean electricity was responsible for volcanic eruptions and earthquakes; a "coup de la foudre intérieure" broke open the earth on such occasions.[17] To Buffon, these eruptions, like lightning, were necessary and natural events, a result of the heat that gave the earth its unique life. Like Marat, he understood electricity to be one of the elements essential for existence, and lightning, like volcanoes and earthquakes, merely its manifestation.

Fads in medical practices attested to the widespread belief in the sustaining powers of electricity, and to the faith in its use in reestablishing equilibrium. Franz Mesmer, who awed the French public in the 1780s with his clinics and controversial healing techniques, sometimes drew upon spectacular displays involving electrostatic machines in his procedures. He posited that disruptions in the balance between the elements could only be returned to equilibrium by a crisis, much like lightning in the atmosphere. Furthermore, the years of Mesmer's popularity also witnessed a widespread discussion about the benefits of medical electricity and the use of shock therapies to heal a variety of illnesses. Marat and his fellow participants in a 1783 Rouen competition entered into a debate about the virtues of electrical shock in medical practice.[18] Although most established scientists dismissed mesmerism as trickery, these popular practices nevertheless bolstered the already-captivating image of electricity in prerevolutionary Paris. The debates about medical uses of electricity also demonstrate that science, particularly in its more popularized forms, often added to, rather than diminished, the mystery of electricity, imbuing it with a universal power whose motions were not yet entirely understood.

As mesmerism suggests, electricity's power was simultaneously purifying and restorative; lightning was a necessary tool for maintaining a balance in the atmosphere or, in Mesmer's case, in social harmony. It stabilized through purgation; as Bernardin de Saint-Pierre stated, nature "used fire to purify, by means of thunderbolts, air that is often filled with toxins during the heat of summer."[19] In the *Encyclopédie* the usefulness of lightning was described as twofold: "1st to refresh the atmosphere...2nd to purge the air of an infinitude of harmful exhalations, and perhaps even to make them useful by diminishing them." The entry continued, "It is claimed that rain that falls while it is thundering is better than others for fertilizing the earth."[20] Thus lightning, even as it retained many of its superstitious connotations as a weapon of gods and kings, was also beginning to be understood as potentially useful for its purgative powers and for its ability to restore balance to the natural world.

The continued fear and awe of lightning, even in the midst of scientific advances, is perhaps best exemplified in a vigorous debate that arose in the 1780s surrounding lightning rods. A young Maximilien Robespierre found himself at the center of these debates as a lawyer in Arras in 1783. Robespierre defended Charles Dominique de Vissery de Bois-Valé, who, in May 1780, had installed a lightning rod atop his home. Within months, fears that the rod could actually *attract* lighting and *increase* the village's dangers had led to a court case, culminating in an order for de Vissery to remove the offending mechanism.

In Robespierre's appeal, he demonstrated a similar understanding of electricity to that held by Marat. A fluid that ran through all living organisms, electricity helped to sustain life. It was an "incontestable principle" held by naturalists that it naturally maintained a certain equilibrium. Once that balance was disrupted in the atmosphere, however, lightning occurred, and would continue until the equilibrium was restored: "As long as this electrical equilibrium between the clouds, the air, and the earth is not troubled, peace reigns in the atmosphere, but if some cause happens to break it, then storms, lightning bolts, [and] thunder are born."[21] These comments reveal some of the key characteristics attributed to lightning in the years surrounding the French Revolution: it was a natural occurrence, caused by some sort of disruption, which allowed for the necessary electrical equilibrium to be reestablished.

Robespierre also used the opportunity of the case to expound on the power of man to control nature, thanks to enlightened advances. In his appeal, he lauded the enlightenment manifested by le Sieur de Vissery and condemned the villagers' ignorance. Lightning rods, he argued, demonstrated the development of man's power over nature:

> A man has appeared among us, who dared to come up with a means of arming man against the fires of Heaven; he said to the lightning: you will go here, and therefore you will distance yourself from these peaceable homes of citizens, and these superb edifices that seem to be the principal objects of your wrath... The obedient lightning recognized his laws; immediately losing this blind and irresistible impulse that strikes, overturns, crushes all that stands in its way, it has learned to discern objects that it should spare, and... is afraid to make an attempt on our lives or to touch our homes.[22]

Man had learned to tame and control nature; he had taken away the arbitrary power of lightning and forced it to spare the innocent.[23] Not only was lightning a natural and restorative event rather than a scourge wielded by gods, it also could be directed through the efforts of enlightened men. It was no longer "blind" and random, but rather was obedient.

Yet not everyone, even in the "enlightened" community, agreed. Marat, for example, countered the idea that lightning was controllable—lightning rods and *conducteurs* had failed to prevent lightning strikes on many occasions. Although they could limit destruction, "it [was]...an error to believe that we can restrain [*enchaîner*] lightning with their help."[24] And although Robespierre's appeal convinced people in the short term—the Conseil d'Artois allowed de Vissery to reestablish his lightning rod in May 1783—it did not win them over on a more widespread level: partly because of fears raised by the debates in the case, the province ultimately chose to ban *par-à-tonnerres*.[25] In science, medicine, and popular culture alike, electricity undoubtedly possessed intense power and potential, either for destruction or for healing. Yet the question of *if* it could be controlled and directed, and, if so, by whom, remained at the heart of debates on the eve of the Revolution.

As Robespierre's appeal suggested, and as Marie-Hélène Huet has argued, the scientific community's attempt to control lightning was represented as a labor of enlightenment, even as an attempt to remove unjust authority from the hands of gods and kings. While popular beliefs, like those discussed by Lanteires, emphasized the justice wrought by lightning striking the guilty, *philosophes* focused on the randomness and injustice of divine or monarchical *foudre*. As Robespierre wrote in a 1785 essay contest, describing despotic government: "It is an irresistible power that strikes without rules and without discernment; it is a lightning bolt that strikes, shatters, crushes everything that it meets."[26] Demonstrating that natural lightning could be trained to be "discerning" could reveal the arbitrariness of despotic government. Thus d'Holbach spoke of taking power away from monarchs by explaining the science behind lightning itself. In *Système de la Nature*, he wrote, "If [the man of reason] wrests *la foudre* from the hands of these terrible gods who make you miserable, it is so that you can cease to walk amid storms on a route that you can see only by the glow of lightning bolts."[27] In effect, he attempted to *naturalize* lightning, stripping it of its superstitious connotations and reducing it to a force of nature instead of a weapon of arbitrary punishment. Similarly, Franklin himself was pictured by Fragonard, in the famous words of Anne-Robert Jacques Turgot, "seiz[ing] lightning from the heavens and the scepter from tyrants."[28] In demystifying lightning and imposing some kind of control over it, the *philosophes* sought to remove the monarch's authority to inflict random and unjust punishment. Only when lightning was rightly returned to its place as a force of nature instead of kings could it be understood and even controlled.

Fig. 3 Marguerite Gérard, after Jean-Honoré Fragonard (1732–1806), *Au Génie de Franklin* (1778). Franklin deflecting lightning; the caption is Turgot's epigram, "Eripuit coelo fulmen, sceptrumque tyrannis." Musée de la cooperation franco-américaine, Blérancourt, France. Réunion des Musées Nationaux / Art Resource, N.Y.

By explaining the causes of lightning, philosophers and scientists hoped to remove its mystique and thereby take away some of the power and awe wielded by monarchs and religion. They sought both to *enlighten* and *empower* the people by tearing the thunderbolt from the hands of kings and

returning it to nature. Yet, as a force of nature, lightning was still powerful: it restored equilibrium and provided life-giving force, even while it
destroyed. Over the course of the Revolution, the language of the thunderbolt began to transform, as authority and control over lightning was
transferred from monarchs to the people. Lightning was used primarily in
three ways in revolutionary rhetoric, all of which merged new understandings of natural lightning with inherited figurative meanings: first, as a signifier of sovereignty; second, as a form of justice that was immediate and
necessary to restoring equilibrium; and, finally, as a synonym for armed
force and, specifically, gunpowder.

The Scepter from Tyrants: Lightning and Sovereignty in the Revolution

On 3 December 1792, as the National Convention debated the question of whether Louis XVI could be put on trial, Jean-Baptiste Drouet
stood before his colleagues in the legislature and listed the king's many
crimes. Drouet, who famously had recognized and stopped the king on
his ill-fated flight to Varennes, demanded to know why, after such a record of traitorous behavior, "lightning remains in [the King's] hands? And
doesn't fall in a salvo upon his head?"[29] In their speeches on the same
day, Jean-Bon Saint André, Pierre Philippeaux, and Alexandre Deleyre all
accused the king of arming himself with lightning against the people of
France.[30] In contesting the king's inviolability, these *conventionnels* questioned his right to wield lightning. Given lightning's figurative meaning
as a "mark of sovereignty," in Furetière's definition, its invocation during
debates over royal authority is hardly surprising. Between 1789 and 1792,
the lightning bolt, previously perceived as the archetypical demonstration
of despotic power—arbitrary, destructive, and instantaneous—came to be
firmly held in the hands of the people. Nature's wrath became something
controlled by the revolutionaries, and directed toward the promulgation
of their cause.

The reattribution of the ownership of lightning was not immediate.
One of its first appearances in revolutionary writing was in a brief pamphlet, which referred to lightning only in its title: *La foudre n'est pas toujours
dans les mains de Jupiter.* Written on 11 July 1789 by an anonymous patriot,
it lauded the French soldiers who refused to turn their weapons against
the French people.[31] Without explicitly saying so, the pamphlet indicated
that force was no longer under the authority of the king alone; lightning

could not be launched at his sole command. Nor, however, was lightning under the control of the people. Significantly, at the storming of the Bastille, *la foudre* was not yet the property of the conquerors. Instead, in revolutionary texts it was the Bastille itself that threw thunderbolts and fired *foudre* from its cannons.[32] The people were the victims of lightning, not its conductors. The event could have some electrifying potential, as an anonymous writer noted in his "Réflexions sur la présente Révolution"; the storming of the Bastille instantaneously spread a revolutionary passion and spirit to all of France. "Conserve, preciously, this handsome fire [of patriotism] that, more prompt in its effects than electrical matter, communicated itself in an instant to all the French on this memorable day."[33] Yet contemporary witnesses to the fall of the Bastille do not appear to have given the power of lightning, even metaphorically, to its vanquishers.[34] The abbé Fauchet, who delivered a stirring and well-received address to commemorate the victims of the Bastille in August, pronounced that the Bastille had "foudroy[é]" the people, and that "[despotism] menaced us unremittingly with all its lightning bolts."[35] Lightning remained a symbol of despotic power, wielded against the people.

Within three years, however, revolutionary rhetoric suggested that lightning had become the property of the people alone. The image was invoked in several accounts of 10 August 1792, the day the monarchy fell. "The people have hurled the thunderbolt of vengeance," proclaimed a self-dubbed "Publicola" Chaussard in a eulogy for the patriot dead; Marie-Joseph Chénier, in another funeral oration, declared that the tree of royalty had been "crushed by lightning."[36] In a play commemorating the event one year later, Gabriel Bouquier addressed the enemies of the nation: "Tremble, oppressors of the world! The children of the earth will, sooner or later, hurl the murderous lightning bolt that will avenge humanity."[37] Between the storming of the Bastille and the proclamation of the Republic, Frenchmen truly had stolen lightning from gods and kings, signifying a fundamental shift in power and sovereignty.

Precisely when and how this shift took place is difficult to determine. However, one of the key events during which the image of lightning, particularly as a contested symbol of authority, was invoked was the debate about war in late 1791 and early 1792.[38] The summer of 1791, with the king's attempted emigration, Leopold II's Padua Circular, and the Declaration of Pillnitz, brought increased fears about the connivances of émigrés and external forces against France—and about Louis XVI's collusion with them. The Padua Circular, issued on 10 July 1791, was an invitation to other European nations to join the Holy Roman Emperor's opposition to revolutionary France; the Declaration of Pillnitz, an agreement between Leopold II and Prussia's Frederick William II made on August 27, declared the two kings' willingness to take action against the French nation. Against this political backdrop, Jacques-Pierre Brissot first appealed for war in October. In the coming months, a series of fiery debates broke out, with Brissot's allies supporting war and many members of the Jacobins, especially Robespierre, condemning it; they feared that war would play directly into the plans of the court and the enemies of France. *La foudre*, a term associated with war from its connotations in weaponry, became a symbol employed by both sides in the debate.

In his speech against the war on 18 December 1791, Robespierre used the language of lightning as a key organizing concept, suggesting that the battle over war was a battle over *la foudre*, and thereby over sovereignty over the people. The question of *who* could launch the thunderbolt of war was fundamental to the question. "I know," he said to the Society of Friends of the Constitution, "that the happy circumstance can arise when lightning can leave [the people's] hands to crush traitors." But he questioned whether this was a moment when that circumstance was in place; instead, he argued, the court and the aristocracy were conniving to draw the people into a war, to again dazzle them with their power, and thereby to seize authority over them. "The ministers and the court seemed to want to direct, for themselves, the lightning against our enemies, so that, having again become the object of enthusiasm and idolatry, the executive power could execute a terrible plan at its leisure and without obstacle."[39] Robespierre retained the belief, manifested in the lightning rod case, that lightning could be directed; what was at stake now was who should control it. Just as kings and theologians had awed the masses with metaphorical lightning and thunder, the court was now attempting to stupefy the French citizenry into submission. This was no way for a republican country to go to war, he declared: war should come, if necessary, by an "explosion" of patriotism within the nation, not from a conspiratorial cabal. If the members of the court were able to "direct the lightning themselves," they would have seized authority from its rightful owners: the people.

On the other hand, Pierre-Louis Manuel, arguing in favor of the war, conjured the image of lightning to emphasize the necessity of war. In a speech at the Jacobin Club in January 1792, he drew upon scientific understandings of lightning as a natural and necessary event, declaring: "Messieurs, I see thick clouds swaying over our heads; nothing but a thunderbolt can disperse them...To war, then! To war!"[40] In the stormy environment of intrigue and external threats, only lightning could clear the atmosphere.

Fig. 4 Barnabé Augustin de Mailly, "Congrès des rois coalisés, ou les tyrans (découronnés)." This image shows a rooster, "emblem of the vigilance of the French Republic," striking with lightning the crowns of the Austrian emperor, Frederick William II of Prussia, Catherine the Great, King Stanislas of Poland, Charles IV of Spain, the "roi des marmottes," or Victor-Amadeus of Piedmont-Sardinia, George III (puppeteered by Pitt), Ferdinand I (the "Neapolitan monkey"), and the pope. The artist, Barnabé Augustin de Mailly, was awarded one thousand livres from the Committee of Public Safety, which demanded the printing of nine hundred copies. *Recueil des actes du Comité de salut public*, 10:187; decree of 11 January 1794. Bibliothèque Nationale de France, Collection De Vinck 4358.

Jérôme Pétion, the mayor of Paris, made that relationship clear in March at the Legislative Assembly, drawing a specific analogy between the natural and political atmospheres: "There exists in the social order, as in the political order, laws whose imposing effect is felt only in memorable times. When the atmosphere that surrounds us is charged with wicked vapors, nature can only break free with a lightning bolt; in the same way, society can only purge itself from the excesses that trouble it with an impressive explosion; and after these great blows are struck, everything is reborn in hope and happiness."[41] As in the natural realm, the political realm demanded great force, and an authority that would channel the energy and the regenerative power of the lightning bolt. Lightning transformed from a weapon *of* kings to a weapon used against them.

The speeches of Manuel and Pétion merged the older figurative understanding of lightning as a signifier of sovereignty with new understandings of the purgative role that natural lightning played in meteorological convulsions. The lightning bolt of war was rhetorically linked with disturbances in the atmosphere. Whereas monarchical lightning had been arbitrary and extralegal, thrown at the whim of the sovereign, revolutionary lightning was both natural—the consequence of "stormy" circumstances—and aimed at deserving victims—the "guilty," the "prideful," the "enemies of humanity." As Pétion maintained in his address to the Assembly, "Far be it from us to seek to strike an individual who is not subject to the law; it is to the law alone that a free people should confer its vengeance."

Yet by Year II, uses of lightning imagery tended to suggest an authority that *transcended* law rather than enforced it. By the fall of 1793 the Constitution over which the Convention had been laboring since the declaration of the Republic, and that had been affirmed at the 10 August Festival of Unity and Indivisibility, had been sidelined. In fact, the Constitution would never be put into effect; on 19 Vendémiaire (10 October 1793), the Convention declared that the government would be "revolutionary until the peace." Yet in September and October 1793 a number of local clubs and societies sent letters to the *conventionnels* urging them to stay at their posts despite the fact that the Constitution would have required new elections. Far from questioning the sovereignty of an assembly without a constitution, however, the letters from throughout France used the language of lightning to reiterate the Convention's authority, and to suggest that the lightning which the people had placed in the hands of the legislature was inalienable.[42]

Although these letters deployed a variety of metaphors in their appeals to the Convention, including comparing the legislative body to a pilot who should not abandon his post during a storm, a number of these addresses referred to the "lightning" the Convention held that still needed to be thrown. The authority of the Convention, the sovereignty conferred on them by the people, had not yet been enacted. Citizens from Finistère requested that, "The Convention...remain at its post until the revolutionary lightning bolts that it holds in its hands have crushed all the reptiles that have dared to act in favor of federalism"; representatives from the Département du Gers proclaimed, "The national lightning bolt is in your hands, use it to strike traitors and conspirators without pity." The lightning bolt was firmly in the hands of the Convention, and they could not abandon their posts until they had exercised their vengeance to its full extent. "[We] invite the venerable Mountain not to disperse until the thunderbolt of the Republic has struck down all the crowned tyrants and their slaves," wrote the Société des Amis de la Constitution républicaine in Couches.[43] The people, having placed "republican," "revolutionary," and "national" lightning in the hands of the Convention, demanded that it be used to annihilate their enemies. These letters suggest that the sovereignty conferred by the people, and symbolized by nature, could even transcend constitutional law.[44] The Convention was not bound by law but by nature; equilibrium would not be restored until the lightning bolt had been released. Even if the people had originally conferred sovereignty on the Convention, they no longer held it themselves; instead, they had delegated the powers of nature to their representatives, and asked them to use that authority to crush sinners. The forces of nature needed to be channeled by the revolutionary government.

Thus the trope of lightning provides insight not only into the perceived transfer of sovereignty and power from the king to the people, between 1789 and 1792, but also, and perhaps more important, from the people to the Convention in Year II. By late 1793, it signified a sovereignty rooted not in law but in necessity. Unlike monarchical uses of lightning, the Convention's lightning was not arbitrary but was directed at specific, and sinful, targets. In this regard, it resembled the lightning of gods more than the random lightning of kings. As the commune of Vaugirard expressed to the Convention in October 1793, "Like another Jupiter...you have lightning in your hand...Do not leave until you have crushed and pulverized all the vultures who daily devour their own children."[45] The people, who had acted as a new Providence in Prudhomme's reading of the September Massacres, had given their divine powers over to the Convention.

The Utility of Destruction: The Victims of Lightning

As the language of lightning transformed to reflect the new basis of authority in the new regime, it also was directed at new victims. Significantly, *la foudre* no longer struck at random, as its usages to describe kingly punishments had indicated, but now destroyed the sinner. Abrogated by the Revolution, the old laws of the Ancien Régime were replaced with new virtues and new crimes. Only the sinners of the new regime—the counterrevolutionary and the aristocrat—needed to fear the lightning bolt. In 1793 images began to appear of *montagnards* aiming lightning bolts at reptiles wallowing in swamps—a symbol of the *Marais,* the Jacobins' moderate counterparts.[46] The targets of lightning were the enemies of the Republic, both within its borders and on the battlefield.

Lightning signified the sinner of the new regime, but it also served to describe how revolutionary justice would operate. The symbolism of lightning is one of *instantaneousness,* both in its judgment and its destruction. It leaves no remains with which to rebuild. Robespierre gestured toward this idea in his speech of 18 Floréal, in which he stated that vice would be "plunge[d] into nothingness" by the lightning bolt of the people. During the trial of Louis XVI he made the immediacy and destructiveness of the people's justice apparent: "A people does not judge as does a court of law," he explained. "It does not hand down sentences, it hurls down thunderbolts; it does not condemn kings, it plunges them into the abyss."[47] By this logic the lightning bolt was again a symbol of authority and justice that *transcended* law: it operated according to a logic that was more divine than mundane. Kingship, for Robespierre and his fellow Jacobins, was a crime against humanity that could not be pardoned or reformed: its only remedy was annihilation. As Saint-Just had concisely stated, "This man must reign or die."[48] The king was beyond redemption and therefore was subject to immediate and utter destruction.

The lightning bolt was a particularly useful image in rhetoric where nothing short of eradication would suffice, and where the population concerned was beyond regeneration; they could no longer be taught or reformed. The *Encyclopédie,* after all, had claimed that lightning both purified the atmosphere and rendered dangerous elements beneficial by

Fig. 5 "Sans Union, Point de Force" (1793). A *sans-culotte* atop a mountain directs lightning bolts at the reptiles of the Swamp. Bibliothèque Nationale de France.

diminishing them; lightning was not merely destructive but transformative. As a result it was a metaphor that figured prominently in Jacobin discussions of the Vendée, which had erupted into a bloody civil war in March 1793, and of the traitorous towns of Toulon and Lyon, where Jacobins maintained that the only way to make harmful elements useful was to destroy them.[49] Toulon had broken out in rebellion against the

Jacobins in July 1793. The uprising culminated in an appeal to the British for assistance in August of that year. To pour salt on this traitorous wound to the Republic, the British aid came at a great cost: the Toulonnais were required to renounce republicanism and to declare Louis XVII their king.[50] When the city fell to republican forces in December following a three-month siege, roughly one thousand individuals were condemned to death for their role in the rebellion.[51]

In these areas, the terrain itself could contain remnants of the counter-revolution and therefore needed to be purged entirely. As Joseph Fouché, the representative on mission in Toulon, wrote in a letter to the Committee of Public Safety member Collot d'Herbois: "Let us exercise justice by the example of nature; ... let us strike like lightning, so that even the ashes of our enemies disappear from the soil of liberty."[52] The idea that even the soil could be tainted by the enemies of the people was also taken up by Bertrand Barère, who in a report of 4 Nivôse (24 December 1793) petitioned that Toulon be renamed "Port de la Montagne" and that all its houses be razed: "It is necessary that *la foudre nationale* crush all the homes of the Toulonnais merchants."[53] Likewise, at a festival in Nevers to celebrate the destruction of Toulon, Aristide Passot delivered a speech reminding his listeners at the Temple of Reason that "once Liberty speaks, her terrible voice is an exterminating lightning bolt that pulverizes the tyrants of the world and returns them to nothingness."[54] This language was reprised in polemics about the Vendée, which was compared to Toulon in a collection of patriotic *chansons*. "Couplets chantés en rejouissance de la reprise de Toulon et de la destruction de la Vendée," included the lines, "La Vendée, forever, / By our generous warriors, / Is purged from French soil.... / Suddenly, a hundred lightning bolts took effect."[55] Lightning became the instrument of this variety of instantaneous, and obliterating, justice, reserved specifically for those who had rebelled against the community of republican France and were no longer worthy, or capable, of rehabilitation. And *this*, according to the Toulon representative on mission, was justice as "nature" had intended it.

The language surrounding the city of Lyon is perhaps most illustrative of this devastating and destructive aspect of lightning imagery. Lyon, which had been the center of a federalist revolt, was the subject of particularly strong venom from Paris, and the Committee of Public Safety sent Collot d'Herbois, as well as Charles-Philippe Ronsin and Joseph Fouché, to carry out its vengeance. The town could not be forgiven, could not be rehabilitated, could not even be *named:* what remained of it became known as *Ville Affranchie.* Over the course of six months, from October 1793 to April

1794, nearly two thousand Lyonnais were condemned to death, some in a particularly gruesome spectacle in December, in which the condemned were merely lined up before open graves and shot.[56] In a report by Collot d'Herbois to the Convention on 1 Nivôse (21 December 1793), he defended these mass shootings, or *mitraillades*, for having spared patriots the sight of continued executions, and for having been particularly humane for those awaiting death. He used language that recalled Robespierre's in describing the death of the king: "The effects of [the people's] justice should be as prompt as lightning, and should leave only nothingness and ashes wherever it has passed: it is with this rapidity that the…executions were enacted."[57] The people's justice was both immediate and entirely destructive. Several weeks earlier, on 15 Frimaire (5 December), Collot d'Herbois had made this very point in a broadsheet written to the neighboring *départements*. In that placard Collot d'Herbois reminded citizens that they had given the *représentans du Peuple* the "thunderbolt of their vengeance"; the placard continued: "they…will not leave until all their enemies are *foudroyés*."[58] The mass shootings merely fulfilled the destiny of the representatives and the executed alike. Again, "thunderbolt" stood for a powerful and decisive authority: when the people handed it to their representatives, they gave them the right to pursue justice at any cost.

Collot d'Herbois made clear the relationship between this *foudre vengeresse* and the total annihilation of the city of Lyon. The representatives' goal in the city was not to reshape but to rebuild completely on its ruins.

> Is it not on the ruins of everything that vice and crime erected that we should establish general prosperity? Is it not on the debris of the monarchy that we have founded the Republic? Is it not with the debris of error and of superstition that we are creating altars to reason and to philosophy? Is it not equally true for ruins, for the remains of edifices of pride and cupidity, that we should raise humble homes for rest in old age or sorrow, for all friends of equality, for all those who have well served the cause of liberty? Is it not on the ashes of the enemies of the People, of its assassins, of all that is impure, that we must establish social harmony, peace, and public happiness [*la félicité publique*]?[59]

Lightning provided an image of a force that destroyed instantaneously, that left nothing but ashes and ruins. And to Collot d'Herbois, that is what made it both necessary and useful: destruction became a positive good, directed at those who could not be saved. Like kingship, like the Vendée, Lyon required a lightning bolt, a terrifying strike from nature itself.

In this sense the image of lightning crystallized a dominant theme of the revolutionary mind-set: the idea of regeneration and the means of achieving it. As Mona Ozouf pointed out in *L'homme régénéré*, an inherent paradox underlay revolutionary notions of regeneration and the creation of a "new man" suitable for republican France. On the one hand was the belief that the Revolution needed to start entirely anew, that in the history of the nation "there was nothing to save, no mooring to find, no assistance to expect in the adventure that was preparing itself."[60] It was this impulse that gave rise to the new revolutionary calendar, and to the rejection of Old Regime history. The counterpoise to this "pessimism," as Ozouf denotes it, was the emphasis on the need to *reeducate*, to continuously reinforce the new model of citizen: in short, to work with the materials at hand to reform a people. Lightning destroyed the material at hand; it embodied the rejection of the past and the embrace of an instantaneous justice, and an instantaneous regeneration.

In this respect Jacobin invocations of lightning imagery seem to distinguish themselves from contemporary political uses in other nations—even revolutionary ones. Given the transatlantic influence of Franklin and of electrical experimentation, it is no surprise that France would not have been the only place where lightning would be used in late eighteenth-century rhetoric. James Delbourgo, in his 2006 *Most Amazing Scene of Wonders: Electricity and Enlightenment in Early America*, established that the language of electricity made its way into the political rhetoric of American patriots during their revolution. In part because of the patriotism surrounding the figure of Benjamin Franklin, but also because of the ubiquitous discussions about the power of electricity, many patriots drew upon electrical similes, particularly to describe the instantaneous spread of republican virtue.[61] While Delbourgo's work is useful in identifying the pervasiveness of natural analogies, it also points to some particularities in the French use of such language during the revolutionary period. Most important, Delbourgo's sources employed electricity and lightning as a simile primarily to describe something that was instantaneous, universal, even natural—but not necessarily destructive. The destructive power of lightning was an essential component of the French use of the metaphor, and was indicative of the relationship between nature and violence posited by many members of the revolutionary community.

Instead of representing tyranny and arbitrariness, lightning signified justice: a justice that was swift and annihilating, and not only punished the sin but cleared the air for a new beginning. Significantly, however, lightning retained an element of the "superstitious" meanings that Jaucourt,

Jean Lanteires, and d'Holbach had condemned. Fusing, first, the scientific community's notion of the lightning bolt as necessary for regeneration and restoring equilibrium; second, the developing belief, enunciated in Robespierre's legal brief, that lightning could be controlled; and, finally, the age-old superstition that lightning struck the guilty, the revolutionaries used the image of lightning to demonstrate a punishment that was immediate, deserved, necessary, and ultimately regenerative.

Nothing illustrates this better than the rhetoric of Robespierre himself, when, in 1794, he inquired of the Convention, "Is it not to strike the heads of the prideful that lightning is destined?" and urged French patriots to "hurl lightning at [their] enemies." These remarks are both distant from, and remarkably similar to, Robespierre's assertion eleven years earlier that lightning was "obedient." Lightning, in Robespierre's brief supporting de Vissery, was obedient, but it was not purposeful. In the language of 1794 it was both controlled by man *and* directed as a means of punishing the guilty. What is more, the image of lightning removed the need to justify violence: it was justification in itself. As Robespierre indicated, it signified the prideful by striking them.

The image of lightning indicates both rupture and continuity in the symbolic language of the New Regime. Between the storming of the Bastille, when lightning belonged to the king's armies and was directed *against* the people, and the king's trial, when the people threw down their lightning bolt at the king, power had clearly shifted in the symbolic realm. This symbolic shift was made possible partly by discoveries of science: lightning, far from being a symbol of arbitrary force, could instead be directed and channeled for positive uses. Increasingly the means of that channeling—the conductor of the people's lightning—was the Convention. Yet we have seen that the symbol also retained certain meanings from the alleged "superstitions" of the Old Regime in that revolutionary actors insisted that, rather than being an accident of nature, lightning continued to signify justice and a punishment for sins, albeit sins against a new providence. In this sense there was an uncomfortable similarity between the *lettre de cachet*, the "lightning bolt of despotism," and the people that judged, not like a court of law, but like a force of nature. More important, the language of lightning inherited by science allowed for the lightning bolt not only to punish the traitor but to create a new equilibrium. The force of *la foudre révolutionnaire* transcended punishment and, instead, cast destruction as part of the natural process of change. "Lightning that brews on mountaintops next to swamps is often necessary to purge the air of the infected vapors that [the swamps] emit," proclaimed a group of emissaries from the département du Mont Blanc to the Convention on 11 August 1793. "Strike when the time is right."[62]

The Saltpeter Initiative: Forging Thunderbolts in Backyards

At the same time as the people of France were claiming to confer the powers of lightning on the Convention, they also were providing the government with the force of lightning through the fabrication of gunpowder, often called *la foudre révolutionnaire*. While the outbreak of war provided a space in which the ownership of sovereignty was contested through the trope of lightning, it also laid the groundwork for a national initiative to encourage citizens to cull saltpeter for use in making gunpowder. This allowed patriots to claim not only to *direct* lightning but also to create it. Gunpowder played a significant role in the revolutionary imagination, particularly after the outbreak of war and the *levée en masse*. In calling for the entire French nation to mobilize in support of the war effort, the August 1793 military levy encouraged women, elderly men, and children to fulfill their respective duties to the nation while France's sons were compelled to the front lines: taking part in medical care, making clothes and weapons, and inspiring patriotism in their fellow citizens. One of the ways in which civilians could take part in the effort was through gunpowder manufacturing or, in the words of one propagandist, "making the lightning bolt destined to pulverize agents of despotism."[63] Significantly, at the very moment at which the people of France seemed to relinquish the power of directing lightning to the constitutionless Convention, they were asked to create that lightning for the nation of France. If the people were gods, hard at work forging lightning bolts, the Convention was the enlightened lightning rod, able to direct the destructive and restorative energy at the proper targets.

If the revolutionary armies were to be armed with "lightning," the French people would need to produce it for them. Instead of planting Victory Gardens, as Americans would during the Second World War, good French citizens of the revolutionary era practiced Victory Chemistry. Zeus's thunderbolts were dug up from backyards, sifted out of sea water, and scraped off stable walls. Following an initiative launched by a decree on 14 Frimaire (4 December 1793), large broadsheets advertised the ease with which one could mine saltpeter from one's own backyard: "The National Convention, by its decree of 14 Frimaire, has invited all citizens themselves to collect *nitre,* or saltpeter, which forms in the earth of their basements, stables, barns, storerooms, sheds, and other areas beneath their houses, as well as that which can be found in the rubble of their buildings."[64] The broadsheet emphasized both the simplicity and importance of the harvest, laying out a procedure of three allegedly simple steps: identifying the earth where saltpeter could be found, leaching that earth, and finally evaporating the wash water to obtain the saltpeter.[65]

Thus citizens were asked to dig in their land, taste the earth for traces of saltiness and bitterness, and then begin the harvest. Several propaganda documents suggested that Nature had endowed France with a particularly vast supply of saltpeter in the earth, simply waiting for the patriotic citizen to bring forth the fiery potential in its depths. Geographically and historically, France was in a unique position to increase production of saltpeter. In his *rapport* of 14 Frimaire, Claude-Antoine Prieur-Duvernois encouraged citizens to take on the task of mining it themselves, but he also indicated that France's coastline provided a special source for the elements of gunpowder. Marine salt, he concluded, could be transformed into soda.[66] Furthermore, France could actually turn its struggles into battlefield advantages, as he chillingly proposed "to reduce to ashes the forests that form the lairs of the brigands of the Vendée and of Lozère." These ashes could then be used in gunpowder production.[67]

Saltpeter harvesting was a necessary patriotic act from which the Revolution, the French, and all humanity would profit. Louis-Pierre Dufourny, the president of the Département de Paris, wrote passionately to his constituents that for the war effort to succeed, "We must have more fire!" But Nature had provided that fire to the Republic: "Nature, whose empire you are reestablishing, offers you all the fire that is hidden in her beneficent bosom, with which to found and maintain your liberty." Saltpeter was nature's unique gift to France, simply waiting to be unearthed and put into motion by the true patriot. Dufourny encouraged French men and women with the words: "Help [Liberty's] birth: bring the machines to life, electrify lightning itself; exterminate the destructors of humanity. Citizens, in the name of the human race in revolution, whose happiness is lodged in *salpêtre,* we beseech you to demonstrate your patriotism by harvesting this precious material until its last atom."[68] France's earth held the fire of revolution, which itself held the happiness of the human race.

Paris sections and provincial departments took up this call to spades with vigor, if their reports to the Convention are to be believed. Bertrand Barère reported, in July 1794, that the sections of Paris had harvested six hundred metric tons of saltpeter in the six months since the passage of the law of 14 Frimaire.[69] Police reports noted the eagerness with which the Paris population took to saltpeter extraction; in Ventôse, a police spy reported, "Everyone is hastening to prepare the elements of *foudre* against the brigands and the traitors."[70] In addition, the French people themselves assimilated the language of *foudre*. The Department of the Marne, for example, issued an address to the Convention on 24 Prairial, Year II (12 June 1794): "And we, too, are scouring the innards of the earth, to draw from it...the lightning that should destroy...the impure hordes of slaves and brigands."[71] Far from a metaphor invoked only by political elites, *foudre* was used by a broader public as a connotation-laden synonym for gunpowder.

In unearthing lightning, the French became endowed with the qualities of lightning—rapidity, force, and both destruction and regeneration. "Be as prompt as the lightning for which you are preparing the materials," wrote the Inspector of Gunpowder in a circular during Year II.[72] In a song lauding *salpêtriers*, this transfer of electrical powers to the revolutionary patriot was reiterated: the good citizen not only culled saltpeter, he *became* it.

> Are we missing cannon powder?
> [The patriot's] heart then becomes *salpêtre*....
> ...To strike down all the tyrants,
> A Jacobin is *salpêtre*.[73]

Through the production of gunpowder, France gathered, controlled, and ultimately *was* lightning, destined to "strike the heads of the prideful."

From the beginning, Paris served as the center of this national production energy, acting as the central point from which education diffused—itself a kind of electrifying process. Antoine François de Fourcroy and Antoine Lavoisier, among the nation's top scientists, taught courses on saltpeter production at the Muséum d'Histoire Naturelle; their acolytes then spread the lessons to remote departments. In Ventôse, Year II, a series of these courses culminated in a Parisian festival celebrating their handiwork; the attendees then dispersed throughout France to educate a broader public. Barère described this educational process in a speech of 17 Messidor, Year II (5 July 1794): "Many, upon returning to their homes, brought with them revolutionary energy and the enlightenment necessary for the fabrication of saltpeter; thus they communicated the movement, which was originally excited here [in Paris], to all parts of the Republic."[74]

Like a circuit, France was connected by education, begun by a spark at its center and transmitted throughout the provinces with near-immediacy. It is significant that Barère used an electrical metaphor to describe the process: "The site of your classes is the electric plate, the districts are the links in the chain, and the shock is felt until the very end."[75] Suddenly, through the process of saltpeter education, France itself became lightning, a positive force capable both of destroying (its enemies) and regenerating (the Revolution).[76]

Although saltpeter had certainly been a matter of concern for the French nation previously—in 1775 the Académie had sponsored an essay contest in an attempt to discern the most efficient and effective means of harvesting saltpeter—this was the first time that it played such a large role in the nation's economic, political, and cultural spheres.[77] Saltpeter rapidly came to be privileged in songs, plays, and even festivals as part of the nationwide educational plan. One patriotic song detailed the process of finding and "harvesting" *salpêtre:* "Let us go down underground, / Where liberty invites us, ... / The earth and water evaporate in a cask, / Soon *nitre* will appear."[78] In glorifying the chemical process of gunpowder production, and in linking its creation with the fight for liberty, the song served as both education and propaganda.

These types of songs were sung at various festivals of the Revolution, but particularly at those that honored *salpêtre* and *salpêtriers* themselves.[79] In Ventôse (March 1794) the city of Paris planned a procession to present the students who had participated in the national saltpeter educational program. Each section would send a commission carrying barrels of saltpeter, decorated with ribbons and garlands, and accompanied by a full parade of other staples at a revolutionary festival—symbols of liberty, drummers, veterans, members of tribunals, representatives of all age groups—along with more particular additions such as eighty workers from arms factories and members of the national agency of *poudres et salpêtres*.[80] At the festival the participants sang, "We have forged the thunderbolt / That will soon purge the earth / Of monsters from all parts." "Animated by a holy rage," the song continued, the French armies would "regenerate the universe."[81] Just as Robespierre had insisted, in the 1780s, that the lightning rod allowed man to allay the arbitrariness of natural forces, so, too, did revolutionary lightning allow nature to be directed toward revolutionary ends.

Salpêtriers and their illustrious product, glorified in Paris's streets, were also honored in her theaters. A saltpeter factory was at the center of Charles-Louis Tissot's play, *Les Salpêtriers républicains*.[82] Dedicated to the members of the Committee of Public Safety, the play opened with a commendation

Fig. 6 Jean-Baptiste Lesueur, "Délégation d'aspirants armuriers de divers départements, se rendant à la Convention à l'occasion de la fête du Salpêtre, Paris, le 20 mars 1794." Note the lightning-bolt insignia on the flag carried by the participants in the saltpeter classes. The caption reads, "Young men sent from various *départements* to Paris to be taught how to make salpeter and gunpowder, and to learn the art of forging cannons. . . . Here they are going to the Convention, carrying the gunpowder and the saltpeter that they made, and a cannon that they cast. 1791 [1794]." © Musée Carnavalet / Roger-Viollet.

of their national educational program: "*Les Salpêtriers républicains,*" Tissot wrote in the introduction, "could never have appeared under any happier authority than that of the Saviors of the Country, who showed the French People the means to make saltpeter, that lightning bolt of war that will help them exterminate the coalition of tyrants."[83] The play's plot centered around the conversion of a lawyer, a tepid observer of the Revolution, who ultimately learned to serve his country by helping to make *salpêtre*. In the process he also transformed from a lecherous and cowardly character into a good citizen who performed his duties to the nation with pleasure. He sang, "Not everyone can be a soldier: / The heavens made me very fearful / But I can serve the state well / by making saltpeter."[84]

Like many of the revolutionary songs praising saltpeter, Tissot's play served as education and propaganda, under the (thin) guise of entertainment. The play was set in a "space like a hangar," where the work of *salpêtre* extraction was conducted. Indeed, during the performance, each stage of saltpeter production was demonstrated onstage, culminating in the appearance of an actual brick of saltpeter at the end of the play. From digging in the dirt to rinsing soil with water to boiling it in cauldrons, the Committee of Public Safety's three-step program was played out on stage.

Just as dirt was turned into lightning, so, too, were all the characters transformed by the creation of saltpeter. In addition to the lawyer Cascaret, who was converted into a good citizen, the other workers in the *salpêtrerie* noted that they had become new people since the opportunity to take part in the military effort. One marveled at having evolved from a common laborer to a chemist. Another, recently returned from war with a wounded arm, noted his transformation from uselessness to productivity: "If I am wounded on one arm, / The other can still make saltpeter."[85] The conversion story was completed by a wedding at the end of the play, between Paulin, the wounded soldier, and Justine, the daughter of the worker-turned-chemist. The ceremony was performed at an altar of saltpeter, which was the result of their labors. Justine and Paulin made their vows over the brick of saltpeter, the "knot that joins them," and they swore to raise their children to be good servants to their country.[86]

In his play Tissot not only reasserted the power of saltpeter to regenerate and transform, but he gave it an almost divine quality as it united a community and imbued its members with proper republican principles. It was the earthly manifestation of the Etre Suprême—the lightning of the *new* divinity—to whom the characters all prayed at the conclusion of the play; not only did the saltpeter unite the patriotic, it also destroyed the enemies of the Republic. In promulgating this message, Tissot strengthened the link between *salpêtre, foudre,* and republicanism that had already been posited in festivals, songs, and political speeches.

Lightning in Crisis: The Explosion of Grenelle

At the center of France's circuit of *foudre* production was the pou-drerie of Grenelle. Barère had noted, in his speech of 17 Messidor (5 July 1794), that Paris was the generative point of electrified France and that the majority of saltpeter production should take place in the capital city. In nature, Barère explained, all things are centralized, and therefore a France that relies on the powers of nature should also be centralized. "By placing the great workshops of saltpeter and gunpowder refining in the center of the Republic and the Government, we will concentrate the revolutionary force more and more, and we will unite, in a single point, all its active powers."[87] Grenelle became the focus of this national "elec-trification." Located in what is now Paris's fifteenth arrondissement, it employed several thousand workers and produced, according to reports, more than thirty metric tons of gunpowder each day.[88]

In the early morning of 14 Fructidor, Year II (31 August 1794), the gun-powder factory of Grenelle exploded. Immediately the joint committees of Public Safety and General Security, still rebuilding from Robespierre's overthrow a mere month earlier, sprang into action. Reports from Grenelle streamed in, followed promptly by *arrêts* from the committees. By the end of the day, more than twenty-one mandates had been issued, all written in urgent, hurried penmanship. Alongside commissions for medi-cal assistance and firemen, transportation to area hospitals, and police surveillance for suspicious behavior, the Committees also mobilized a bat-talion of *afficheurs,* or poster hangers, to publicize their various decrees.[89] Indeed, the revolutionary government was facing both a human disaster, which claimed the lives of hundreds of Parisian workers, and a public re-lations crisis. The center of its circuit, and of the rhetoric of *foudre,* had self-destructed: lightning, as it turned out, could strike not only the guilty, but also the laboring patriot.

The Convention first strove to reassert the patriotism and, indeed, the martyrdom of the workers in the Grenelle factory. In fact, the rhetoric of gunpowder production as civic duty had made its way into the language of the workers themselves, as evidenced by numerous letters of appeal written to the revolutionary government. In a letter of 11 Brumaire (1 November), a Citizen Dumas, injured in the explosion, appealed for aid based directly on the particular service he and his fellow factory workers provided for the state. Because his injuries after the explosion rendered him unable to work, he asked for additional assistance: "Does this position differ somehow from that of a *défenseur de la patrie*, who risks his life on the front line? And does not each of them have equal rights to the benevolence [*bienfaisance*] of the Nation?"[90] Dumas presented himself as a civil servant, motivated by the same patriotism, faced with the same risks, and worthy of the same treatment as a soldier in the Republican Army. Clearly, the notion of making arms as a service to the country had permeated the mind-set of the workers.

The Convention did not disagree with this characterization. Indeed, upon receiving word of the explosion, the Convention immediately decreed that its victims would be considered *défenseurs de la patrie*. Before 9:00 on the morning of the tragedy, the *Journal de la Montagne* reported, the legislators had adopted a proposal by Jean-Baptiste Treilhard allowing for the same compensation of the wounded and the families of the dead as that received by soldiers of the Republic.[91] By treating the *ouvriers* as defenders of the Nation, and by compensating their families accordingly, the National Convention affirmed the notion of arms production and gunpowder manufacturing as a patriotic service, worthy of merit and honor. It elevated the Grenelle workers from tragic victims to martyrs for France. In death, saltpeter transformed laborers into heroes, just as they had been transformed into chemists and warriors in Tissot's play.

In addition to reinforcing the idea of patriotism through saltpeter and gunpowder production, the explosion of Grenelle was portrayed as creating the prospect for national unification and renewal. Like a lightning strike, it was presented as a phenomenon that could transform and regenerate even in the wake of tragedy. One wounded victim of the tragedy, a Citizen Dobigny, even insisted to the legislators in a letter that the accident had provided the nation with a unique opportunity to demonstrate its justice toward the suffering. In fact, he suggested, it seemed that a small number of workers were spared precisely for this purpose. "Our number is so small," he wrote to the Convention, "that it seems that nature and Providence allowed us to escape to signal to France, and to Europe, your justice."[92] This remnant could serve as a constant reminder of the force of gunpowder, and of the generosity and integrity of the French government.

Indeed, the explosion led to an outpouring of support not only from the government but from fellow citizens as well. On 30 Fructidor, the

Guillaume Tell section of Paris held a benefit concert for the relief of the families of those who had died in the explosion. It was presided over by Pierre Trassart, who frequently gave "sermons" to citizens of the neighborhood on occasions of the *décadi,* the day of rest that replaced Sundays in the revolutionary calendar. At the benefit, Trassart attempted to rally support for the victims themselves, and also to raise the patriotic spirits of those in attendance. The two impulses, sorrow and unity, generosity and patriotism, were inextricably linked: "Aid to the needy! Hatred and war to tyrants!" he proclaimed, fusing the sentiments of benevolence and animosity. He continued: "That is, in effect, the prerogative of this tableau: while it should excite in us bitter and sharp sadness, it should also simultaneously, by the reflections that it provokes and the memories drawn out by its facts, electrify our souls, and imprint on them, if it is possible, even more deeply,…the generous sentiment that tyrants dread: love of country."[93] The factory explosion left a scar on the people of France, one that reminded them of tragedy but also excited their patriotism. Just as lightning bolts left scars on their victims, so, too, did the explosion of *la foudre révolutionnaire* electrify the body of the French population.

Trassart retold the events of 14 Fructidor, emphasizing the immediacy of the explosion: "O deplorable destiny! In an instant, the workshop of national vengeance became a volcano that consumed and devoured a number of our brothers. In an instant, in this plain where, on all sides, the venerable activity of labor that is useful to the country was taking place, one could see only the debris of the most hard-working men…, and everywhere the image of death or sorrow." Yet immediately after the event, Trassart noted, the earth moved again—this time by the rush of patriots to the site, eager to defend and offer relief to their compatriots. "What a sublime spectacle! A terrible and terrifying explosion was the work of an *instant,* and in another instant, good-will [*la bienfaisance*] took hold of this great theater of sorrow: the number of helpful citizens far surpassed the number of those in need of help."[94]

The gunpowder at Grenelle was capable of instantaneous, untrammeled force. Yet the explosion also released another immediate, and equally powerful, impulse: unity, benevolence, and regeneration. The *coup de foudre* had a secondary effect that not only counterbalanced but overtook the initial tragic one: instead of returning France to an equilibrium, the explosion of Grenelle laid the foundation for a new sentimental union, a goodness that surpassed the tragedy, and a national rebirth. Not only did the victims of Grenelle die while in service to the country, their *deaths themselves* were a service to the nation, by setting an example of patriotic behavior and creating the opportunity for unity and growth.

The Grenelle tragedy provides a unique example of how useful naturalized language could be to the revolutionary government, especially in times of war and crisis. The language of lightning provided a powerful metaphor for changing notions of sovereignty; it also applied the language of science to the rhetoric of political revolution. As eighteenth-century naturalists had explained lightning as a necessary result of, and remedy to, disequilibrium in the atmosphere (or, in the case of practitioners of medical electricity, imbalance in the body), so, too, did revolutionaries like Collot d'Herbois, Robespierre, and Barère use the image of *la foudre* to describe a force that was both necessary and regenerative. "Lightning" could, with instantaneous power, either slay the enemy or heal the body of the Revolution—or both. As the explosion at Grenelle demonstrated, nature, even in the wake of apparent tragedy, was on the side of the Revolution. As Bertrand Barère expressed in his speech of 17 Messidor (5 July) to the Convention, France and Nature were in a coalition with each other; she provided lightning bolts in the earth for France to throw at its enemies; she organized revolutions in the natural world that would be models for the political one.[95] These revolutions could sometimes be violent—their storms destructive, their lightning bolts lethal—but they were *natural*, they were *necessary*, and ultimately, they were beneficial to all mankind. Lightning, in the hands of revolutionaries, could strike the guilty and redeem the innocent; it could restore the equilibrium of the political universe.

4

PURE MOUNTAIN, CORRUPTIVE SWAMP

On 28 Nivôse, Year II (17 January 1794), a play called *Les Petits Montagnards* started its run at the Théâtre de la Cité-Variétés. Popular enough to garner large crowds and have its songs sung again at festivals and reprinted in collections of *chansons patriotiques*, the play translated the mythology of the Mountain, the popular nickname for the Jacobins, into song and dance. The play centered around two young children, Petit-Jacques and Georgette, living on a "volcanic mountain named the Puy de Montagnard," whose poor father Gervais had come upon difficult times.[1] Having lost his wife years earlier, Gervais had fallen into inescapable poverty. To assist him, his two children set out to find their mother. Drawing on a trope common in sentimental novels, the radical playwright Aristide Valcour arranged a chance meeting between the mother and her children: during a terrible storm, they encountered a poor and lonely woman who had been turned away from an inn because she could not pay for it. They offered her their last two *sous*, giving her the chance to find shelter for the evening. Predictably enough, the woman turned out to be their long-lost mother, with whom Gervais was reunited at the jubilant conclusion of the play.

Although Valcour refrained from direct political allusion throughout most of the play—the Mountain served as much as a geographic site as a political metaphor—the closing scene made explicit the link between Gervais's mountain of struggle and virtue and the Jacobin Mountain of patriotism and incorruptibility. The play ended with a chorus in which all the actors, and apparently much of the audience, joined. The song put the image of the Mountain in a historical context:

> It was on the ancient Mountain
> That man was born free and proud.

> It was from the Helvetian Mountain
> That Tell pulverized Gessler;
> In the plains, slaves
> Groveled at Caesar's feet.[2]

Historically, mountains were the place from which freedom emerged. In keeping with that tradition, the modern Mountain was the locus of liberty, virtue, and happiness. However, the plain—a nickname given to the moderates of the Convention—was the locus not of freedom but of slavery. Playing with the geographic and political meanings of the word, the song began, "Happy inhabitants of the Mountains / Liberty reigns among you / In all times, she has as companions / Innocence and truth."[3] The play, like its eponymous song, glorified both *montagnards,* the virtuous people living in mountainous regions, and *Montagnards,* the political bastion of liberty.

On 6 Ventôse (24 February 1794) a police spy noted that after the production the audience demanded that the "couplets in praise of the Mountain" be sung again, and applauded heartily.[4] The audience's response suggests that the political and geographic conflation was not only posited by the playwright but was recognized by a broader public. The *Journal de Paris* reported that the play, and particularly its concluding vaudeville, met with great success, and the newspaper, too, reprinted the patriotic song.[5] Indeed, Valcour's song could be found in numerous patriotic collections, signifying both its popularity and its political currency, as some of the collections were financed or printed by the Jacobins themselves.[6]

Despite the ubiquity of the terms "Montagne" and "Montagnard" during the Revolution, little work has been done to investigate the rationale behind, or the meanings associated with, the appellation used by the Jacobins. The genesis of the term refers to the radicals' seating position in the Convention, near the rafters of the assembly hall. Yet, as Ferdinand Brunot noted in his exegesis of language during the Revolution, the term "mountain" seemed to designate more than mere seating order: "There were others just as high on the right side."[7] Brunot offered a few cultural markers for the use of the term, yet he did not fully illuminate the choice, or the popularization, of the term, particularly among Jacobins themselves. What began as a partially mocking term for the radical faction in the Convention was embraced as an appellation to signify all emissaries of the true Revolution: bastions of incorruptibility and political virtue. In fact, natural histories, travelers' accounts, and literature all provided a wealth of useful referents that the Jacobins and their supporters could, and did, deploy in their rhetoric, especially in songs and plays intended for a broader audience. For its various meanings in natural history as well as the Scripture's Mount Sinai and the myths of Mount Olympus and Mount Parnassus, the term "Montagne" connoted a sublime space, a place of unspeakable power and of purity achieved through struggle.[8]

What is more, a rich scientific literature of the eighteenth century provided a language with which to vilify the political antithesis of the Mountain, namely, *le Marais* or the Swamp, for its insidious, corruptive, and unnatural presence.[9] The mountain came to be deployed by individuals in power as a means of aligning the work of the Revolution—and, specifically, the Jacobin Revolution—with the operations of nature, or of "return[ing] nature to itself."[10] As a result, it nullified opposition to the radical revolution, making enemies of the Mountain enemies of nature. The Festival of the Supreme Being of 8 June 1794, with an elaborate simulacrum of a mountain at its center, exemplified this synthesis of the mountain, the sacred, and the natural world. By invoking nature as an agent of the revolution, the Festival revealed the extent of the "secular providentialism" of natural language. The *Fête à l'Etre Suprême* did not erase violence.[11] Far from it. Instead, it naturalized violence; nature's force was revolutionary, just as revolutionary force was natural.

The Natural and Political Mountain

Perhaps one of the reasons that the idea of the Mountain has not been more thoroughly analyzed is that it is easy to consider it a mere abstraction, a name whose referents were quickly subsumed by its political denotations. Yet, in revolutionary discourse, the geographic mountain and the political Mountain were intimately tied, as the responses to Valcour's play suggest. As indicated in a stanza from a patriotic song of Year II titled "La Montagne," the "mountain" was placed in the context of other geographic spaces, and treated as an aesthetic as well as a political choice over the city, country, or plain:

> We have a thousand different tastes,
> We make a thousand choices in this world;
> One always wants to run through the fields,
> And the other, to travel over waves;
> He in the city loves noise,
> While another loves the peace of the countryside;
> This one heads to the plains, and the other runs from them;
> As for me, I love the Mountain.[12]

Fig. 7 The Mountain at the center of the Festival of the Supreme Being. "Vue de la montagne élevée au champ de la Réunion." Paris: Chez Jacques-Simon Chéreau, 1794. Bibliothèque Nationale de France, Collection de Vinck 6301.

Letters to the National Convention compared the defense of France's mountains to the defense of la Montagne; in July 1793 the members of the first battalion of Calvados encouraged the *conventionnels* to complete their work on the Constitution, promising that they would, "defend with all their power the Mountain of the Convention against the maneuvers of federalists, just as they defend, with all their strength, the mountain of Cassel against the attacks of the coalition of tyrants."[13] Even at the Festival of the Supreme Being, discussed in more detail below, the rendering of the mountain at the center of the festival was no mere abstraction; instead, it was a representation that evoked a natural peak.

What is more, representations of mountains in political spaces became *more* natural over the course of the early Revolution. The uses of the symbol at the height of the Jacobin ascent to power emphasized the relationship between the image of the mountain and the natural world far more than did its earlier enunciations. At the first Festival of Federation, on 14 July 1790, some eyewitness accounts referred to a "mountain" having been erected on the Champ de Mars. One engraving described the "metamorphosis" that took place there, as "suddenly, in a vast and superb amphitheater,…arose a mountain upon which the altar of Federation would be placed." The awestruck engraver continued, "One would say that a magic wand touched the earth and brought forth from nothing the Palace of Liberty."[14] Yet the scene portrayed in his depiction, like those in other representations of the festival, bore no resemblance to the depictions of the "mountain" at the center of the Fête de l'Etre Suprême; instead, they showed merely elevated terrain, populated by a crowd of citizens swearing oaths. The naturalized mountain as a political symbol was a product of the radical Revolution.

From its first usage in political speech, "mountain" referenced man's experience with natural, geographic mountains. As Brunot points out, the first documented use of the term in political speech was on 27 October 1791, when Joseph Lequinio sought to respond to the unrest in the *départements* resulting from conflict over the Civil Constitution of the Clergy. Lequinio proposed a stance of toleration—surprising for someone who would later become an ardent dechristianizer—and emphasized freedom of religion, but also proposed the removal of anyone who had not sworn allegiance to the Constitution from national payrolls. Before offering his decree to the deliberation of the Assembly, however, he attempted to address the population at large. He began, "Citizens of France, you have honored us with your trust, and your esteem has carried us to the top of the mountain, from which our gazes stretch over the entire kingdom."[15]

This statement gave rise to murmurs, and to a riposte by Michel Mathieu Lecointe-Puyraveau, who snidely remarked, "We cannot be worried that M. Lequinio has us headed toward the mountains, but that he is rushing to place us in a temple." The language of the "mountain" was a source of scorn and even ridicule for the members of the Législative; Lecointe-Puyraveau's response suggested that the image of the mountain was steeped in religious, even sanctimonious connotations. Lequinio, however, explained that he had learned how to speak the language of the people (and specifically the language of those who were "overcome by fanaticism") and that this language was appropriate for addressing them.[16] He continued: "You, French citizens, see nothing but the narrow space that surrounds you; but we, we perceive in a single glance the general situation, and the evils that sadden and trouble the Empire, the source from which these disorders flow and the means to apply effective remedies."[17] He positioned the legislators in an almost divine position; Lequinio proclaimed that the legislators had a perspective that allowed them a greater clarity than the narrow view of the citizen, who was reminiscent of Leibniz's man who could see "scarcely beyond his nose" and could not condemn divine judgments.

It is noteworthy that Lequinio invoked the mountain *specifically* as a means of appealing to the broader population. The natural metaphor became a way to illustrate the legislator's position to the public at large. Albert Soboul, in his *Dictionnaire historique de la Révolution Française*, found that the term was largely used in extra-parliamentary venues, including festivals, petitions, and iconography. It was also widely recognized as a popular epithet; as Soboul notes, Robespierre wrote in his *Lettre à ses commettans* in December 1792 that the upper corner of the Assembly was, "what is commonly [*vulgairement*] known as the Mountain."[18] "Mountain" became a common theme in popular songs and in images; it was a "popular" appellation in both senses: its use was widespread, but also commonplace among non-elites in particular.

Furthermore, Lequinio's suggestion that the mountain was a space of clarity and comprehension, that the heights of the mountain granted legislators the ability to take in vast terrains in a mere *coup d'oeil*, was a position that, before the eighteenth century, was largely unknown, save to the actual inhabitants of mountainous regions. But in the 1700s recreational and scientific mountaineering had granted travelers, and their readers, new insight into the vistas afforded by mountaintops. The mountain itself was the object of a new fascination and admiration in the years prior to the Revolution. As Donald Geoffrey Charlton and Philippe Joutard have suggested, the European public grew increasingly captivated with mountains over the course of the eighteenth century. Once symbols of obscurity, of divine anger, or of demonic power, Europe's mountains became objects of curiosity, discovery, and wonder.[19] The two scholars posit similar causes for the development of the cult of the mountain, including scientific discovery, the role of the Alps in the increasingly popular Grand Tour, and the rise of an aesthetic taste that "unites sentiments of horror and beauty."[20] The second half of the eighteenth century witnessed a veritable explosion in the number of travelers to the Alps. In 1786 Mont Blanc was finally climbed by Gabriel Paccard and Jacques Balmat, who received a fair amount of press attention; the *Mercure de France* reported on it in September and again in November. The passionate naturalist Horace-Benedict de Saussure climbed Mont Blanc in 1787 to even more attention, publishing *Rélation abrégée d'un voyage à la cîme du Mont Blanc* that same year.

Saussure, among the most widely read of the century's mountain explorers, emphasized the *difficulty* of mountain exploration. One had to rid oneself of modern conveniences, of carriages and even horses, to traverse treacherous lands, in order to gain a broader view of the mountains.[21] Fatigue would no doubt set in, but the mountaineer would press on, inspired by the hope of what he might see. Yet nothing short of enlightenment awaited the intrepid traveler: "He arrives: his eyes, both blinded and fascinated from all sides, do not know at first where to settle; slowly he grows accustomed to this great light…But what expressions could excite the sensations, and depict the ideas, with which these great spectacles fill the soul of the Philosopher! It seems that, looking over this Globe, he discovers the springs that put it in motion, and that he recognizes…the principal agents that carry out [*opèrent*] its revolutions."[22] From the summit, the disoriented traveler could see the very mechanisms that perpetuated life on earth. The earth's "revolutions" were suddenly understandable from this vantage point.

Saussure also noted that, from the top of Mont Blanc, his perspective was uniquely clear and edifying. After having spent years struggling to understand the geography of the Alps, he grasped the organization of the land in a single instant. From his heightened perspective, the view was simultaneously illuminating, clarifying, and stupefying: "I could not believe my eyes," he wrote. "It was like a dream to see, beneath my feet, these majestic peaks and these formidable summits."[23] This may come as no surprise to the modern reader, but in an era in which very few individuals had ascended to the highest mountain peaks, the clarity provided from the summit was nothing short of wondrous. It was this singular perspective, which allowed the mountaineer a unique clarity of vision, that provoked the first political use of the term "mountain" in Lequinio's speech. Far from a space of obscurity, the mountaintop was a site of clarity and comprehension. As Joseph Fouché would write in 1793, "Yes, I am a Montagnard, in the sense that I am high enough to see only the good of my country."[24]

The travel literature born out of mountain journeys gave rise to other referents from which the revolutionary generation could, and did, draw. In addition to Mont Blanc and the Alps, other mountainous regions, including the Auvergne and the Pyrénées, had entered the public discourse in the eighteenth century. The Auvergne became the focus of much writing and exploration after the discovery of the region's volcanic origins in 1752; through 1794 the Committee of Public Instruction continued to press for a detailed map of the area to uncover its volcanic past.[25] Pierre Jean-Baptiste Legrand d'Aussy's *Voyage d'Auvergne* expressed the sublimity of the topography of the extinct volcanoes in 1788. Legrand d'Aussy noted the overwhelming sensory experience provided by the sweeping vistas. "Never before had my eyes seen a theater so rich, so vast, so nobly designed...My view went from the plain to the mountains, and from the mountains to the plain. In vain I tried to fix [my gaze] on a single object, and another object even more beautiful called it toward it, and next to this object I would discover twenty others that seemed even more striking." The sensory experience was almost too powerful to absorb in a single moment; it created a "disorder of senses and ideas."[26] The Auvergne landscape, with its steep mountains plunging into plains; its weather, with torrential downpours lasting days followed immediately by sunlit serenity; and its people, who lived in poverty yet seemed always to be happy, all provided studies in paradox. Joy and sorrow, want and plenty, beauty and slovenliness, all combined on the steep slopes of the Auvergne. It was a space of sublime and awesome beauty.

In the south of France the Pyrénées also became the object of both leisure and study during the eighteenth century. Their thermal baths were beginning to attract elite visitors, but at the same time they reminded tourists of the volatility of mountain life. According to Serge Briffaud, the explorers of the Pyrenées in the second half of the century noted two conflicting, but related, phenomena: both convulsion and chaos, and regeneration and fertility. "The two images, however, could not be dissociated from each other: the valleys owed their picturesque quality to the troubling proximity of 'the other mountain,' which allowed so many dangers to hover over them and which poured into the valleys the product of the convulsions that moved it: its torrents, its landslides, its avalanches."[27] Indeed, the Pyrénées experienced so many floods and avalanches during the decades prior to the Revolution that Louis XVI considered making an emergency fund available to their inhabitants.[28]

In the Alps, the Auvergne, and the Pyrénées, then, the mountains were spaces of conflict, of beauty made possible by destruction. They were also sites of sensory revitalization, and sources of both literal and moral clarity, uncovered by a new generation of mountain explorers such as Legrand d'Aussy, Saussure, and Ramond de Carbonnières. These lessons were reiterated in natural histories and philosophical texts written by savants who preferred a less adventurous approach to their research. Buffon gave mountains a role of foremost importance in his theory of the earth, claiming, in his *Époques de la Nature*, that all Nature originated in mountains.[29] Bernardin de Saint-Pierre opened his *Etudes de la Nature* with an engraving of a mountain, which he hoped would demonstrate "elementary harmonies" that could be found only on islands and in alpine regions.[30] As his idea of harmony was particularly important to one of the foremost goals of his text—namely, to correlate nature's diversity with a divine plan— the mountain was a site of unique importance. According to d'Holbach, mountains were not only spaces of virtue and aesthetic wonder; they were beneficent reminders of Providence's wisdom. His *Encyclopédie* article on mountains compared mountains to the bones of the human skeleton, equally necessary for the earth's survival. D'Holbach suggested that mountains, instead of having been formed by the Flood, as some posited, had always existed:

> In effect, it seems that *mountains* have been necessary to the earth since the beginning of the world; without them it would have been deprived of infinite advantages. It is to mountains that we owe the fertility of the plains, the rivers that water them, for which mountains are the inexhaustible reservoirs. The waters of the heavens, in rolling over the inequalities that form like so many inclined planes, will carry to valleys the nourishment so necessary to the growth of vegetation; it is in the bosom of mountains that nature has deposited metals...It can therefore be presumed that Providence, in creating our earth, adorned it with mountains that were useful for [*propre à*] giving support and solidity to human habitation.[31]

In addition to their aesthetic and intellectual benefits, mountains also provided material vital for survival: fertile soil, sources of water, and metallic ores.

In the naturalist literature of the day, mountains represented a space of struggle and virtue, and of paradox and beauty, as well as a repository of staples necessary for human existence. However, as Philippe Joutard rightly points out, no text had a more significant impact on the image of the mountain in the eighteenth century than Rousseau's *La Nouvelle Héloise*.[32] Mountains were important images in several of Rousseau's texts; the Savoyard Vicar's sentimental profession of faith in *Emile* took place on a hilltop facing the mountains, where, "Nature spread out all her magnificence before our eyes to offer us the text for our discussion."[33] Furthermore, his *Lettres écrites de la montagne,* written in response to the calumny of Jean-Robert Tronchin's *Lettres écrites de la campagne,* defended not only Rousseau himself and his texts but also, in his own words, "religion, liberty, justice."[34] While the mountains play no visible role in the *Lettres,* it was from their heights that Rousseau was able to gain access to the truths that would redeem him. Yet it was in *La Nouvelle Héloise* that the mountains became a space of particular virtue and beauty. Rousseau's passionately beloved novel was set in a small village at the foot of the Alps, and early in the text, Saint-Preux retreated to the mountains to find tranquility in his love Julie's absence. Saint-Preux's account of mountain life reinforced some of the key characteristics provided by natural historians' and travelers' accounts of mountains: the moral virtue of the mountain dwellers, the paradoxes inherent in mountain vistas, and the sublime effect on his senses. To Rousseau's Saint-Preux, the mountain was a space of paradox: "Nature seemed to take pleasure in putting itself in opposition with itself, so much so that one saw the same place differently from different perspectives!"[35] These oppositions gave rise to an almost unspeakable beauty, just as they would for Legrand d'Aussy, traveling in a real mountain range years later.

The experiences of both real and fictitious mountaineers diffused a powerful and positive image of mountains and their inhabitants to the eighteenth-century reading public. These characteristics came to the fore in the various uses of the "mountain" in revolutionary imagery and discourse. While in December 1792, as Robespierre had mentioned in his *Lettre à ses commettans,* the word "mountain" was still a "common" term, it had, in fact, been used within the Jacobin Club for months as a self-referential cognomen, often tinted with naturalized hues. As early as 3 April 1792 Brissot was already referring to deputies who sat "on the mountain" in the Legislative Assembly.[36] Soon after the convocation of the Convention, Collot d'Herbois referred to the "patriots who inhabit the Mountain"; as discussions of trying Louis XVI began, Billaud-Varenne noted that "the majority of the Convention has arranged itself on the side of the Mountain."[37] François Chabot suggested, on 19 December 1792, that the term was used to distinguish true revolutionaries from the Brissotins who had once sat within the Jacobin Club: "Even if there were only ten of us on the mountain, we would remain at our post. We will unveil all the crimes of Brissot and of the Girondin faction," he proclaimed, "and all the waves of the sea will break against the rock where we sit, because it is supported by the unmovable bases of justice and truth."[38] In separating the "mountain" from the moderate factions, and in fusing the image of the *conventionnels* seated high above the moderates with the naturalized image of a strong and impenetrable boulder, Chabot hinted at some of the reasons why the Jacobins may have embraced with such enthusiasm what had begun as a satirical appellation: the durability of the mountain itself and the hardiness of the mountain dweller. By the spring of 1793 the term was ubiquitous; in June the Jacobins launched the *Journal de la Montagne*, formalizing the relationship between the mountain and the radicals. As the Jacobins gained power and currency, they drew upon the various connotations of "mountain" prevalent in the eighteenth century to refer to their virtue, to sacralize their authority, and ultimately to present their policies as being in accord with, or even dictated by, nature.

The Virtuous Montagnard

Not only were mountains themselves the subject of naturalistic study in the eighteenth century, so, too, were their inhabitants. In an era in which moral characteristics were deemed linked to physical and geographic characteristics, *montagnards* themselves became objects of the naturalist's gaze. Saussure, like many of his fellow aspiring mountaineers, attributed the wonder of mountains to both their physical *and* moral qualities. In his *Voyages dans les Alpes,* he wrote, "The morality in the Alps is no less interesting than their physical qualities…If one can hope to find, somewhere in Europe, men civilized enough not to be ferocious and natural enough not to be corrupt, it is in the Alps that we must search for them."[39] The mountain communities were the ideal nexus between the state of nature and the state of civilization. Saussure envisioned the mountains as spaces of equality and purity, free from luxury and corruption.

Louis-Sébastien Mercier, in his *Tableau de Paris,* also praised the morality of *montagnards* in an entry on "Vue des Alpes." "Happy is the habitant of the Alps," he wrote, "elevated on a rock between earth and the heavens.

He breathes pure air, he sees the sun in all its glory, he possesses moderation, he is satisfied, and, unaware of the shortcomings and follies of opulence, he believes himself to be rich." According to Mercier, the *montagnard* lived in the present moment, pleased with his station in life and unsusceptible to the fears and anxieties of Parisian life. Mercier attested to a relationship between the mountain dweller's physical surroundings and his moral character, and again between his moral character and his physical appearance: "And since everything is linked, since moral and physical realms are interdependent, the tranquility of the countryside is reflected on his calm face."[40] At the end of 1789, looking back on the wonders and miracles that the year afforded, Mercier compared the "new Paris" to the mountains as a space of happiness and freedom: "You have changed *my Paris*, it is true; it is something altogether different today; in just a little more time, it will be the residence of liberty and happiness. I already breathe the mountain air of Switzerland there."[41] The Revolution had brought changes in the atmosphere of Paris, so that the air was purer, the people more virtuous, and the nation more jubilant.

The ideas both of mountainous regions as spaces of sacrifice and integrity, and of their inhabitants as archetypes of virtue, were commonplace in the eighteenth century and were emphasized by the political actors claiming the name "Montagnard" during the Revolution. Virtue, of course, was at the center of revolutionary discourse about both civic and moral responsibility. Robespierre, in his speech on revolutionary religion of 18 Floréal (7 May 1794), suggested that the Revolution was the transformation of the nation into a state of purity and virtue. Among Robespierre's proposed festivals for inculcating civic virtue was one devoted to *désintéressement*, a virtue that Robespierre's muse, Rousseau, had praised effusively as a characteristic of the *montagnards* Saint-Preux met in *La Nouvelle Héloise*.[42] In Rousseau's novel, mountain inhabitants were simple, lived in relative equality and liberty, but above all they were "disinterested," a term that for Rousseau indicated an authenticity unmitigated by self-interest or *amour propre*. This quality was almost indescribable to the young Saint Preux: "But what I could not depict to you, and what can hardly be imagined, is their disinterested humanity, and their hospitable zeal for all foreigners."[43] In a space where neither profit nor luxury corrupted the people, *montagnards* could act out of pure humanity.

Yet this virtue was not easily won; instead, it required constant vigilance and sacrifice. "O sublime people!" Robespierre exclaimed in his address concerning the festivals of the Republic. "Receive the sacrifice of my entire being; happy is he who is born amidst you! Even happier is he who can die for your happiness!"[44] His program of festivals sought to cultivate a spirit of civic virtue and communal responsibility. Similarly, just as Saussure had struggled to reach the summit of Mont Blanc, and had assured a clarity of vision to those who attained such heights, Aristide Valcour represented the mountain in *Les Petits Montagnards* as a place of difficulty and struggle but, ultimately, of virtue. Gervais noted that he did not always live on the mountain, that he had previously had a life of "honest ease."[45] His life as a *montagnard* was one of hardship and poverty, but ultimately it brought him joy and completion. With this portrayal, Valcour gestured, wittingly or not, toward a motif in contemporary mountain literature: the virtuous and often risky lives of mountain dwellers.

In both revolutionary and prerevolutionary discourse, the mountain was a symbol of moral purity, and indeed its very name became an important mark of a purified group: the Theater of Montansier became the Théâtre de la Montagne after its proprietress was imprisoned; the section of Butte-des-Moulins (previously Palais-Royal) became the section de la Montagne in August 1793, after completing a purge of its unpatriotic members.[46] And, perhaps most famously, the city of Toulon was renamed Port de la Montagne following its reconquest in 1793. On the other hand, the term *marais* was eliminated from political speech, particularly after the removal of the Girondins from the Convention. On 6 June 1793 the Section du Marais asked to be known henceforth as the Section de *l'Homme Armé*, a declaration that the Commune "welcomed with emotion."[47]

Taking the name of the Mountain evinced a new, rarified civic and moral life, just as being a *montagnard* indicated a shared set of values with not just the political Mountain, but with the quintessential literary mountain dweller, namely, disinterest, modesty, and purity. For example, in an address to the National Convention on 22 Ventôse, Year II (12 March 1794), a group of *sans-culottes* from Montmirail credited the Mountain with the expanding dominion of Reason over France.[48] In addition to the rather typical sycophantic language flattering the generous and "august" legislators, the *sans-culottes* added that they were themselves *montagnards*. "Nature has made us *montagnards* for all time," they wrote, and this required a certain moral discipline to which they adhered. "We have proven that we are morally worthy of this glorious title," they continued, by their devotion to the Temple of Reason.[49] Both *montagnards* and *Montagnards* were expected to be bastions of virtue and morality. As Robespierre himself said, "Any representative of the people who sincerely loves liberty, any representative of the people who is ready to die for the nation, is from the Mountain."[50] Robespierre attempted to define the Mountain as a moral as well as a political community, as a congregation that was willing to act virtuously, indeed to sacrifice their very lives, for the good of the nation. The mountain thus made its way into popular parlance as both a political appellation and a metaphor for purity and virtue.

The Sublime and the Sacred Mountain

In addition to being a space of virtue, and of a uniquely clear perspective, the mountain was also a place where humans confronted the sublime. In *La Nouvelle Héloïse*, Saint-Preux had found that the mountain was a place of transformation, of an encounter with something that transcended the natural. "The spectacle has *je ne sais quoi* of magic, of the supernatural, that ravishes the spirit and the senses; one forgets everything, one forgets himself; one no longer knows where he is."[51] Legrand d'Aussy's "disorder of the senses," or Saussure's "excited sensations," were reminiscent of descriptions of the sublime in aesthetic literature of the eighteenth century.

Edmund Burke, in his *Philosophical Enquiry into the Origin of Our Ideas of the Sublime and the Beautiful*, described the sublime: "Whatever is fitted in any sort to excite the ideas of pain, and danger, that is to say, whatever is in any sort terrible, or is conversant about terrible objects, or operates in a manner analogous to terror, is a source of the *sublime*."[52] Significantly, for Burke, the *sublime* often could be found in nature—in storms, in the ocean, in a starry night—in things that exceeded the limits of the human imagination and hinted at infinity.[53] Although the notion of the sublime dates back to the classical period, it experienced a renaissance in the late seventeenth and early eighteenth centuries, in part because of Boileau's 1674 translation of Longinus's *Traité du Sublime*, and was linked explicitly to the natural world not only in Burke's *Essay* but also in Diderot, Mercier, John Baillie, and Alexander Gerard.[54] A stormy sea, to Diderot, was "sublime" in a way that a calm ocean was not.[55] In Mercier's words: "The great and the sublime are not rare; they abound in nature; our eyes tire of them. The sublime...soars on the wings of tempests; it rises with this volcano whose red and somber flames set clouds on fire; it accompanies the majesty of these vast floods, it reigns on this ocean that joins the two worlds; it descends into these deep caverns where the earth reveals its open and shredded entrails."[56] Descriptions of natural disasters over the course of the century helped to fuel this new language of the sublime, but so, too, did scientific discovery and naturalists' expeditions.

The new discoveries of science and the new aesthetics of the sublime seemed to go hand-in-hand. As Lacépède told his class at the Muséum d'Histoire Naturelle at the end of the century, "What an aid for the historian of human societies...is the view of these sublime annals that Nature has engraved on the summit of mountains, in the depths of the seas, and in the bowels of the earth!"[57] Naturalists who sought to discover nature would also find sublimity. This was particularly true of mountain travelers; in fact, the very things that made mountain vistas aesthetically "sublime"—their perception of infinitude, their variegated forms, their juxtapositions—made them important for scientific study. In Saussure's words, "High mountains, [unlike vast plains], are infinitely varied in their materials and in their form, and provide natural cross-sections of a large size, in broad daylight, from which one can observe with the greatest clarity and see in a single glance the order, situation, direction, thickness, and even the nature of the foundations of which they are composed."[58] Saussure went on to explain that a true naturalist could not expect to learn anything by staying on the beaten paths, but rather needed to "climb atop elevated summits, from which the eye can take in a multitude of objects at once."[59] In this sense the naturalist's gaze and the aesthete's were one and the same.

By invoking the language of the sublime, revolutionaries created a vision of a force that transcended human imagination, and one that was meant to terrify, awe, and inspire. As Edmund Burke posited in his *Philosophical Enquiry*, the sublime gave rise to "admiration, reverence, and respect."[60] The *Encyclopédie* entry on the sublime, written by Jaucourt, defined it as, "Everything that elevates us above what we were, and that simultaneously makes us aware of that elevation."[61] Saint-Preux's experience atop the mountains paralleled this description precisely; he was transformed into something transcendent, while also being cognizant of his metamorphosis.

Both Daniel Arasse and Marie-Hélène Huet have noted the importance of the sublime in descriptions of the revolutionary spectacle.[62] For Huet, the revolutionary sublime invited the individual to merge his sentimental experience with the collective, essentially subsuming himself within the general will.[63] The festival was the quintessential space for this collective experience, which makes the rampant invocations of nature that took place at both the Festival of Unity and Indivisibility and the Festival of the Supreme Being of particular import. In fact, upon witnessing the Festival of Unity and Indivisibility, Jean-Joseph Pithou described a kind of drunken stupor that lulled the crowd. "Citizens," he wrote, "the touching voice of the nation has made itself heard, it has penetrated and subjugated all hearts; all, in the thrill [*transports*] of a sweet drunkenness, swore love and fidelity to it."[64] The sublime does not spur action, but instead inspires awe.

Alexander Gerard's *Essay on Taste,* translated into French in the 1760s, echoed these ideas; his essay drew largely on John Baillie, whose 1747 *Essay on the Sublime* had cited mountains as sources of sublimity, as they were evocative of infinity.[65] Gerard concurred, and expanded on the feeling that such sublime sights would give rise to, namely, astonishment, terror, and immobility: "Hence the raging of the sea in a storm, and the loud roaring thunder, which inspire an awful sedateness, are termed sublime. Objects exciting terror are...in general sublime; for terror always implies astonishment, occupies the whole soul, and suspends all its motions."[66] In aesthetic theory the sublime was not intended to provoke action, or even reflection, but rather to stir emotions and often to stupefy—a result Saint-Preux described in his moment of self-forgetfulness. In Burke's words, "No passion so effectively robs the mind of all its powers of acting and reasoning as fear," aroused by the sublime.[67] The linking of the sublime and the Mountain may have betrayed an attempt to stifle dissent and expression.

The Committee of Public Safety's policy toward the Festival of the Supreme Being demonstrated clearly the relationship between sublimity and stifled expression. As Marie-Hélène Huet has emphasized, the "sublime" festival itself was declared un-representable: the Committee of Public Safety made reenactments of the festival illegal. In their decree of 11 Messidor (29 June 1794), they stated, "[At the festival] the Eternal was there, Nature was there in all its magnificence...It is only in memory that we can regain the deep impressions that moved our hearts: to search for them elsewhere is to weaken them; to bring to the stage this sublime spectacle is to parody it."[68] It was inappropriate to use groups of individuals to represent the collective of the French people; it was pastiche to use simulacra to depict Nature. Despite their good intentions, therefore, playwrights were asked not to represent the festival onstage. In an explicit affirmation of the ineffability of the sublime, the spectacle of the Supreme Being was declared un-representable.

References to mountains and *montagnards* as "sublime" in revolutionary rhetoric emphasized the suppression of opposing voices, just as they celebrated the unifying morals and virtues of the mountain. For example, the song concluding *Les Petits Montagnards* included the verse:

> From the unshakeable Mountain
> The most terrible of volcanoes
> Has struck the guilty crowd
> Of tyrants' dependents.
> Lightning has struck down crime,
> It no longer sullies our vision,

> And since this sublime moment,
> All the French are *Montagnards*.[69]

In piling natural image upon natural image—mountain, volcano, lightning—Valcour created an almost overwhelming effect. The forces of nature conspired to slay France's enemies, and to purge the Republic of vice and crime. And the result was a "sublime moment" of unity, wherein "all the French are *Montagnards*."

Similarly, on 24 Prairial (12 June), Year II, Robespierre gave a speech in which he expounded on the image of the Mountain. A mere four days after the Festival of the Supreme Being, Robespierre sought to align the Mountain with the Convention and the Committee of Public Safety alike, refuting the idea that the Mountain was a mere faction by stating that any representative willing to sacrifice his life for the nation was a Montagnard.[70] The mountain was a place that required sacrifice—indeed, the sacrifice of one's own life—but also a place that provided sanctuary and sanctity. When the conspiracy of the Girondins was uncovered, he said, the Mountain became a place of respite and purity: "Thus the name of the Mountain, which served as an asylum amid the tempest, became sacred, because it designated the portion of representatives of the people who fought against error." Tested in a moment of turmoil, the mountain became sacred, a sanctum of truth. He continued: "The Mountain is nothing but the heights of patriotism; a Montagnard is nothing but a patriot: pure, reasonable, and sublime."[71] Those who chose not to climb to such heights were the impure, the corrupt, the treasonous.

In these uses, "mountain" and "sublime" were linked to describe moments in which opposition had been silenced, and in which a collective became united by a single sentiment. These examples demonstrate the ardent wish of Robespierre and many of his followers for a single voice and a single sentiment shared by the entire nation, uninterrupted by discordant individuals or groups. Indeed, this elevation of the collective above the individual—if not to say the erasure of the individual voice for the unity of the multitude—was itself emblematic of the sublime. Baillie's aesthetic theory maintained that the sublime was necessarily the replacement of the individual with the collective: "Love to any of the Individuals, nay, to *all* of them, when considered as Individuals, and one by one, has nothing of Exalted; it is when we love them *collectively*, when we love them in vast Bodies stretching over large countries, that we feel the Sublime rise."[72] Certainly this had been at the crux of the criticism of the Committee of Public Safety concerning representations of the Festival of the Supreme Being: the plays, "in breaking [the people's] unity with an artless copy...in substituting groups for the mass of the people, in insulting its majesty,...diminish the progress of art, suffocate talent, and corrupt taste."[73] Factionalism, opposing voices, and individual wills disrupted the unity of the citizenry, dividing the impression of infinitude and purging an event of its sublimity.

Amid their protestations against representations of Nature and of the Festival of the Supreme Being, the Committee seemed to forget that the centerpiece of their festival was itself a simulacrum of nature: a mountain, covered in trees and caves, on which "the people" could clamber.[74] Surrounding the mountain, rocks were inscribed with phrases such as, "The Revolution is the daughter of heaven." The mountain erected at the center of the festival was not only evocative of virtuous *montagnards* and of sublime nature; it was also a monument to an additional connotation of the mountain inherited, not from natural histories, but from religious faith. Rhetoric about the Mountain often gestured toward a more famous ancestor: Mount Sinai.

Indeed, the biblical Mount and the Jacobin Mountain were conflated as sources both of law and sacrality. The interplay between the Mountain as the locus of law, and Mount Sinai, was exhibited in a text titled the *Décalogue Républicain*. In a section called "The Commandments," the text cried out to the "Revolutionaries of the Mountain, the Sinai of the French."[75] Similarly, the patriotic hymn "La Montagne" proclaimed,

> When the Eternal One handed down the laws
> That would make man wiser,
> He did not go to the countryside
> To pronounce his edicts
> No, he dictated his decrees
> From the heights of the Mountain.[76]

The mountain was a privileged site, from which law descended. Significantly, in syncretizing the Mountain with Sinai, these metaphors diminished the role of the legislator; law was not created but instead was handed down. It was not the work of human hands, but the gift of the "Eternal," of the Mountain, or of Nature. The voice of the people, and even the notion of the general will, was replaced with sacred law.

In August 1793, members of the Tenth Batallion of Pas-de-Calais, addressing the Convention, described the process of constitution building under the Republic: "France was missing a free and republican Constitution.... This wish was made manifest to you, when suddenly lightning burst forth from the holy Mountain which, amid the storm and through the thunderbolts, gave us this immortal work: the sacred rights of man and of the human race."[77] The Constitution was not the product of deliberation or of the coalescing of the general will, but of a sort of divine intervention through

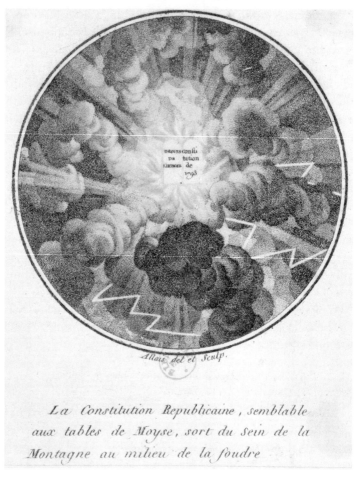

Fig. 8 Louis-Jean Allais, *La Constitution Républicaine.* Engraved for the Festival of Unity and Indivisibility, 10 August 1793. Bibliothèque Nationale de France, Collection de Vinck 6170.

the medium of the Mountain. A collection of hymns created for primary schools also adopted the iconography of Moses: "May the Tablets of the Rights of Man, descended from the Holy Mountain, be conserved for all future races so that they may never lose sight of the dignity of man and of his duties toward...the nation."[78] Those who opposed this sacred authority, of course, were akin to heretics: as petitioners from the town of Saint-Mère-Eglise expressed to the Convention, "If new fools dare to sacrifice to a golden cow, with an indefatigable arm, throw the tablets of the law from the heights of the sacred Mountain and you will pulverize the idol and its adorers."[79]

Merging the Mountain with Mount Sinai made it possible to give more responsibility to the Jacobins than they merited politically, particularly regarding the Constitution and the Declaration of Rights. In treating these laws as divine edicts, and in attributing their "manifestation" to the Mountain, this rhetoric made the political Mountain the locus of a new law. Furthermore, its sacrality even allowed it to postpone the law—or the Constitution—until peace made its enactment possible. Rousillon, a Paris Jacobin, addressed the Jacobin Society of Perpignan in Pluviôse of Year II: "The mountain, palladium of liberty and the terror of tyrants, thus has taken the initiative to place the Constitution in the holy ark until the moment when all the conspirators and satellites of tyrants have eaten dust."[80] Referring to the suspended Constitution of 1793, Rousillon held that until the social covenant could be fully instated, the Constitution would be placed in a sacred ark. (In fact, the actual Constitution was ordered to be placed in an ark and housed within the Assembly Hall, as per a decree put forward by Jacques-Louis David—he had helpfully provided drawings of the tabernacle—and passed in the immediate wake of the Festival of Unity and Indivisibility, on 11 August 1793.) Just as the heights of the Mountain allowed Lequinio to see things that his constituents could not, and the purity of the Mountain bolstered Robespierre's reputation as an "incorruptible," the holiness of the Mountain and its legacy as the source of divine edict granted legislators the ability to take radical measures under the auspices of the common good.

Nature Returned to Itself: Purging the Marais

While rhetorical allusions to the Mountain merged the purity of the Jacobins with the purity of mountain air or waters, popular rhetoric simultaneously distinguished both from the "miry swamp" of the moderates and conservatives. The counterpoint to the Mountain in the Convention's seating order was the Plain, the vast middle ground, which, over time, came to be known as the Swamp, or the *Marais*.[81] This provided an illustrative contrast evoked in songs, engravings, and radical newspapers. In the patriotic song, "The Mountain," the swamp was not only dangerous—full of insects, venomous reptiles, and poisonous fumes—it was also corruptive:

> In a swamp that is always miry
> With black poisonous vapors,

A thousand venomous reptiles
And biting insects abound,
A thick and dark atmosphere
Often obscures the countryside;
But for a clear view and pure air,
There is only the Mountain.
Who can stop the rapid course
Of this benevolent brook?
Who can corrupt its waters,
If not this fetid swamp?
It changes it into a fatal bog
For the inhabitant of the countryside.
[The brook's] waters were like crystal,
When they emerged from the Mountain.[82]

The river that was pure on the mountaintop became fetid and undrink-able; furthermore, its victim was the innocent inhabitant of the coun-tryside, who was faced with this "fatal bog." The political *Marais* had the power to turn even the purest of ideas into stagnant and poisonous ones; they endangered the people of France with their corruptive influence.

Indeed, government policy shared this dangerous view of swampland. For much of the eighteenth century, concerns over the mephitic air around swamps had permeated academic essay contests, philosophical writing, and natural histories. The stagnant air and water of swamplands were believed to pose a health risk, as air was understood to be a primary conveyer of noxious vapors and pestilence. Thinkers as diverse as Voltaire and Bernardin de Saint-Pierre promoted the draining of swamps as a means of restoring health to the neighboring areas; *marais* were spaces of stagnation that needed to be destroyed wherever possible.[83] On the other hand, mountain air was lauded for its health benefits; Ramond de Carbonnières, the noted student of the Pyrénées, believed that toxic ema-nations "took place only on the horizontal plane" and that mountains could provide freedom from noxious air.[84]

Policy debates that took place on the floor of the Convention and the Legislative Assembly drew upon that language as legislators attempted to increase the amount of arable farmland by proposing initiatives for draining swamps. With the Revolution came attempts to better the health and economies of communities near swamps and other sources of stag-nant water. And it was within the Legislative Assembly and the National Convention, during policy debates over swampland, that the malevo-lence of literal *marais* was reinforced, providing a significant and nefari-ous vocabulary for discussing the political *Marais*. The language that was developed in conversations about *literal* swampland was redeployed in popular songs, plays, and images that described the *political* Swamp. Calls for the destruction of the Swamp that echoed legislative debates over the elimination of swampland naturalized opposition to—and the eradication of—both literal and political swamps.

Legislation in 1790 aimed at drying out marshlands, but largely to no avail. In the following years various deputies and concerned citizens drew upon a long legacy of anti-swamp literature to fight for the draining and destruction of swampland, arguing that swamps were dangerous legacies of aristocratic privilege and perilous cesspools of corruption and degeneration. Likewise, *étangs*, usually understood to be private ponds used for fishing, were ordered to be destroyed in a (largely unenforced) decree of 14 Frimaire (4 December 1793), in an attempt to increase the amount of usable farmland and destroy terrestrial vestiges of noble privilege.[85]

Drawing on language inherited from the nascent field of chemistry, Louis-Etienne Beffroy, a deputy from Aisne and a member of the Committee of Agriculture, explained in 1793 that swamplands were the sources of corrupted air; laden in *air fixe*, the swamplands' atmosphere was heavier and therefore held the vapors longer, posing an increasing danger to inhabitants of the land. Calling swamps "receptacles of homicidal poison," he insisted on the necessity of their destruction.[86] Beffroy went on to explain that, in addition to improving the health of the citizenry, destroying the *marais* would also prove a boon to commerce by making available new land for growing crops and by providing more wood and peat as additional heat sources.[87]

Beffroy was not alone in holding these views of the health and commercial risks of *les marais*. Citizen Duchosal, a member of Paris's *section de la Bibliothèque*, addressed the patriotic society of his section in May 1791, describing in some detail the malfeasant consequences of life near swamps. He recounted an episode in 1789 in Roye-sur-les-Mats in which nearly all the inhabitants fell ill, "victims of the pestilential exhalations of their swamps."[88] A post-*marais* world looked utopian in his vision: "The state would be tranquil, independent, instead of its present agitated and precarious existence;...far from being debtors, we would be the creditors of neighboring peoples; we would rarely need to fear offensive war, or if by chance we were obliged to defend ourselves, history would no longer pass down stories of treaties concluded by the misery that the dearth of grains has so often thrown us into."[89] He criticized deputies on the right for sabotaging the benevolent efforts of the National Assembly in 1790 and encouraged the current legislature to look to the well-being of their citizenry in seeking to end the curse of the *marais*.[90]

Under the Convention, Jacques-Antoine Boudin, a deputy and former farmer from the Indre, published his *Du dessèchement des marais et terreins submergés* as a supplement to his proposed decree to do away with "unnatural" swamps. Complaining that the decree of December 1790 had done little to destroy swampland, he argued for a thoroughgoing demolition of marshes and their corruption. Most important, to Boudin, a world without *marais* would not only provide a utopian future, as Duchosal had predicted; it would return France to its original, natural state. In his opening pages, Boudin inquired, "Is the submersion [of these lands] a scourge of nature or one of the first divergences of sociability? Everything is good when it emerges from the hands of the author of all things, said Jean-Jacques; everything degenerates in the hands of man."[91] *Marais*, according to Boudin's history, were the product of man's greed and aggression; war prompted aggressive peoples, led of course by "nobles and priests," to attempt to "increase and perpetuate" the submersion of enemy lands. "Dams, roads, retaining walls for hunting and fishing [grounds], fortifications [*abatis*], destroyed bridges, would have necessarily obstructed, little by little, the natural course of rivers."[92] Yet it was the development of waterwheels that made swamplands permanent fixtures of the French countryside. As waterwheels were the exclusive property of nobles in Old Regime France, the swamps created by them were unnecessary and unnatural remnants of aristocratic self-interest. Thus, Boudin determined, *marais* were products of privilege and legacies of man's destructive intervention in the true plans of nature.

Like Duchosal and Beffroy, Boudin insisted on the unhealthiness of swamplands; they literally corrupted not only the air but the very bodies of the people who resided near them. "On the banks of stagnant rivers and miry swamps, one finds only pallid faces and frail bodies, destroyed by all kinds of incurable and recurrent illnesses."[93] Indeed, proximity to these unnatural and stagnant waters impacted both the physical and the moral well-being of their inhabitants; it "changes the essence of individuals," rendering them hopeless and fatalistic.[94]

Joseph Eschassériaux, presenting a decree in the name of the Committee of Agriculture in 1794, shared Boudin's sentiments about the privileged origins of swamplands; he argued that "their destruction would be the last blow against feudalism; it would restore a free path to these waters that the interest of some men had held in chains; it would return nature to itself."[95] Nature itself had been imprisoned and enslaved to particular interests; the revolutionary government could finally liberate it through its beneficent legislation. Like other campaigners against *les marais,* he emphasized their destructive impact on the health and well-being of citizens and farms residing near them: "It is in these imprisoned and stagnating waters that an infinitude of animal and vegetal substances live, die, and decompose; it is in their depths that murderous exhalations, which devastate and corrupt harvests, are formed; the terrains that they cover are lost to cultivation and have become a dwelling place of putridity for man and animal alike."[96]

Thus, in the policy debates over physical *marais*, swamps were described as unnatural, as remnants of a privileged order and of private interests, and as corruptive and potentially lethal. Swamps needed regenerating; they needed to be destroyed and converted into spaces of production and patriotism. Although the policy debates themselves do not seem to have been infiltrated with the language of factionalism, they did provide a vocabulary regarding the *Marais* that was deployed in popular songs and images.

It was not only the corruption but the divisiveness of the swamp that made it a particularly useful image in the wake of the 1793 federalist revolts. After the purge of 29 Girondins from the Convention in the early summer of 1793, several cities throughout France rose up against the Jacobins to protest the dismissal of their representatives and to argue for a less centralized authority.[97] The Jacobins portrayed these revolts as counterrevolutionary attempts to fracture the unity of the nation. Like geographic swamps, which impeded the natural flow of waters, the political *Marais* had attempted to impose false divisions on the nation of France. In the words of the president of the National Convention, speaking at the commemoration of the suppression of the federalist revolts at the Festival of Unity and Indivisibility, "This monster, . . . whose criminal hands are trying to separate what nature has united, is federalism."[98] The revolts threatened to break up the natural boundaries of the *patrie*.

Thus it was in specific reference to the revolts and to the purge of the Girondins that the nickname of the Marais was most common. Aristide Valcour, whose verses in *Les Petits Montagnards* paid homage to the Mountain and expressed revulsion for the Swamp, again drew on these opposing images in a speech celebrating the anniversary of the start of the Girondin purges, on 31 May 1794. Addressing the citizens of the commune of Nogent-sur-Marne, he described the dangers posed by federalism: "Impure federalism vomited its poisons in the *départements*. This eight-headed hydra rose up proudly, strongest even in the heart of the national representative body; and, amid a miry swamp, it launched its poisoned darts at everything that surrounded it. But these darts could not reach the summit of the mountain."[99] The swamp provided a safe haven for the monstrous hydra of federalism; similarly, in an allegory of the Revolution penned by Valcour, he accused "reptiles hidden in the rushes of the miry swamp" of attempting to corrupt and dirty the pure waters flowing from the fountain of regeneration with their "poisonous scum."[100] At the Festival of Unity and Indivisibility, this interplay between mountain and marsh was played out before Les Invalides. There, Jacques-Louis David commemorated the *journées* of May and June 1793 that destroyed the Girondin threat. At this fourth station, David planned an elaborate drama between the *peuple fran-çais*, perched atop a mountain, and federalism, "emerging from its miry swamp." The people struck down the federalist beast, "forcing it back into the stagnant waters, never to emerge again."[101]

A series of letters from republican societies throughout France likewise commemorated the destruction of federalism and of the Girondins by using the language of corrupted swamp air. The Montagnard Society of Cahors regretted the former influence of a Girondin deputy in their midst who had since been purged, calling him "a deputy covered in the dirty exhalations of the Marais."[102] Another address to the Convention thanked the Mountain for purging "the political atmosphere of France of all the mephitic and contagious exhalations that emerged from the depths of the swamps and that distressed the Republic."[103] And the Société populaire de Guéret made clear the juxtaposition between the diseased air of the swamps and the rar-efied air of mountains, saying, "The miry mists that rose from the *marais* have not, since [the events of 31 May and 2 June], been an obstacle to the expansion of the pure and healthy air that *montagnards* breathe."[104]

This juxtaposition became a part of the revolutionary catechism, with the purity of the Mountain defeating the corruption of the Swamp in plays, festivals, and songs. A "litany of *sans-culottes*" published for the use of school-children positioned the "holy mountain" in opposition to the Swamp: "O Holy Mountain, do not ever change, and from your majestic summit, hurl lightning, and crush…the reptiles of the miry swamp."[105] The Mountain was permanent and unchanging; in the context of the debates about swamplands, the timelessness of mountains—their potential status as the origin of all life, as posited by Buffon and d'Holbach—contrasted sharply with the artificiality and contingency of swamps, which had been created largely through manipulation of, and diversion from, the plans of nature.

If songs, plays, and letters reinforced the conflation between the divisive and corruptive (literal) swamp and the federalist and poisonous (politi-cal) Marais, they also proposed the same remedies that policy debates in the legislature had suggested. Legislators' recommendations for eliminat-ing swamps often focused on simply allowing nature to take its course.

Because swamps were dangerous and unnatural, Boudin insisted that their elimination would be both simple and necessary. Draining the swamps required only allowing nature to again take its rightful path: "Nature, violated for thousands of centuries, does not demand great efforts from us...; she only asks to be restored to herself: it is not against [nature] that we must fight unceasingly but against the greed and ignorance of men."[106] Thus destroying the *marais* would be a return to the earth's natural state and a reclamation of a more healthy existence. The revolutionary moment allowed for nature to be restored to its rightful state.

Eschassériaux did not offer a concrete suggestion for how to destroy the *marais*, unlike Boudin, who proffered the natural reclamation of the earth, or Etienne Légier, who in 1792 had suggested an elaborate series of canals to eliminate the scourges; tellingly, he simply called for a "regeneration."[107] "The republican government should be a second providence," Eschassériaux declared, urging the *Conventionnels* to pass legislation that would benefit future generations of French men and women; they had the unique opportunity to right the wrongs committed against nature.[108] Like Boudin, he saw the revolutionary moment as one that could liberate nature from the strictures that had been placed on it by misuse and greed; that restoration of nature would be the work of a new "providence," namely, the revolutionary government. Eschassériaux's *rapport*, presented a mere eight days before the Festival of the Supreme Being, revealed a belief that the Revolution could work on behalf of nature; as I argue below, the Festival suggested that nature was returning the favor.

This language proved extraordinarily powerful when describing the destruction of the moderates and federalists in France. For nature to be restored to its proper state, the political Marais, like the physical one, needed to be destroyed, regenerated, purged of its corrupting influence; that eradication was simply allowing nature to take its course. The political Mountain was to be the counterpart to this cesspool of counterrevolution, an exemplar of purity, virtue, and patriotism. A Year II theatrical commemoration of the young martyr Barra set in the Vendée featured a song sung by the young protagonist. In it he praised the Mountain for its destruction of the reptiles inhabiting the swamps:

> It is there [on the mountain] that a pure atmosphere
> Allows the view to go on forever
> And that a just and sure glance
> Can see in the plain and in the valley,
> The Python, infesting and ruining the countryside
> From his stinking swamp.

The song continued:

> A lightning bolt stopped [the python's] progress,
> And was launched from the tops of mountains.[109]

The mountain—again the locus of wise perspective—was uniquely able to stop the "infesting" swamp from continuing to ravage the countryside. The mountain's weapon of choice, lightning, was also significant; it did not need to draw on *unnatural* means to accomplish its goal, but instead harnessed natural forces to destroy the *marais*.

This position was particularly common in revolutionary theater. In Citizen Thiébaut's tribute to the revolutionary effort against rebels in the Vendée, he penned an allegorical scene in which Liberty, seated on a throne, claimed a representative from the Mountain as her chosen child, saying to him, "The Mountain that I cherish, and where you are seated, will fill in the swamps in which all my enemies are wallowing."[110] In another play of Year II, François Cizos-Duplessis's *Les Peuple et les Rois,* which premiered in Germinal (April 1794), the destruction of the swamp symbolized the return to nature promised by legislators like Boudin. The scene of the fifth act called for a large rock to be placed at center stage, spewing flames intermittently; in front of the rock was a swamp "covered in rushes."[111] Suddenly "a terrible explosion takes place; the swamp and the rock disappear." From the destruction rose a Mountain, labeled "The Temple of Nature."[112] The *mountain itself* would replace the swamp. Lightning and the earth were the tools of eradication; no unnatural intervention was required to eliminate the swamps of France.

This textual symbolism was replicated in numerous images of the revolutionary period as well. A revolutionary calendar, printed in Year II, featured the image of a mountain striking a swamp with thunderbolts, a host of toads and snakes lying belly-up in the stagnant water (see figure 9). While Hébert reviled the "toads of the swamp" in his radical newspaper *Père Duchesne,* engravings showed the monarchist and federalist frogs encountering a watery grave at the foot of a mountain.[113] With imagery that was sometimes humorous and always illustrative, revolutionary publications juxtaposed the pure and powerful mountain with the corruptive, and ultimately lethal, swamp.

Both eighteenth-century scientific debates and legislative discussions provided a language with which to vilify and de-naturalize literal swampland as well as the metaphorical Swamp. And it was the Mountain, and its virtuous inhabitant, that destroyed the reptiles there. The Mountain in

Fig. 9 *Gloire immortelle à la Sainte Montagne.* Detail from revolutionary calendar. Paris: Chez Citoyen Quéverdo, graveur, and Citoyen Picquet, graveur. Bibliothèque Nationale de France, Collection Hennin 11955.

this opposition became not merely a space of virtue and purity but also the locus of destructive authority. It was the natural phenomenon that would fill in the abscesses left by the swamp and that would supplant the unnatural and the aristocratic. This juxtaposition between the Mountain and the Swamp not only reveals the political battle between Jacobins and their opponents, however; it also reveals an important coalition, namely, the alliance between nature and the radical revolution. The thunderbolts launched at the Girondin moderates, and aimed at the reptiles of the *marais*, were, according to this language, not unnatural aberrations, but natural processes and important steps for the return of nature.

The Convention's passage of the law to eliminate *étangs*, or artificial fish ponds, in fact coincided with the promulgation of two other laws that suggest that the "return of nature" was not just a rhetorical flourish, but instead a revolutionary policy. On 14 Frimaire, Year II (4 December 1793), alongside the law about the *étangs*, which called for their stagnant water to be removed and the land made usable for cultivation, the Convention also put the soil of France under requisition: the law inviting citizens to take part in the harvest of saltpeter passed that very day. And, simultaneously, the National Convention famously created the revolutionary government, an emergency government not bound by the Constitution whose stated purpose was to usher in the end of the Revolution. These extraordinary times of revolution required extraordinary measures.

Although the coincidence of these three laws may well be, in fact, coincidental, their simultaneity suggests a moment of possible transition, from

nature serving as a metaphor for revolution to becoming an active partici-
pant in it. In addition to serving practical purposes (eliminating remnants
of feudal privilege and contributing to arable land in the case of the pond
legislation; increasing gunpowder production in the saltpeter laws), these
decrees asked French citizens, first, to model nature in their idea of just
governance and, second, to deploy nature as an arm of the Revolution. In
Billaud-Varenne's address to the Convention describing the revolutionary
government, he explained:

> In government, as in mechanics, anything that is not combined with preci-
> sion…gives rise to infinite breakages. Strangling resistance, and destructive
> friction, diminish as we simplify the cog. The best civil constitution is the one
> that is nearest to the processes of nature, which itself only admits three prin-
> ciples in its movements: the impelling will [*la volonté pulsatrice*], the being
> that this will brings to life, and the action of this individual on surrounding
> objects; thus any good government should have a central control, levers
> that are immediately attached to it, and secondary bodies that these levers
> act upon, so as to extend the movement to the very extremities. Through
> this precision, the action loses none of its force and none of its direction in
> a communication that is more rapid and better regulated. Anything beyond
> this becomes excessive and parasitic, without vigor and without unity.[114]

A government, in other words, should be as simple as possible: it should
have a single center and effective mechanisms by which to transmit information to any dependent region. The decree of 14 Frimaire made
clear what the central impulse of the Republic would be: "The National
Convention is the unique center of the impulsion of the government."[115]
While this may sound despotic or even absolutist, Billaud-Varenne did not
use political theory to make his point. He used the laws of nature. He
wanted to align the revolutionary government with the self-regulating and
harmonious natural world.

In addition to making the government more closely aligned with nature,
the Convention's decrees on that day also asked French citizens to deploy
the powers of nature on the nation's behalf. Prieur de la Côte d'Or, in
his discourse on gunpowder and revolutionary lightning, suggested that
saltpeter had been given to France as a gift of nature and that the citizenry
needed only to bring it forth.[116] The discussion over the *étangs* made clear
that by eliminating the stagnant waters of fish ponds—leftover and corruptive remnants of feudalism and aristocratic greed—France would both
make nature more fruitful and productive and eliminate unnatural and
destructive spaces.[117] Nature not only provided a model for revolution, but
could be marshaled in support of revolution.

The language of eradicating the Swamp through natural means, and specifically of "return[ing] nature to itself," is therefore suggestive of a broader phenomenon in the Jacobin revolution. Nature was not just a metaphor for revolution, it was an agent of it. If, as Boudin and the Committee of Agriculture suggested in their proposals for eradicating swampland, and as plays and songs about the Marais concurred, the Revolution provided a unique moment that made possible the return of nature, then the Revolution not only worked on behalf of nature, but nature worked on behalf of the Revolution. To revolutionize and regenerate France was to recall nature from its exile, as Robespierre would suggest at the Festival of the Supreme Being.

The Festival of the Supreme Being: A Theology of Terror

A sacred mountain, bastion of virtue and symbol of the collective, formed the centerpiece of the Festival of the Supreme Being on 20 Prairial, Year II (8 June 1794). No hollow symbol, the mountain was, in the words of R. R. Palmer, "executed with careful naturalism," decorated with shrubs and rocks, and tall enough to allow the Conventionnels to climb to its peak and numerous women and children to clamber on its flanks.[118] Villages were encouraged to hold their festivals outdoors, "on a 'natural hillock,'" amid decorations of flowers, vines, and plants.[119] Mountains had played a role in a number of other festivals as well but never before with such an eye toward a realistic, naturalistic representation. A festival in Bellevue a month earlier, for example, centered around the image of nature as it celebrated revolutionary martyrs, and featured a miniature mountain in its procession. Carried by a *sans-culotte,* it bore the inscription, "from my summit emerges the lightning that pulverizes the enemies of the people and the republic," and on the other side, "Frenchmen, rally to me, and you will never die."[120] Echoing songs and images that combined mountains with other natural imagery, these slogans also gestured toward some of the broader themes of the Festival of the Supreme Being, namely, the associations between the mountain and sacrality, and between the Revolution and a divine mission.

The Festival of the Supreme Being was intended to pay homage to the author of nature, as well as to nature itself. In his discourse of 18 Floréal, laying out his program for national festivals, Robespierre had proposed a combined festival honoring the Supreme Being and Nature, saying, "The true priest of the Supreme Being is Nature; his temple, the universe; his cult, virtue; his festivals, the joy of a great people assembled together under his eyes to tighten the sweet bonds of universal fraternity, and to pay him the homage of pure and sensitive hearts."[121] The priests of the Old Regime had sullied the name of the true God, but the cult of the Supreme Being of the New Regime represented a return to the genuinely divine, made possible by the Revolution. It also signified a step away from dechristianization and atheism, which, according to Robespierre, had sapped civic life of its meaning and transparency. Robespierre suggested that the cult of the Supreme Being would provide a sense of order amid possible chaos; addressing the nation's dechristianizers, he asked, "What advantage do you find in persuading man that a blind force presides over his destiny, and smites at random [both] crime and virtue; that his soul is but a soft breath that is extinguished at the gates of the tomb?"[122] Worship of the Supreme Being signified a restoration of order and faith, and a return to religion as it was intended to be: an homage paid to nature and to the natural world.

Robespierre's sentiments from his proposal were brought to life at the festival itself; direct quotations from his speech were engraved on rocks surrounding the mountain on the Champ de Mars. A statue of atheism was symbolically burned, set alight by Robespierre's "torch of truth," and nature was praised in song, speech, and symbol. The Festival was a celebration of nature, *returned to its rightful place,* made possible by the Revolution. "May nature now reclaim all its splendor," declared Robespierre.[123] In the same way that drying out swampland could, after centuries of oppression and privilege, restore the natural order, so, too, did Robespierre claim that the establishment of the cult of the Supreme Being returned the world to its natural state. The obstacles of monarchy, aristocracy, and priesthood were being removed, the last vestiges of privilege purged, to allow for nature's dominion. A few weeks earlier, in a speech urging vigilance before the Convention on 7 Prairial (26 May 1794), Robespierre had expressed a similar belief: the representatives of the people, he said, were working "with one hand to bring the homage of a great people to the feet of the Eternal, the Author of all things; and, with the other, hurling lightning at the tyrants conspiring against it, founding the first republic in the world, and returning liberty, justice, and nature, which had been exiled, to mortals."[124] Nature had been *exiled* from the Old Regime; the Revolution had returned it to its rightful station. The Mountain, the natural center of the Festival, symbolized that restoration.

In this way the Revolution had paved the way for rightful reverence to be paid to both Nature and its Author, and Nature would repay the devotion of the French. Indeed, Nature had ordained the work of the Revolution. In Robespierre's address to the crowd assembled in the Jardin National for the Festival of the Supreme Being, he asked, "Is it not [the Supreme Being] whose immortal hand, in etching the code of justice and equality in the hearts of men, there wrote the death sentence of tyrants? Is it not he who, since the beginning of time, decreed the Republic, and put liberty, good faith, and justice on the agenda for all time and for all people?"[125] Nature and Revolution were in coalition with each other—and this included the violence of Revolution.

Mona Ozouf has argued that violence was almost entirely removed from the festival that took place on the day of Pentecost in 1794.[126] Ozouf sees violence as constantly being *deflected* in the revolutionary festival; it is the silent and suppressed backdrop, the unmentioned. Yet a martial spirit certainly penetrated most of the festivals that took place throughout France that day: a procession in Strasbourg featured several military bands, armed adolescents paying homage to Agricole Viola and Barra, military men carrying a miniature Bastille, and salpêtriers, who bore "emblems announcing that the heavens protect the people who prepare the fall of kings and of the earth's oppressors."[127] Although most of the participants in the Paris festival were unarmed, youth between the ages of fourteen and eighteen were asked to carry sabers, pistols, and pikes; what is more, the hymns that were sung were distinctly military. The crowd assembled on the mountain repeated in a refrain: "Before we lay down our triumphant swords, let us swear to annihilate crime and tyrants."[128]

Amid the utopian images of the people atop the mountain, of mothers holding their young and the aged moved to tears, violence was not displaced, but instead was ordered, sacralized, and naturalized. The French were called upon, and in fact were assisted by, Nature to purge the earth of kings, tyrants, and traitors. First, they were fulfilling the vision of the Supreme Being and of Nature. As Robespierre declared, "The author of nature has linked all mortals with an immense chain of love and happiness; may the tyrants who dared to break it perish! French Republicans, it is up to you to purify the earth that they have sullied."[129] The peristile erected in the Jardin National, the site of the festival's joyous beginning, bore the inscriptions, "To honor the divinity and to punish kings are the same thing," and "The Divinity has condemned tyrants; the French people have executed his decrees."[130] A collection of prayers published after the festival, intended for use in primary schools, attributed the revolutionary goals to the Supreme Being: "You gave us liberty; you etched in our hearts this august and terrible vow: Live free or die! War on tyrants!...Long live the Republic!"[131]

Furthermore, Nature was facilitating their efforts. Deschamps's hymn to the Divinity, sung at the festival, thanked the Supreme Being for "cover[ing] our weapons with glory and our fields with rich harvests." "You make the seasons fight for us," the stanza concluded.[132] Two songs planned for the festival seconded this sentiment; the program for the festival called for participants to sing the official Hymn to the Supreme Being, which asked "the sacred motor of nature" to "join the avenging fires of thunder to the lightning bolts of the French," while Chénier's proposed hymn for the *fête*, printed in a revolutionary hymnal, proclaimed, "Your invisible arm guided our courage; your lightning bolts marched before us."[133] In a play of Messidor celebrating the military and civic virtues of *paysans* in the French countryside, a soldier noted the fair weather, saying, "One could say that nature is working on our behalf," and his compatriots agreed, citing a good harvest and a mild winter: "When all the kings make war on us, all the elements are with us."[134] Nature acted in coalition with the Revolution and could even enact violence and destruction on behalf of the Revolution. One of the engravings of the mountain at the center of the festival (see figure 10) echoed this coalition of Nature, Supreme Being, and Revolution: The "proud mountain," the caption read, "crushes the factious / Just as volcanoes scorch the countryside [*foudroye la Campagne*]." The Mountain, as a symbol of nature protected by the Supreme Being, was capable of destruction for the good of the Republic.

The Festival of the Supreme Being thus evinces a far more theologically nuanced belief than a naturalistic or deistic interpretation would belie. The festival gave credit to the divinity himself for the unfolding of the Revolution. The Supreme Being and Nature alike were not merely mechanistic, but could be interpreted as *providential.* The festival and the cult replaced the supernatural miracles of Christianity with natural miracles, such as lightning striking down the treasonous or fair weather facilitating the march of the French armies. Nature, as it was portrayed in the Festival of the Supreme Being, acted as *particular* providence; not only did it operate with a purpose and a teleology, but it also could intervene in its own processes to promote the Revolution's path.

The festival also revealed the possibility of imposing a kind of theodicy upon the Revolution and its violence. As explained in a catechism of the Supreme Being published just after the festival: "If some fleeting evils afflict us here below, it is doubtless because they are inevitable; moreover,

Fig. 10 "Vûe du côté orientale de la montagne élevée au Champ de la réunion pour la fête célebrée en l'honneur de l'être Suprême." Paris: Chez Coustellier, 1794. Despite the pastoral image, the caption threatens the "audacious tyrants" and compares the mountain to a volcano, ready to "crush the factious." Bibliothèque Nationale de France, Collection de Vinck 6306.

you [the Supreme Being] wish for it, and that is enough for us; we submit to you with faith, and we hope for your infinite mercy."[135] Similarly Sylvain Maréchal—despite being an avowed atheist and the author of numerous incendiary irreligious texts in the prerevolutionary period—offered a providential view of the Supreme Being in his *Décades des cultivateurs,* a text intended to appeal to peasants.[136] Addressing the Supreme Being, he wrote: "You control [the world's] events in such a manner that those that seem to us to be the most inauspicious nevertheless contribute to our happiness."[137] Maréchal assured his audience that everything, from the most ordinary event to the "grandes révolutions," was brought about by the divinity with a good end in mind.[138] The cult of the Supreme Being made possible a faith in a sense of order, the very thing that Robespierre accused the dechristianizers of having stolen from the French people.

The Festival of the Supreme Being, and the elaborately naturalized mountain at its center, thus linked the political and natural revolutions. Just as the "great revolutions" in the natural world were undertaken by the divinity with a particular end in mind, so, too, was the political revolution a part of a providential design, overseen by the Supreme Being. In this sense, Mona Ozouf correctly identified the Festival of the Supreme Being as being "homogenous with the discourse of the Revolution," not only because it affirmed a utopian vision or asserted an Enlightenment model of religion, as she suggests, but because it was an affirmation of the secular providentialism that bolstered the revolutionary justification of violence.[139] The mountain, as a symbol of purity, the antithesis to the noxious swamp, evocative of the sublime, and reminiscent of the sacred, was a polyvalent image that ultimately facilitated the asserted relationship between Revolution and Nature. Far from being a metaphor stripped of its prerevolutionary connotations, the political Mountain utilized the many meanings inherited from literary and scientific sources, ultimately allowing the Jacobins to lay claim to a political space of virtue, unity, and authority sanctioned by the operations of Nature herself.

5

"MOUNTAIN, BECOME A VOLCANO"

*L*e *Jugement dernier des rois,* a play written by Sylvain Maréchal, opened to enthusiastic reviews at the Théâtre de la République in Vendémiaire of Year II (October 1793). "The Theater of the Republic...has never better fulfilled its title than since it has been putting on a play of an original genre, which has as its title, *Le Jugement dernier des rois,*" extolled Prudhomme's *Révolutions de Paris* on 28 October 1793.[1] The *Père Duchesne* exclaimed, "There [at the Théâtre de la République] is a fit spectacle for republican eyes."[2] The play gave an account of the exile of all Europe's monarchs, as well as the Pope, to a remote volcanic island. The radical Théâtre de la République, subsidized by the revolutionary government, was also given a special bequest from the Committee of Public Safety for this especially patriotic production: a donation of twenty pounds of saltpeter, an extremely valuable commodity, to create the spectacular explosion that marked the play's conclusion—a volcanic eruption that would "launch stones and burning coals" into the theater.[3]

Maréchal subtitled his play, "a prophecy in one act." The future foreseen by the playwright and hoped for by the supportive Committee of Public Safety was also embraced by Prudhomme. "The theatrical fiction will not take long to become historical fact," he wrote.[4] The overthrow of Europe's kings, their return to an "uncivilized" state, and their ultimate destruction by natural forces was a fiction that was presented to, and patronized by, a broad French public, playing in Beauvais, Compiègne, Grenoble, Le Mans, Lille, Metz, and Rouen.[5] And the volcano, symbol of revolutionary fervor and destruction, became the ultimate demonstration of nature's justice, annihilating the monarchs in a single, terrifying, and glorious moment described in the play's liner notes: "The explosion takes place: the fire attacks the kings from all sides; they fall, consumed in the innards of the opened earth."[6] The quite literal fall of the monarchs, although enabled by the Revolution itself, was portrayed as the work of natural forces.

The image of the volcano, so dramatically evoked by Maréchal, provides an illuminating case study for the fusion of the language of natural history with the rhetoric of political transformation, revealing the simultaneous politicization of the natural world, and the naturalization of political rhetoric.[7] Like the images of lightning and mountains, revolutionaries drew on the symbolic language of volcanoes in ways that demonstrated shifting ideas about authority, justice, and political virtue; in even more striking ways than the previous images, the volcano's connotations transformed with changes in the political realm. During the early years of the Revolution, it symbolized the potential for unbridled force and destruction; it represented volatility, and a fear of cataclysm, playing a crucial role in the revolutionary language of watchfulness and surveillance. Yet, for a brief period that began with the call for terror as the order of the day, the volcano became a *positive* symbol of revolutionary transformation, emblematic of patriotic passion and republican virtue. The image of the volcano was deployed as a symbol of constructive and purgative change at the very moment at which "terror" itself became a positive and regenerative concept.

Volcanoes in Scientific Inquiry

Natural histories of the eighteenth century allowed for the positing of volcanic eruption as a potentially constructive and purifying event, despite its destructive capabilities. As the eighteenth-century philosophical community struggled to understand and explain the natural world, volcanoes proved both fascinating and troubling. Key discoveries of the period facilitated the century's enthrallment with volcanic activity, including the excavation of the ruins of Herculaneum and Pompeii in the 1730s and 1740s, and, an event of far more regional importance in France, Jean-Étienne Guettard's 1752 pronouncement that the mountains of the Auvergne were extinct volcanoes. Sylvain Maréchal, whose fascination with volcanoes was apparent from his revolutionary play, had previously published a book on the antiquities of Herculaneum in 1780; Winckelmann's letters written from Herculaneum and Pompeii were published in French in 1784.[8] Furthermore, both Etna and Vesuvius erupted in the 1770s and 1780s, and paintings of both volcanoes, often stunningly

Fig. 11 Vesuvius's 1754 eruption. *Encyclopédie,* "Histoire Naturelle: Règne Minéral. Sixième Collection," Plate II (23:6:2). ARTFL *Encyclopédie* Project.

realistic portrayals, began to appear. The *Encyclopédie* contained spectacular images of Vesuvius's 1754 eruption and Pierre-Jacques Volaire made
a sustainable income selling violent images of both Italian mountains in
fiery explosion.[9] Aesthetically, volcanoes were simultaneously wondrous
and devastating, capable of annihilating entire villages and leaving only
artifacts for later centuries to study.[10]

As both real and fictional volcanoes captivated the public imagination,
their inner workings became the subject of debate among amateur geologists and natural historians: the questions of their origins, their purpose,
and their consequences were all heated points of discussion. Research on
volcanoes in the late eighteenth century marked the start of a divide between theories that would come to be known as *vulcanisme* and *neptunisme,*
one arguing that the earth's topography was determined by fire, the other
by water.[11] Bernardin de Saint-Pierre favored a "neptunist" rationale in
part because it allowed him to align his geological findings with the biblical Flood. His *Études* suggested that the incendiary potential of volcanoes
was a result of "vegetal and animal fermentation;" after the Flood, "the
remains of so many forests and so many animals, whose trunks and bones
can still be found in our quarries, floated on the surface of the ocean and
formed monstrous deposits…in the basins of mountains. It is likely that
they burst into flames by the simple effect of fermentation, as we see bales
of damp hay catch fire in our grasslands."[12] Instead of being a source of
fire, or having an internal heat of their own creation, volcanoes merely
were susceptible to combustion because of the detritus within them.

As Kenneth Taylor has argued, most naturalists and nascent geologists
in the eighteenth century attributed geological formations to some combination of the elements, and were able to accommodate both fire and
water in their theories of the earth. Buffon even changed his mind on
the matter over his lifetime, arguing in 1749 for the importance of water
in shaping the earth's surface and in 1778 for the existence of a "central
heat" within the surface of the earth.[13] But the contested claims about
volcanic origins highlight the fundamental problem posed by volcanoes:
how to make sense of something so violent, destructive, and apparently
anomalous within the order of nature. The unique rock formations of
the Auvergne further problematized the purported destruction of volcanic eruption: the legacies of the region's volcanic past were *not* traces of
devastation but, rather, were well-ordered columns of basalt, as depicted
in figure 12.

Popularized in part by the findings of William Hamilton, the British
ambassador to Naples, the idea that volcanoes possessed an inherent
heat was starting to take hold in France by the 1780s. Hamilton reported

Fig. 12 Basalt columns of the Auvergne. *Encyclopédie*, "Histoire Naturelle: Règne Minéral. Sixième Collection," Plate VII (23:6:3). ARTFL *Encyclopédie* Project.

on the eruptions of Vesuvius and Etna to the Royal Society; rather than being mere remnants of a historic flood, he argued, volcanoes had a force all their own, and therefore could themselves play an important role in earth's history of creation, destruction, and regeneration. In Hamilton's words, "Volcanoes should be considered in a creative rather than a destructive light."[14] Déodat Gratet de Dolomieu, who had written about the Messina and Calabria earthquakes, advanced the idea that volcanoes were ignited by an internal heat.[15] In his study of Mount Etna he stated, "Lavas enclose deep within them a combustible material, which burns and smolders in the manner of other combustible materials; however, in addition to the borrowed heat that they have acquired in the hearths of volcanoes, they also have a heat that is their own and that develops by a true combustion."[16] There was an internal, inextinguishable fire contained in volcanic matter that both contained and caused heat. Similarly, Nicolas Desmarest maintained that the basalt surrounding the Auvergne region had been created by fire, arguing that the presence of ordered prismatic rock—not ruins or devastation—was the clearest record left by the operations of volcanoes on the earth's surface.[17]

Some natural historians hypothesized that this internal fire was the result of a kind of electrical force. Indeed, the widely read Buffon, in his *Epoques de la Nature*, suggested that both earthquakes and volcanic eruptions were caused by electrical energy. Noting the similarities between the sound of thunder that accompanied a lightning strike and the rumblings of the earth during an earthquake or eruption, Buffon attributed both to the same cause. Buffon believed that "the basis of electrical material is the terrestrial globe's own heat," and he determined that this invisible force could be released by movement within the earth.[18] Buffon was far from unique in holding this belief; Marat, in his writings on fire and electricity, took steps to refute suggestions by the abbé Pierre Berthelon de Saint-Lazare that volcanic eruptions were caused by electrical outbursts.[19] Instead, Marat posited that volcanoes were, in fact, mountains made of sulfur, prone to combustion but holding no internal heat of their own.[20]

In addition to the question of where the incendiary power of volcanoes came from, eighteenth-century naturalists also debated whether volcanic eruptions were extraordinary events that *disrupted* the natural order of the earth or, instead, were necessary parts of the earth's cycle. Natural historians strove to distinguish the "natural" from the "accidental." In the words of Kenneth Taylor:

> According to such a viewpoint, events or objects that stood outside what was thought to be the ordinary course of nature, ... could not be expected to serve the purposes of the seeker after genuine knowledge, which consisted centrally of an understanding of the general case. By this way of thinking, *extraordinary things*, which in a literal sense stand outside rule, could not represent the fundamental order of nature.[21]

Volcanoes, which could create both well-ordered basalt columns and devastation of an unthinkable magnitude, seemed difficult to define. The century marked a struggle to align the "disorder" of volcanoes with the "order" of nature, with many savants ultimately concluding that the violence of volcanic eruption was itself a necessary part of the natural order. Above all, their purgative powers made them essential to the operations of the earth.

D'Holbach's article on volcanoes in the *Encyclopédie* certainly demonstrates this vision of volcanic activity. Also the author of the article on *tremblemens de terre*, d'Holbach understood the two phenomena to be linked—and benevolent, despite appearances to the contrary. He compared volcanoes to chimneys that evacuated toxins and destructive substances from the earth's interior: "Volcanoes are...a kindness of nature; they provide a free passage to fire and air; they stop them from pushing their ravages beyond certain limits, and from completely disrupting the face of our globe."[22] Although d'Holbach and Bernardin de Saint-Pierre agreed on little else, the sentimental writer who so loved final causes offered a similarly beneficent view of volcanic activity. In his *Études de la Nature,* Bernardin de Saint-Pierre wrote, "Nature purges water by the fires of volcanoes like it purifies the air with lightning, and, just as storms are more common in warm nations, nature has created multiple volcanoes there for the same reasons. Nature burns the filth of the sea on its shores, as a gardener burns the weeds of his garden at the end of autumn."[23] Likewise, Pluche maintained the beneficence of volcanoes, suggesting, like d'Holbach, that they provided a necessary release for "imprisoned air." "We may see how these volcano's [*sic*]," he wrote in the third volume of his *Spectacle,* "which are looked upon as so many plagues and calamaties in those countries where they are, are appointed by God for their safety and preservation."[24] Whatever the volcano's origins, its purpose was clear to these naturalists: to preserve the purity and order of the globe.

Scientific inquiry made possible this beneficent vision of volcanic activity; the first generation of field scientists, exploring and observing volcanic terrain at both active and extinct sites, were able to ascertain particular benefits arising from the terrestrial legacy of eruptions. Eighteenth-century travelers and naturalists had begun to recognize that volcanic activity, despite its obvious destructive potential, could lead to increased fertility and regeneration. William Hamilton, in a letter describing his travels to Etna that was translated into French in 1773, attributed the fertile soil on the mountain's slopes, and the grapes that thrived there and produced such strong wine, to the admixture of ash and earth.[25] "May not subterraneous fire be considered as the great plough...which Nature makes use of to turn up the bowels of the earth, and afford us fresh fields?" he asked in a letter to Matthew Maty, the secretary of London's Royal Society.[26] Louis de Jaucourt, who authored the entry on Vesuvius in the *Encyclopédie,* noted that "scientists [*physiciens*] claim that the type of ashes that Vesuvius emits dissolve little by little, and intermingle with the earth, enriching it and contributing to its fertility."[27] Though most paths to Vesuvius were scarred by its destruction, the verdant plains nearby were testaments to its abundant potential. As Patrick Brydone, a Scottish traveler in the Messina and Calabria regions that would be struck by devastating earthquakes in 1783, noted, "Nature employs the same agent for creation and destruction."[28] With destruction came new opportunities; creation and obliteration were but two sides of the same incendiary mountain.[29]

In philosophical as well as scientific literature, the volcano could serve an important and productive purpose in human communities. For Rousseau, as he indicated in his *Second Discourse,* the volcano played a crucial role in the progress of man, inspiring him to create fire and attempt metallurgy. Not only were human communities themselves the product of catastrophes, including volcanic eruptions and earthquakes, as he had suggested in his *Essai sur l'origine des langues,* but the spectacle of eruption taught early man the creative value of fire.[30] These crises—"happy accidents," as Rousseau described them—were entirely random but also inextricably linked with the development of human civilization.[31] Metallurgy was first imagined as a result of "the extraordinary circumstance of some volcano that, vomiting fused metallic matter, would have given to observers the idea of imitating this operation of nature."[32] Volcanoes were hypothetical sources of both community and technology, essential to both natural equilibrium and human progress.

In aesthetics, philosophy, and natural history, volcanoes represented a powerful and destructive, yet potentially beneficial, force to the eighteenth-century public. Volatile and terrifying, they captured the imagination. It was this volatility and vigor that made them particularly useful and vivid images during the revolutionary period. An analysis of the uses of the image of the volcano in revolutionary rhetoric indicates that, despite the debates in the geological community, the idea that volcanoes contained their own heat and fire, rather than being merely subject to combustion, seemed to prevail in the public space. That internal incendiary potential made them, initially, symbols of danger and warning, and then, later, symbols of passion and vengeance. What is more, theories about volcanoes provided a metaphor for transformation which posited that violence could bring constructive and regenerative possibilities.

Volcanic Volatility

It has long been recognized that counterrevolutionaries used the volcano as a symbol for the supposed instability and self-destructiveness of the revolutionary regime.[33] Indeed, during the early years of the Revolution, figures on all points of the political spectrum continued to use the volcano as an ambiguous, threatening symbol of potential violence and disruption. Hidden troubles, and latent evil, could be denoted by the metaphor of *le volcan.* In January 1792, as the nation turned its attention to the possibility of war, the deputy from the Département de Var, Honoré-Maximin Isnard, cautioned the Assembly against believing the peaceful overtures of Europe's kings. "As for me, I fear that the current state of Europe resembles the menacing tranquility of Etna. Silence reigns on the mountain, but open it up suddenly and you will find an abyss of fire, torrents of lava that are preparing the next eruptions."[34] The subterranean lava, waiting to burst forth and destroy the people of France, was a secret cabal of international conspirators.

Similarly, in a pamphlet titled *La Juste vengeance du peuple*, written in the immediate wake of the September Massacres, the author stated that France "is on a volcano more terrible than Vesuvius."[35] He used this image as a call for increased surveillance, reminding the people of France of the volatility of their situation and of the ubiquity of enemy forces *within* France itself. The volcano not only hid its power until the moment of its release, it also contained within it its own obliteration. Drawing on the image of volcanoes as inherently combustible because of their own heat and internal movement, these revolutionary writers warned against the appearance of safety that cloaked a lethal danger. Just as the beauty and calm of the Auvergne, the order of its basalt columns, disguised the latent force within it, so, too, did the apparent tranquility of Europe belie the potential for destruction and violence.

After the fall of the monarchy on 10 August 1792, Pierre-Jean-Baptiste Chaussard praised the revolutionaries for having uncovered a conspiracy within France. According to Chaussard, the mayor of Paris Jérôme Pétion and his fellow patriots had "follow[ed] the sulfurous trail of the volcano kindled beneath our feet." There they found "fanaticism stirring up poorly extinguished ashes with a dagger."[36] The image of a volcano made incendiary by fanaticism—by passion taken too far—was one that Chaussard had perhaps inherited from the prerevolutionary years.[37] For Chaussard, however, the fanatical rumblings of counterrevolutionaries had alerted Paris's leaders to the dangers beneath their feet; they defused the risk by overthrowing the monarchy.

The volcano as a possible source of passionate and ruinous violence was also evident in the rhetoric surrounding the Glacière Massacres in Avignon. The criminal tribunal's report in 1792 noted the widespread discontent in the surrounding area, saying, "The same passions and the same interests that bloodied Avignon also silently stirred in the towns of the Comtat; too close to the volcano of public dissention, they were soon covered in its burning lava."[38] The rumblings of discontent were not only incendiary but were also damaging to the region as a whole; mere proximity to such a "volcano" posed a threat and portended destruction. Even if that destruction was inadvertent, stoked by "passions," it was nevertheless dangerous; the example of Avignon suggested that volcanoes needed to be closely watched and, if possible, extinguished. As Isnard suggested in

his speech on war in January 1792, if there were volcanoes of passion inside of France, then true patriots should "rush to them en masse to put
out [their fires] with wisdom and moderation."[39]

By using the volcano to urge vigilance and surveillance, revolutionaries aligned the symbol with a period of increasing fear and watchfulness
inside of France. Potential dangers both within and outside of France
were escalating; the civil war in the Vendée broke out in March 1793, and
the federalist uprisings of that summer threatened to shatter the unity of
the young Republic. The Revolution seemed to be at its breaking point.
As Prudhomme wrote in March 1793, "For three years the fires have been
smoldering, but the moment of explosion has arrived. Citizens! You are
walking on volcanic earth."[40] The volcano was not merely susceptible to
combustion, as Bernardin de Saint-Pierre had indicated, but itself held
a heat that was a source of constant danger and required unremitting
vigilance. Therein lay both its danger and its force.

With the political changes of 1793, however, the connotations of the
volcano radically transformed. Just as lightning shifted from the hands of
the king to the people and then to the Convention, so, too, did the image
of the volcano transfer from a metaphor for potential dangers of counterrevolutionary forces to a symbol of revolutionary strength and fervor. The
volcano became an agent of the Revolution, able to destroy its enemies
and purify France's terrain. Its destructiveness and fearsomeness became
its beneficent attributes, at the very moment in which the Committee of
Public Safety turned to violence and terror to solidify its regime. Though
prior to 1793 the volcano typically indicated forces that were potentially
destructive to the Revolution itself, between September 1793 and July
1794 the volcano came to refer primarily to revolutionary force, power,
and passion.

During this crucial period of French politics, the volcano could still re-
tain some of its old uses; for example, an ode by Chénier, written for the
Festival of the Supreme Being (which was not, in fact, sung during the
festival) continued to mention the menace of volcanoes to signify monarchical powers.[41] Saint-Just, reflecting on the stages of revolution on
11 Germinal (31 March 1794), condemned the conspiracies against liberty under the Constituent Assembly, saying that the "popular revolution
was the surface of a volcano of foreign plots." In addition, his planned
speech of 9 Thermidor also invoked the image of the volcano; this time he
turned the alleged words of Billaud-Varenne against him: "Billaud often
repeated these words, with a false fear: 'You are walking on a volcano.' I
think so, too, but the volcano on which we are walking is his dissimulation

and his love for domination."[42] Despite these negative uses, Year II is the only moment of the Revolution, based on my research, when the image could equally—and even dominantly—be invoked as a positive, productive symbol.

Passion, Terror, and Virtue: The Volcano in Year II

In December 1793, Committee of Public Safety member Bertrand Barère addressed the National Convention on the subject of Toulon, where an anti-Jacobin revolt had begun in July. Quoting a letter from Joseph Fouché, the representative on mission there, he proclaimed, "On all sides, the perfidious and terrible English will be assaulted, the entire Republic will form a single volcano that hurls upon them a devouring lava; the despicable island that produced these monsters will no longer belong to humanity, and will forever be buried beneath the tides of the sea."[43] In imagery reminiscent of Maréchal's play, the entire island would be destroyed by the volcanic eruption, by the coalescing of all the passions of the French people that would burst forth with annihilating vigor. Barère used the volcano as an image of immediate destruction, invoked to represent collective violence—violence not only against a group of traitors but enacted by the nation as a whole.

Remarkably, the image of the volcano as *politically* constructive and purgative became predominant simultaneously, and coterminously, with the positive connotation of terror. The image of the volcano was invoked as a constructive, pro-revolutionary metaphor on 5 September 1793, the very day the Commune of Paris called for terror to be made the order of the day.[44] On that day Pierre Gaspard Chaumette, the president of the Paris Commune, challenged the Committee of Public Safety to embrace the passion and violence of the revolutionary moment. Chaumette was himself the product of a scientific background, calling himself a "student of medicine" in 1791 and dabbling in botany and naturalistic writing.[45] On the morning of the 5th he approached the National Convention to appeal for a revolutionary army of the people. He made an appeal to the Mountain by exhorting, "Mountain, become a volcano."

Chaumette's speech, rich in both passion and imagery, indicated that there was a latent force hidden within the Mountain that needed to burst forth. He asked the hardy Mountain to allow its violence to be freed, to destroy forever the enemies of the Republic.

And you, mountain, forever celebrated in the pages of history; be the Sinai of the French; hurl among the lightning bolts eternal decrees of justice and of the will of the people. Unwavering amid the storms, gather up the aristocracy and be stirred by the voice of the people. For long enough the concentrated fire of the love for the public good has boiled in your flanks; let there be a violent eruption. Holy mountain, become a volcano, whose burning lava will destroy forever the hopes of the villain, and will reduce to ashes [*calciner*] the hearts where an idea of royalty is still found.[46]

While the Mountain is the source of eternal law, it is also the source of a passionate fire. Its lava was "the love of public good," waiting to burst free and purge the nation of the Revolution's enemies and the lovers of aristocracy. Chaumette's speech continued, "No more quarter, no more mercy to traitors...The day of justice and of anger has arrived."

Chaumette's use of *emotions* to describe the motivating forces within the mountain is significant. The burning liquid that will destroy the enemies of the revolution is *passion*—it is simultaneously *love* (of country) and *anger* (against the enemies of France). The volcano as an image of passion and unbridled fervor was drawn upon frequently in literature of the eighteenth century; the Marquis de Sade used the volcano as a symbol for repressed passion that could finally be released in his novels written during and after the Revolution.[47] As a symbol of unreflective action, the volcano signified passion overcoming reason, or even, in the case of de Sade, subverting traditional morality. Chaumette's deployment of this particular enunciation of volcanic potential aligns with a shift in the dominant revolutionary beliefs about the importance of emotion, and a transversal of moral standards brought by the Terror.

Significantly, the more passionate an individual during this phase of the Terror, the more *authentic* his actions were interpreted to be. Much of this faith in emotion developed from the legacy of sentimentalism, the dominant genre of late-eighteenth-century literature. Sentimentalism emphasized the creation of moral communities based on emotional experience; virtue could be attained through shared suffering or communal joy.[48] These ideas informed the spectacle of the revolutionary festival, in which citizens joined in a celebration that ideally evoked the same sentiments and heightened both their sense of community and their passion for the nation.[49] As William Reddy has indicated in his *Navigation of Feeling*, the Terror marks a moment in which "politics was emotional."[50] An individual could be judged by the strength and veracity of his emotions. Those who did not burn with an ardent, and manifest, patriotism might be suspected of counterrevolutionary sentiment. After the passage of the

Law of Suspects on 17 September 1793, anyone not holding a certificate of patriotism could be prosecuted as a potential traitor to the nation. The Paris Commune included among the individuals who could be refused such a certificate "those who received the republican constitution with indifference," and "those who, having done nothing against liberty, have also done nothing for it."[51] With the criminalization of indifference and inactivity, an *unrevealed* emotion was itself proof of guilt. A dormant volcano, still holding its fiery potential within, was far more dangerous to the revolutionary cause than a volcano that destroyed with its passions, and that created a more fertile soil on which the Republic could prosper.

Thus revolutionary sentiment and passion were portrayed as both useful and necessary by several Jacobin leaders. On 19 Vendémiaire, Year II (10 October 1793) Saint-Just, in his "Rapport sur la nécessité de déclarer le gouvernement révolutionnaire jusqu'à la paix," emphasized the importance of passion among the French, and particularly within the French Army. The two passions he noted—love of country and hatred of the enemy—were precisely those that Chaumette suggested were boiling within the volcano of the nation. Saint-Just stated: "If the French nation is driven in this war by all the strong and generous passions, love of liberty and hatred of tyranny and oppression; if, on the contrary, her enemies are mercenary slaves, automatons without passion, the system of war for French arms should be *l'ordre du choc*."[52] An army driven by passion could—and indeed *should*—defeat the enemy.[53] Similarly, Robespierre explained in his discourse of 5 Nivôse, Year II (25 December 1793): "Patriotism is ardent by its nature. Who can love his nation coldly?"[54] Although heat and its inherent movement could sometimes cause instability, a nation of overzealous patriots was far better than one of passive "cadavers." As a result, Robespierre exhorted his countrymen to "protect patriotism, even in its errors," while simultaneously looking for ways to limit "excesses."[55] In this sense the volcano—potentially unstable and destructive but at the same time full of fire and force—was not only a symbol of, but a *model for* Revolution. An authentic and passionate love of country and hatred of the enemy, even if impetuous, could lead to the success of the French Republic.

In addition to being a symbol of the new legitimacy of passion, the volcano was terrifying—just as the Revolution itself should be. In 1782 Marat had described volcanic eruption in vivid and violent language:

> By this terrible explosion, all the elements are merged, thrown with an unbelievable rapidity far from their center of activity, bowling over everything opposing their passage; boulders tumble, the supports [*voûtes*] of these

deep dens are destroyed, and, in this sudden action and reaction of elements, unleashed and seeking to open the passages towards the top where
they find the least resistance, the earth moves and opens; torrents of flame
flow from it, immense abysses open up in which entire towns are swallowed
up with their inhabitants.[56]

The detritus from volcanic eruptions were "traces of terrible blazes."[57]
Vesuvius's eruption was described as "terrible," its lava said to "imprint
a profound terror on souls."[58] Saint-Just, in his 1789 epic poem *Organt,*
had evoked the terror of Etna, saying, "[Organt] contemplated these wa-
vering boulders / the burning entrails of Mount Etna / pompous debris
where Terror resides."[59] The linkage of the idea of terror and the image of
volcano is particularly important given the genesis of its positive connotations: the moment in which terror itself became a positive and productive
notion in revolutionary rhetoric.

The idea of terror as a beneficial strategy for the revolution had circulated since July 1793, soon after the death of Marat.[60] Prior to that moment, "terreur" had been almost universally understood as a negative
phenomenon or feeling, often linked to unseen forces and rationales.
George Armstrong Kelly, in his analysis of prerevolutionary uses of the
word "terror," determined that it was used primarily to describe moments
of helplessness, confrontations with infinitude, the wrath of "arbitrary
government," and an aesthetic sentiment aroused by tragic scenes.[61] The
transfer of this ominous word, described in the *Encyclopédie* as fear that
"breaks our spirit," into a political program intended to regenerate and
purify France, marks an extraordinary moment of linguistic revolution.[62]

Robespierre, in his speech of 17 Pluviôse, Year II (5 February 1794),
outlined the new principles of the Revolution under the rule of terror:
"If the mainspring of popular government during peacetime is virtue, the
mainspring of popular government in revolution is at once *virtue* and *terror:* virtue, without which terror is tragic; terror, without which virtue is impotent. Terror is nothing but prompt, severe, and inflexible justice."[63] This
new morality marked a transmutation of traditional ideas of both virtue
and terror—even for Robespierre himself. In 1785 he had used the idea
of "terror" to condemn arbitrary punishments under despotic regimes. In
an essay competition for the Royal Society in Metz, the young Maximilien
described "terror" as the product of the "horrible spectacle" of an innocent man sent to the scaffolds. This vision, he had stated, "brings terror
into the soul of each one of us, for nothing guarantees that we will never
be its deplorable victims."[64] Ten years later, terror had become a necessary

component of a revolutionary regime. As the Société populaire d'Evreux wrote to the National Convention in September 1793, "Terror, in seizing the despots that surround us, will liberate the soil of liberty from their bloodthirsty hordes." Likewise, the Jacobin Society in the département du Doubs praised the Convention, saying, "The Convention...is the terror of enemies both inside and outside [France]."[65] This new regime of virtue and terror sheds light on the redefinition of volcanic eruption during this particular moment in revolutionary history: that which was terrifying could suddenly be virtuous.

By supporting passion and terror, the Jacobin Mountain did indeed become a volcano in the Year II. This transformation was replicated in festivals and onstage. The mountain at the center of the Festival of the Supreme Being could, according to the engraving shown in figure 10, "crush...the factious / Just as volcanoes scorch the countryside." Another particularly dramatic image titled *The Triumph of the Mountain*, likely produced in late 1793, featured a fiery mountain emitting flames and lightning, striking reptilian creatures emerging from the swamp (see figure 13).[66] The Jacobin Volcano was particularly terrifying to counterrevolutionary figures. In Charles-Louis Tissot's play, *Les Salpêtriers républicains*, discussed in chapter 3, a good patriot asked, "What is this Mountain, then?" and immediately answered his own question: "It is a volcano, the horror of the tyrant." His fellow laborers in the saltpeter workshop then repeated the line after him.[67] *La Veuve du républicain ou le calomniateur*, a highly lauded play that premiered on 23 November 1793, concluded with a promise to all the enemies of France: "Saxons and Castillians, Germans, English, and Batavians: Gather together!...France is marching, and, like a volcano, will devour you all."[68] In *Les Petits Montagnards*, not only did the virtuous family at the center of the action live on a volcanic mountain, but they praised, in song, the volcanic eruption that emerged from the (political) Mountain: "From the unwavering Mountain / The most terrible of volcanoes / Has struck the guilty mob / Of tyrants' dependents."[69] From the start of Year II the Mountain became the Volcano—not of volatility and danger, but of strength and terror for the enemies of the Revolution.

That Volcano, moreover, was associated with the same pulverizing and purifying force that eighteenth-century naturalists had discerned in literal volcanoes. Chaumette used the term *calciner* to describe the effects of revolutionary lava on counterrevolutionary hearts, referring to the chemical process of applying fire to stones and metal. Buffon, in his *Epoques de la Nature*, had described the eruption of "ash, calcinated stones, and burnt earth" from the innards of volcanoes.[70] An October letter from the town

Fig. 13 Pierre-Michel Alix, *Le triomphe de la montagne*. In commemoration of the events of May and June 1793. The images of volcano, mountain, and lightning are all united; the force of the mountain strikes reptiles in the swamp while patriots dance on the slopes. Bibliothèque Nationale de la France, Collection de Vinck 5012.

of Saint-Yrieux to the National Convention reminded their legislators of the fertilizing powers of the volcano, asking them to remain at their posts, "until after you have proven to Europe... that the flames of volcanoes only work to fertilize the soil that they seem to devour."[71] The volcano also was cathartic; in February 1794, a patriotic member of Paris's Section des Piques appealed for a purge of the section's counterrevolutionary members, saying, "When terror is the order of the day, when the revolutionary volcano hovers on the horizon of liberty, let the blade of the law sever the heads of the guilty." He clarified the process of purification by suggesting that the section take an "emetic... and expel all those who carry the mark of condemnation."[72] Likewise, another letter to the Convention offered "eternal gratitude to this holy Mountain that, by the eruption of its sacred fire..., has purified the political atmosphere of France of all the mephitic and contagious exhalations that emerged from the depths of the swamps and that distressed the Republic."[73] Suddenly the very impetuousness and volatility of the volcano became a revolutionary weapon that could be used against its enemies. The volcano, whose cathartic powers had been lauded by Bernardin de Saint-Pierre, could purge the earth of counterrevolutionaries and of the disease-ridden *Marais*.

A number of letters to the Convention in September and October 1793 echoed this language; for example, the Société Républicaine de Rochefort wrote of the time when the "sacred volcano emerged from the depths of the Mountain... [and] exterminated the infernal hydra." An address of the Société Républicaine de Saint-Servan, dated 25 September, hoped that "the volcano of vengeance will erupt from the depths of the Mountain; may the traitors be struck down." Destruction was always linked with regeneration; in the words of the Société Populaire de Grenoble, "a vigorous explosion has announced the age of the well-being of the Republic: daily we see regenerative fires flowing from this crater of pure republicanism and spreading over the horizon of France."[74] The productive powers of the volcano were lauded not just by revolutionary elites, but also by republican societies throughout France.

The people of France were encouraged to boil like the lava inside the volcano of the Republic. In a circular sent to the *sociétés populaires* throughout France, in February 1794, the Committee of Public Safety praised the societies for their work in gathering saltpeter and manufacturing arms for the nation, as per the decree of 14 Frimaire the previous December. "Friends and brothers," the letter urged, "warm your fellow citizens to this idea..., so that popular societies, like the true hearths of the Revolution, may bring forth the volcanic eruptions that should soon swallow up all our enemies." As Chaumette had urged the Committee of Public Safety to enable eruptions, the Committee went on to echo this message to the citizenry, asking them to stoke the fires of the republican volcano. "It is necessary," the letter concluded, "that the free French destroy all the hordes that surround it in a single instant."[75] With the same immediacy as lightning, volcanoes could demolish their surroundings instantaneously; the entire nation was to be volcanized through their participation in revolutionary activities.

It was in this context that Maréchal's play *Le Jugement dernier des rois* premiered at the Théâtre de la République. The play was set on a half-volcanic island, where a single Frenchman, exiled long ago by a "tyrant," lived in peace alongside a group of "gentle savages" who communicated through gesture alone. Behind the exile's *cabane* was a white rock inscribed with the lines: "It is better to have as a neighbor / A volcano than a king / Liberty, Equality."[76] From the opening scene Maréchal set the tone for his patriotic play: In a time of war, volcanoes—both as destructive nature and as an emblem of radical revolutionaries—made better neighbors than did kings.

The debasing and vilification of kingship was both a stated goal and a perceived effect of the play. In Maréchal's comments to the audience at the first performance, he reminded the spectators of the ridicule that the common people had endured in theaters under monarchs. "I thought it was time to return the favor," he explained. "I thought it was time to make them [the monarchs] the laughing stock of the public."[77] The play's impact, however, surpassed ridicule: it kindled a passionate hatred of kings. The *Journal des Spectacles* raved that "everything assures the long success of this work, made to attract the public and to fuel the republican spirit and the hatred of kings."[78] The *Feuille du Salut Public* noted that the audience was transformed, animated by a spirit entirely unlike the "blasé" atmosphere at other theaters. The crowd was overcome with fury against monarchs; after the play, "the *parterre* and the entire room seemed to be composed of a legion of tyrannicides."[79] The audience shared in the judgment pronounced by the volcano: death.

The *Jugement Dernier* played out like an authentic sentencing. The kings, escorted in chains by *sans-culottes* from all over Europe, were presented to the island as criminals, their various crimes announced and their sentence pronounced. "Nature, hasten to finish the work of the *sans-culottes;* blow your breath of fire over this scum of society, and return the kings to nothingness forever, from which they never should have emerged," proclaimed the French *sans-culotte*.[80] Significantly the judgment, though pronounced by the people, was carried out by natural forces; nature confirmed and ratified the revolutionaries' decision. In the words of the English revolutionary, "The hand of nature will hasten to ratify and sanction the judgment declared by the *sans-culottes* against the kings."[81]

Jean-Marie Apostolidès, in a thoughtful analysis of Maréchal's play, sees three levels of interpretation to the volcano itself: as a reminder of the calamitous explosions on Vesuvius that had captivated the European imagination; as a representation of the Mountain; and as a metaphor for the guillotine.[82] Indeed, the imagery in the play, like most rhetorical uses of natural phenomena, drew upon symbols and understandings of both real and metaphorical volcanoes. However, whereas Maréchal's play demonstrated the shift from the Mountain to the Volcano in political parlance, Apostolidès' equation of the volcano with the guillotine fails to convey the full harshness of the judgment carried out in the play. In fact, instead of the guillotine, the volcano represented a far more torturous and naturalized form of punishment. One of the *sans-culottes* explained the punishment to the exiled Frenchman:

> Their punishment would have been too mild and would have finished too quickly [had we hung or guillotined them]; it would not have fulfilled the goal that we intended. It seemed more useful to offer to Europe the spectacle of its kings detained in a *ménagerie* and devouring one another, no longer able to release their rage on the brave *sans-culottes* that they dared to call their *subjects*. It is good to give them the leisure to reproach one another for their crimes, and to punish one another with their own hands. That is the solemn judgment that was pronounced against them unanimously and without appeal.[83]

By returning the kings to a state of nature, they would endure a punishment far worse than the "humane" guillotine, which killed instantaneously and (allegedly) without suffering.[84] Indeed, in fulfillment of the *sans-culotte*'s prophecy, the monarchs began to berate one another, with Catherine of Russia going staff-to-scepter against the Pope in a particularly comical bout.

In subjecting kings to a fate more terrible than that imposed on common criminals, *Le Jugement Dernier* reflected a belief, nascent in Louis XVI's trial, in the status of kings as enemies not merely of the nation but of humanity writ large. The Montagnard rhetoric of the 1792 debates focused on the exceptionality of the king, and on his monstrosity. His very inviolability, attested to by his defenders, in fact determined his necessary destruction; in the words of Antoine de Baecque, "Since Louis is an exceptional being, a 'body outside the nation,' the Republic [could] only be installed by annihilating him."[85] As Dan Edelstein has argued, several Jacobins maintained that Louis had been returned to the state of nature precisely *because* of his exceptional status. Because a king was outside the bounds of constitutional or positive law, only the laws of nature could determine his fate.[86] For Maréchal, nature alone could properly and justly end the lives of kings; they were monsters unworthy of a humane—or human—death. The French *sans-culotte* said to the enchained kings, "Crowned monsters! You should have all died a thousand deaths on the scaffolds: but where would we have found executioners who would have consented to sully their hands in your vile and corrupt blood? We leave you with your regrets, or rather with your impotent rage."[87] Maréchal's play was simply a spectacular performance of what nature itself demanded: the immediate and merciless destruction of kings and other enemies of the human race.

Maréchal's play not only garnered critical praise and passionate audiences; it also was a source for other playwrights in France, who shamelessly plagiarized his story in more local iterations. A citizen Desbarreaux authored a play titled *Les Potentats foudroyés par la Montagne et la Raison, ou La Déportation des rois de l'Europe* that premiered in Toulouse in Nivôse of Year II (December 1793), following a nearly identical plot. In Desbarreaux's more Rousseauian version, the island was inhabited by a French exile, Julie, and her child Emile; the eruption—accompanied in this instance by thunder and lightning—that brought the kings to their death, as suggested by the title, was enacted by Reason. "Reason, which shares [the rage of the people of Europe], lights this very volcano with its torch." Reason, the heavens, and the natural world coalesced their forces to bring about their fate:

> The heavens are accomplices in this terrible decree;
> This volcano will swallow you up.
> This judgment is not severe;
> It is just, it is merited.[88]

Reason and nature alike required the destruction of the tyrants; they operated according to the same laws and acted in coalition.

It is worth comparing Maréchal's play to another, premiering in 1792, with a similar plot: *Les Émigrés aux terres australes*, by a Citizen Gamas.[89] In Gamas's play, a group of aristocrats and priests were exiled to a remote island; like in *Le Jugement dernier des rois*, the choice of exile was made because death would have been too mild a punishment for their crimes. "Death would be a favor to you," the captain of the National Guard explained to the émigrés. "We would prefer to condemn you to live, consumed with guilt and remorse. This is delivering you into a constantly renewing torment."[90] The exiles interacted with the native people, who bore a striking resemblance to the wise islanders portrayed in Diderot's *Supplément au Voyage de Bougainville,* learning from them. Ultimately the cast of *ci-devants* was transformed, recognizing the laborer among them as their leader, and employing themselves usefully for their survival. In the 1792 play, nature did not "ratify" the judgment of the *sans-culottes,* it reformed the exiles; by 1794 nature no longer reformed, it destroyed.

While the state of nature forced the kings' penance in *Le Jugement dernier des rois,* the "hand of nature" issued their punishment.[91] In a dramatic conclusion, featuring a stunning explosion, the volcano consumed the exiles. Without making the point explicitly, however, Maréchal also destroyed another race of people in his volcanic eruption: the gentle "savages" who lived in peace and harmony on the island.[92] Even the just punishment doled out to the tyrants of Europe had unattended consequences: collateral damage that could not be avoided as nature's wrath coincided with revolutionary vengeance. Unwittingly Maréchal gestured toward a tension inherent in the metaphor of the volcano, namely, an eruption's indiscriminateness. At a certain point eruption, even if desired, was uncontrollable; Julie, in Desbarreaux's play, had explained to the *sans-culottes* that "the volcano that you see, whose eruption can neither be calculated nor predicted, will soon swallow up the scourges of the human race."[93] Yet this unpredictability of the volcano was silenced during this period in the image's history; Maréchal, like Chaumette, Barère, and other revolutionaries who drew on the metaphor in a positive way, allowed the potential benefits of eruption to outweigh its possible transgressions. The beneficent vision of volcanoes as purgative, regenerative, and necessary to the natural order, made possible in part by a century of study among naturalists, found a sinister enunciation in the rhetoric of the Terror.

The tension of a powerful, revolutionary, and yet ultimately uncontrollable volcano was brought to the fore by Robespierre on the very eve of his fall. On 8 Thermidor (26 July 1794) Robespierre invoked the volcano, an image he used only rarely, in a metaphor that revealed his own ambivalence toward popular violence.[94] In an address to the Convention, the "Incorruptible" attempted to allay criticism of his alleged tyranny. He stated that atheism had cast France into mourning prior to 18 Floréal, the date on which Robespierre himself had proposed a series of festivals culminating in the Festival of the Supreme Being. He proclaimed that "a just indignation, compressed by terror, fermented silently in all hearts; a terrible, inevitable eruption boiled in the entrails of the volcano, while small philosophers played on its peak with great scoundrels." Terror had fostered the development of a boiling passion, "fermenting"—Saint-Pierre's precise word for the sources of volcanic fire—within the people. Yet Robespierre, far from calling for the eruption to take place, instead recognized its potential dangers: "whether the people consented to suffer tyranny, or they violently shook off their yoke, liberty was lost either way."[95] He maintained that only the return of the French people to their rightful religious faith, through the Festival of the Supreme Being, had allowed the eruption to be avoided, and the nation to be saved.

Like Chaumette, Robespierre attributed the force of the volcano to emotions and even to terror; he likewise saw a certain justice in the people's eruptive power. Unlike Chaumette or other advocates of the purgative and constructive force of the volcano, however, Robespierre claimed to want to quell its potential violence. Yet the eruption was, in his own words, "inevitable." Robespierre's language reveals the ambiguity of the volcano as a political metaphor. A volcano was forceful, purifying, and regenerative, but it was also ultimately uncontrollable. Its eruptions could neither be predicted nor contained. Robespierre exemplified the shift in volcano rhetoric from a counterrevolutionary force to a revolutionary one motivated by passion and justice, but he also indicated the limits of its use as a positive metaphor and, indeed, gestured toward its demise. With the end of the Terror came the end of the volcano as a symbol of constructive revolutionary transformation.[96]

The Terrible after the Terror

On 27 Prairial, Year II (15 June 1794), nature's destructive power moved from rhetoric to reality, when a literal mountain exploded: Vesuvius burst into flames, devastating the town of *Torre del greco* and showering ash on Naples. Nearly every French newspaper reported on the eruption, vividly describing both the explosion and its destruction, and portraying it as one of the most violent eruptions in the mountain's history. "Lava and stones were thrown great distances," reported the *Mercure Universel* in July; "lava swept away all the homes it met in its path, and entirely devastated the hills and mountains through which it passed."[97] The *Feuille de la République* reminded its readers of Vesuvius's long history, stretching back to the obliteration of Herculaneum and Pompeii.[98]

Bertrand Barère, addressing the National Convention on 17 Messidor (5 July), used the incident to demonstrate the coalition between Nature and the Revolution. "Nature, from the heights of Vesuvius, has just commanded Naples not to release its fleet that was going to join the English on the shores of the Mediterranean." He continued: "The eruption of this volcano was stronger than ever before; the suburbs of Naples have been burned by lava, and the town and its ports were covered for three days with smoke and ashes." Nature's destructive power had allied with the Revolution to facilitate its success, damaging Italy to a historic extent at precisely the moment when France would benefit most. This put France in a far better position than any of its European enemies; with Nature as an ally, what chance did the Counter Revolution have? Comparing this alliance to that between Leopold II and Frederick William II, he proclaimed: "This coalition between Liberty and Nature, lightning…and lava…is well worth the Treaty of Pillnitz." With Nature acting on France's behalf, the political Mountain and the physical Vesuvius were aligned: "The revolution of this *other mountain* has delayed the plans of the Italian governments," he declared.[99]

The positive image of the volcano, of course, could not be dissociated from the image of the Mountain. As a result, its currency faded along with the Mountain's. After Thermidor, and the fall of the Jacobins from power, the "volcano" again became a symbol not just of volatility but of anarchy and fanaticism. The possible slippage between "mountain" and "volcano" was embraced by counterrevolutionaries and moderates as a warning against the radicalism of the Jacobins. Dominique Joseph Garat, the former minister of the interior who managed to survive the Terror despite his Girondin leanings, wrote in his 1795 justificatory memoirs:

> We gave to the [left] side the name of the *Mountain,* and I said often that they needed no other name but the volcano; it was a volcano, in effect, from which burst, in torrents, all the passions set ablaze by the sudden appearance of a great Republic amid the human race, of a revolution that, in restoring all rights, shattered in an instant all restraints. But, in this lava, pure and precious metals ran, melted by the flames that threatened to devour everything. All the materials were flammable; not all were incendiary. If we could have separated them, the blaze could have been avoided.[100]

With this vivid imagery, Garat painted the picture of a nation inspired and unbridled by the sudden Revolution, but whose passion led to a mixing between pure and impure elements. The fires of the Mountain melted distinctions but also made it impossible to separate those who would destroy the Revolution from those who would save it. Of course Garat, in his post-Thermidor attempt to differentiate himself from the Jacobins, implied that he was one of the elements that could have saved—indeed, could *still* save—the Revolution.

Just as, prior to 1793, the volcano had been used to warn of potentially insidious counterrevolutionary plots, after Thermidor it became a warning of overzealous revolutionaries who could ignite the fragile Republic—and particularly against dormant Jacobins who might again prompt an eruption. After the closing of the Jacobin Club, the *Messager du soir* compared their empty chamber to "a volcano whose crater is extinct, and that attracts the attention of the traveler."[101] The *Reveil du peuple,* a popular song among re-actionaries, appended a new verse in the spring of 1795 that warned: "O you guilty egoists / and you cowardly idlers, / If you save yourself alongside terrorists / You will sleep on volcanoes. / It is not enough to hate crime/ You must destroy it: / if you don't close up the abyss, / the abyss will swallow you up."[102] "Volcaniser"—a term born in the Revolution itself—was to make unstable and dangerous, as a 1795 satirical pamphlet indicated. In the anonymous pamphlet, the Devil and a reincarnated Marat conspired to wreak havoc on Paris. "Will he again pillage, volcanize, massacre?" an "honest man" asked of the Devil, to which the answer was a definitive "oui."[103] Similarly, in a Year VII festival commemorating the king's death—a festival against both monarchy and anarchy, the twin tyrants of Louis XVI and Robespierre—the president of the Departement of Orne described anarchy as "a volcano that destroys all virtues, both public and private."[104] The volcano, for its associations with the Mountain, but also for its connotations as something destructive, passionate, and terrifying, again became a symbol used to inspire watchfulness and warning. The period of untrammeled passion and explosive patriotism had ended.

With the fall of the Mountain, then, also came the fall of the volcano as a positive image of revolutionary transformation. Tracing the metaphor throughout the revolutionary period demonstrates several important details about both revolutionary political culture and understandings of the natural world. First, it exemplifies the politicization of natural language. The brief yet powerful moment of the volcano's positive uses coincides directly with the calls for terror to be made the order of the day. Its usage, far more than that of any other natural metaphor, was determined by specific political moments and movements. Just as "terror" shifted from a destructive and destabilizing notion to a constructive political strategy, so, too, did the terrifying volcano transform from a sign of volatility to one of just vengeance, which allowed for the creation of a new political order. Furthermore, the shifting meanings of the image of the volcano suggest an idea of a revolution that, in the eyes of its actors, was beyond their control. While Robespierre struggled to assert his power over the natural forces of the Revolution, as he indicated in his discourse on 8 Thermidor, he recognized that, despite his efforts, the French still "walked on volcanoes."[105] And he, of course, fell prey to the forces of Revolution a single day later. Even in the most contrived circumstances, as on Maréchal's fictional island, revolutionary violence could spiral beyond human control, as his benevolent native islanders were killed alongside Europe's exiled monarchs.

For a brief moment the volcano, long a symbol of fear and power, became an instrument of Terror, an emblem of patriotic passion. A force of nature, it both aligned with and superseded the efforts of revolutionaries. Yet its fires burned too brightly, its passions too ardently. With the emergence of a new regime that aimed to distance itself from both the Terror and the Mountain, the image of the volcano largely faded from use in political language. In justifications of revolutionary action, however, it persisted. Two decades after the Terror, memorializing the Revolution from his exile on Saint Helena, Napoleon declaimed, "The most well-founded revolutions destroy everything in a single instant, and do not rebuild [*remplacer*] until the future. Ours seemed to be the result of an irresistible fatalism; it was a moral eruption that was just as inevitable as a physical eruption, a true volcano: when chemical combinations that produce the latter are complete, it explodes; the moral combinations that produce a revolution had arrived in France, and she erupted."[106] Like so many before him, Napoleon turned to nature to understand the phenomenon of revolution. The volcanic eruption, impetuous, destructive, and above all inevitable, illustrated a revolution that surpassed human control.

CONCLUSION

Revolutionary Like Nature, Natural Like a Revolution

The period from 1793 to 1794 marked the height of the relationship between pro-revolutionary violence and nature in revolutionary rhetoric. Soon after the Jacobins fell from power, the terms "mountain" and "volcano" both shed many of their positive connotations; volcano again became a term that signified rampant and uncontrollable destruction, and Edme Petit called for the word "Mountain" to be banned from the Convention floor a mere month after Thermidor.[1] A decree of 20 February 1795 mandated the dismantling of symbolic mountains across France, and two weeks later the saltpeter program came to an end.[2] Revolutionary forces could still strike like thunderbolts or flow like torrents, but the purgative, restorative, and constructive connotations of these images were largely subsumed by other meanings. As cultural, social, and political contexts changed, so, too, did the basic analogies assumed by the metaphors.

The metaphorical relationship between the natural and political realms posited by revolutionary leaders unveils a French nation that, by the end of the eighteenth century, was deeply attuned not only to the natural world, but to a nascent scientific discourse that infused plays, songs, and even policy. The rhetoric of the French Revolution both affirmed the efforts of the Enlightenment to educate a broad public about the natural world, and extended that education despite the dissolution of some of the stalwart Old Regime institutions dedicated to natural knowledge. Instead, plays, poems, and songs carried on the popularizing traditions begun by Bernardin de Saint-Pierre, who sought to combine natural history with sentimental literature, and the physicist Perrin, who entertained audiences with a physics show (complete with a problem-solving pet spaniel) near the Boulevard du Temple throughout the 1780s.[3] During the Revolution

French men and women could learn about the process of saltpeter extraction by attending a state-sponsored class taught by Antoine François de Fourcroy, but also by seeing a performance of Tissot's *Les Salpêtriers républicains* or singing along with the rousing song "Saltpeter." The educational efforts of the eighteenth century had already succeeded in many respects, as leaders assumed a certain amount of knowledge among their audiences as they referred to electrical circuits or the miasmas around swamps. As Jean-François Féraud wrote in his 1787 dictionary of the French language, metaphors must "be just and natural, [and]...be understandable to the average reader."[4] The persistence of analogies to the processes of the natural world suggests that they were, in fact, transparent enough to the audience to make them tenable. What is more, those analogies were shared by popular societies throughout France that likewise referred to regenerative volcanic eruptions, lightning bolts that restored an atmospheric equilibrium, or the corruptive "exhalations" emitted by swamps.

Yet the patterns of use of these images demonstrate more than a society that could draw allusions to recent scientific discoveries. Between 1789 and 1794 the connotations of natural imagery changed (lightning transformed from an arbitrary weapon of despots to a symbol of directed, immediate, and purgative justice; the volcano shifted from an image of destruction to one of regeneration). As the simultaneous decrees of 14 Frimaire suggest, nature also became a rhetorical ally of the Revolution. Although in the wake of the 1792 September Massacres, the people had moved like a torrent (irresistibly, regeneratively) and embodied a providential purpose, as Prudhomme had suggested, it was nevertheless the *people* that were an agent of revolution. By 1794 nature itself was revolutionary, and vice versa: in May 1794, Barère proclaimed that France was revolutionary like nature, on the very day Robespierre suggested that nature had been returned from exile. At the Festival of the Supreme Being Robespierre preached that nature had reclaimed its splendor, and, less than a month later, Barère portrayed Vesuvius as operating on behalf of the Revolution. Nature, rather than the people, became the revolutionary and providential force. Nature became a space of *particular* providence, not just a regulating system.[5]

Revolutionary uses of natural metaphors therefore transformed the meanings of nature and revolution alike. While nature had, in eighteenth-century science and literature, been an exemplar of an ordered, beneficent, and self-regulating system, philosophers and naturalists attempted to strip the natural world of its superstitious connotations. D'Holbach had tried to wrest lightning from the hands of gods and kings and render it a purely natural phenomenon, and the Lisbon earthquake was treated as a necessary convulsion in the operations of the earth rather than a scourge of God. Miracles had no place in the naturalist worldview. Yet by the time Chaumette urged the Mountain to become a volcano in the fall of 1793, nature was not merely a model of good governance; it was an active partici-pant in revolution, providing thunderbolts with which to "strike the heads of the prideful," as Robespierre said in his speech on revolutionary gov-ernment in Pluviôse.[6] The lightning bolt's function for Robespierre was clear: it was not a result of an electrical imbalance in the clouds. Instead, it was created to strike the prideful, just as Lisbon's bay was destined to drown Jacques the Anabaptist in *Candide*. Neither Robespierre nor the French Republic nor the Committee of Public Safety were the bearers of such power; rather, that power was borne by an untrammeled force of na-ture, acting with a justification and a logic beyond the grasp of man.

These changing connotations force us to reconsider a number of assumptions about both revolutionary sovereignty and revolutionary violence. The natural history of the Revolution reveals a notion of gov-ernance in which human will and agency were often neglected. As chap-ter 2 demonstrated, the term "revolution" could be used to describe an event that was inevitable and destructive but was also benevolent and concerned with the public good. Revolution was not always a guaran-tor of individual agency or a product of human will, but instead was a part of the natural process of change. Indeed, Billaud-Varenne's "revo-lutionary" government was modeled on nature and natural processes but was completely devoid of any will, or *volonté*, save that of the small coterie at its center. In fact, by 1793, nature seemed to have overtaken the general will as the legitimation of governance. Letters encouraging legislators to hold fast to the "lightning bolt" of sovereignty even in the absence of a constitution flooded into the Convention in September and October 1793. Even revolutionary law was not created; it was discerned, descending from the mountaintop like the Mosaic Commandments. As Wordsworth would write, in 1805, about the Revolution, "To nature, then, power had reverted."

The substitution of the general will and constitutional law with refer-ences to the natural world reinforces the conclusions reached by Dan Edelstein, who argues in his *Terror of Natural Right* that a "natural republi-canism," with nature alone as the source of law, was at the heart of Jacobin politics. In his rigorous and groundbreaking analysis of Jacobin political language of the Year II, Edelstein determines that appeals to constitutional law and to the general will were replaced by calls for natural law and self-regulating institutions. In his words, "What set [the Committee of Public Safety members] apart from this [republican] tradition was their belief that natural right, rather than a constitution, should serve as the foundation for laws and *moeurs*."[7] Natural law became the new source of legitimacy for the radical republic. Yet the insertion of the natural world into political life that I outline here suggests that natural law itself was inflected by eighteenth-century discussions of and inquiries into the natural world. That which Edelstein traces in part to the *weakness* of republicanism in the legal tradition in France, I attribute to the *strength* of the natural world in scientific and literary discourse.[8]

Whether approaching revolutionary language from the perspective of jurisprudence or of natural histories and responses to natural disasters, however, the recognition of this Jacobin move toward nature as a legitimation of revolutionary government challenges François Furet's reading of Terror as nascent in the revolutionary obsession with the general will. Instead, the Terror seems to have escalated amid calls for nature to rule; it was, in fact, the *removal* of will and agency from revolutionary rhetoric that is emblematic of the most radical period of the Revolution. As a result, the narrative of natural history suggests a reassessment of the relationship between revolutionary leaders and the citizenry that is focused less on attempts to discern and represent the general will, and more on civic participation in extra-institutional venues.

As Lequinio noted when he first used the image of the mountain, the natural world was a space that elites and the "common man" alike could relate to. Indeed, the natural world was the subject of much legislation: the use of previously restricted forests, the cultivation of fish ponds, and the draining of swamps all aimed to make nature more accessible and more productive for the French citizen. However, Roland's suggestion that the legislator must build dams to restrain the torrents of the people after the September Massacres reveals his ideal of an enlightened leadership of, rather than by, the people. Robespierre used the language of nature to demonstrate a continued faith in the ability of leaders to control the passions of the people: he never abandoned his belief in the lightning rod, as demonstrated by his calls to hinder the volcanic eruption on 8 Thermidor.

Nature could be a way of excluding the people from politics even while maintaining the illusion that they were active participants. If the revolutionary wars were, in fact, the first "total wars," as David Bell has argued, the saltpeter initiative is fascinating proof of a total requisition: even

French soil was called upon to serve the nation.[9] In elevating *salpêtriers* to the status of soldiers, the Convention demonstrated its deep commitment to the idea of an entire nation in service. According to this logic, a nation was built not by reasoned participation at the polls but by the more visceral experiences of digging up earth for the war effort, taking part in festivals, or comprising the revolutionary "torrent" that the Festival of Unity and Indivisibility praised.

Even as the will of the people was evacuated from the natural history of revolution, violence was integrated into that narrative. The notion that violence was an inherent part of the Revolution was a rhetoric born in the revolution itself, by the very actors taking part in it. It was not a way of de-legitimizing the Revolution, or a post-Thermidor attempt to exonerate Terrorists;[10] rather, it was accepted as fact by Louis XVI, who in his request for amnesties referred to the "damages that a great revolution always entails," and by leftists stepping to the defense of the Glacièristes. In addition, the forward-looking justifications of violence so dominant in the Terror emerged early in the Revolution: as early as the spring of 1792, in the debates over the Glacière Massacres, violence that was born *from* the Revolution was considered necessary to the outcome *of* the Revolution. Violence was not legitimated based on vengeance alone, but rather was un-punishable because it was a product of "effervescence" and *"secousses"* that were an inherent part of revolutionary activity. With the September Massacres, and the assumption that the Revolution was not yet over, the justification of crowd violence was pushed forward, into the future: just as the Lisbon earthquake could only be understood by an all-knowing and benevolent God, the task of judging the massacres was left to later generations and, in the meantime, covered with a "religious veil." The rhetoric of the Glacière and September massacres not only made the people a natural and providential force, it made doubting the justice of their actions a counterrevolutionary (if not heretical) stance.

What is more, naturalized rhetoric turned the very spontaneity, disorder, and collectivity of crowd violence into proofs of its necessity and therefore of its justice. The naturalization of violence allowed for the creation of a *rational ordered world* whose order was paradoxically maintained by occasional outbursts of disorder. This finding turns some of the theories of violence established in the last thirty years on their heads; whereas theorists of violence, including Sergio Cotta, and historians of revolutionary violence, including Howard Brown, have made the distinction between order and spontaneity one of the primary differences between legitimate force and illegitimate violence, revolutionary rhetoric demonstrates that spontaneity and untrammeled passion were, in fact, *legitimizing* factors in violent acts.[11] Brown, in his recent illuminating study of violence in France between 1794 and 1802, suggested that there are two types of violence: communicative, which abides by certain socially and culturally conditioned rules, and solipsistic, which "is essentially an outburst of un-regulated passion, a sudden anger unleashed, or a categorical refusal of the 'other.'" Such violence, Brown continues, "achieves little more than a unilateral affirmation of the individual or group."[12] Yet, in many accounts of revolutionary violence, it was the apparent disorder, alleged unpredictability, and passion of the violent act that themselves made it "revolutionary," and guiltless.[13] As Brian Singer has argued, revolution problematizes such measures of "rational" violence by throwing into question the very societal rules by which a group is expected to operate.[14] In fact, during the Revolution, spontaneous violence—far from being understood as anarchic or "solipsistic"—was portrayed as inevitable, natural, and constructive of a new order. Demonstrating that violence was spontaneous was the most effective way to make it "revolutionary" and legitimate.

Thus, by naturalizing revolutionary violence, its advocates also made it seem a *necessary* step in the regeneration and future progress of the Republic. Understanding the violence of the Terror as inevitable was not an innovation of François Furet's; rather, it was present in the very rhetoric of the revolutionaries themselves. By comparing it to storms and sublime tempests, and by invoking the language of Providence through their future-oriented justifications, they removed human agency from the revolutionary equation. In this regard, the natural history crafted by revolutionaries not only calls us to reconsider the rhetoric of the French Revolution; it asks us to examine the ways in which language is used to stifle action in any space or time. The specific way in which revolutionaries crafted their narrative of violence, invoking particular images derived from inquiries into the natural world throughout the Enlightenment, was unique to the moment of the French Revolution, but rhetorical attempts to cloak responsibility and limit dissent can be found in nearly all moments of crisis.

Analogies conceal even as they allude; they seek to make familiar what is otherwise unrecognizable. In conflating two events or phenomena, we may lose sight of the utter novelty of each one or miss the opportunity to assess responsibility and enact change. And in establishing a metaphorical relationship between manmade events and natural ones, we risk replacing agency with complacency. Invocations of the sublime natural world may have awed revolutionary audiences (Pithou de Loinville described the

"sweet drunkenness" of the crowd at the Festival of Unity and Indivisibility),
but those who are awed by mystery are often condemned to stand complacently by in its midst, accepting what is occurring around them as both
natural and necessary. In Arendt's words, "So long as we talk in...biologi-
cal terms, the glorifiers of violence can appeal to the undeniable fact that
in the household of nature destruction and creation are but two sides
of the natural process, so that collective violent action...may appear as
natural a prerequisite for the collective life of mankind as the struggle for
survival and violent death...in the animal kingdom."[15] In their allusions
to the natural world, revolutionaries fused the realm of uncontrollable
nature and inevitability with political action. Crafting a natural history
of Revolution meant leaving individual agency, responsibility, and will as
mute bystanders to the march of Nature.

In a 1790 satire of revolutionary optimism, an anonymous pamphleteer
resurrected Voltaire's Pangloss and Martin to debate the virtues of the
Revolution. For every problem raised by Martin—murders, fires, priests
who had their throats slit, individuals who had lost all their belongings,
the risk of civil war—the revolutionary Pangloss argued that all was, in
reality, for the best.

> Any time that there is [*qu'il s'opère*] a change in government, the passage
> from the old to the new is necessarily a moment of anarchy. What can go
> against [*s'ensuivre contre*] the change, if it is proven that it was necessary,
> indispensable, and that it took place for the good of the nation?...Because
> the sun causes pestilential exhalations to arise from an infectious cesspool,
> is its warmth any less beneficial? Do we not still owe to it the dews that fertil-
> ize the earth?[16]

Although the pamphlet mocked this thoroughgoing optimism, by late
1792 this language was not uncommon. Indeed, the Revolution seemed
to cultivate a Panglossian attitude: revolutionary activity, even if violent,
was ultimately for the best. This providential attitude, exemplified by
Prudhomme's comparisons between the Terror and a hailstorm or the
September Massacres and the Lisbon earthquake, relied on the vision
of an ordered but secular universe made commonplace by eighteenth-
century natural histories. The revolutionaries did not maintain that God
was punishing the aristocrats for their sins (as, indeed, Joseph de Maistre
would in his 1796 *Considerations on France*); nor did they require a deity to
make sense of their sorrows. Nature could provide all the theodicy they
needed.

With the (political and rhetorical) collapse of the Mountain, the vogue for images of nature as mechanisms for political change seemed to fade. Prudhomme himself apparently reversed his opinion on both the Lisbon earthquake and the September Massacres, resurrecting the victims and responding with neither adoration of providence nor silence. In his 1797 *Histoire générale et impartiale des erreurs, des fautes, et des crimes commis pendant la Révolution française,* he detailed the many atrocities that had taken place during the early Revolution, attributing them not to the providential masses but to a conspiratorial faction that manipulated the people. He included a list of the dead, inspired by lists generated in the wake of Lisbon: "In the disaster of Lisbon, 100,000 citizens of every age, rank, and sex died in a few minutes. A few months later, alphabetical lists of the names of the unfortunate victims were created, for the use of families who survived the physical revolution. Why not follow this example in regard to the political revolution in France?"[17] Prudhomme continued to see an analogy between political and terrestrial revolutions, but this time without the redemption or justice he had lauded in the wake of the September Massacres. If the revolutionaries were Panglosses for much of the early years of the Revolution, by the end of 1794 France was a nation of Candides, weary of final causes and ready to cultivate their garden (even if they continued to search for saltpeter in it).

NOTES

Introduction

1. *Procès-verbal des monumens, de la marche, et des discours de la fête consacrée de la Constitution de la République française, le 10 août 1793* (Paris: de l'impr. Nationale, Year II [1793]), p. 2. The festival is also described in Jean-Joseph Pithou de Loinville and Jacques-Louis David, *Description Générale de la Première fête républicaine de la réunion, cette fête a été célébrée en mémoire de la fameuse journée qui s'est passée au Tuileries, le 10 août 1792, et à l'occasion de l'acceptation de la constitution par le souverain* (Paris: n.p., n.d.); *Détail de la fête de l'Unité et de l'Indivisibilité de la République qui a eu lieu le 10 août* (Paris: de l'impr. de Chaudrillié, n.d.); and the program, *Ordre et marche de la fête de l'Unité et de l'Indivisibilité de la République* (Paris: de l'impr. de Chaudrillié, n.d.). All translations by the author unless otherwise noted.

2. *Détail de la fête de l'Unité et de l'Indivisibilité de la République qui a eu lieu le 10 août*, p. 5.

3. *Procès-verbal*, p. 5.

4. Ceremonies were also held at a sixth station to commemorate the republican dead. See James A. Leith, *Space and Revolution: Projects for Monuments, Squares, and Public Buildings in France, 1789–1799* (Montreal: McGill-Queen's University Press, 1991), p. 134. See also Marie-Jean Hérault de Sechelles, *Recueil des six discours prononcés par le président de la Convention Nationale, le 10 août l'an 2me de la République aux six stations de la fête de l'Unité et de l'Indivisibilité de la République* (Paris: de l'impr. de Chaudrillié, n.d. [1793]).

5. On the significance of this statue as the Egyptian goddess of nature, Isis, see Dan Edelstein, *The Terror of Natural Right: Republicanism, the Cult of Nature, and the French Revolution* (Chicago: University of Chicago Press, 2009), pp. 184–185.

6. *Procès-verbal*, p. 12.

7. Ibid., pp. 16–17; Pithou and David, *Description Générale*, p. 23.

8. Mona Ozouf, *Festivals and the French Revolution*, trans. Alan Sheridan (Cambridge, Mass.: Harvard University Press, 1988), p. 84.

9. My research on this rhetoric of the natural world is based primarily on texts intended for public consumption that discussed revolutionary events and revolutionary violence. I have used word searches wherever possible (the database of the Project for American and French Research on the Treasury of the French Language [ARTFL] has been particularly helpful in uncovering the broader eighteenth-century context for these terms), but most of my findings from the revolutionary period have come from close readings of revolutionary plays, songs, festival accounts, political speeches, and newspaper articles.

10. The French Revolutionary calendar was used from 1793 until 1 January 1806. The calendar marked the Republic's break with its Old Regime past by starting at Year One,

which began with the start of the Republic in 1792. It replaced weeks with ten-day *décades,* which culminated in a secular festival on the tenth day, and the Julian months with seasonal names that were meant to evoke agricultural images. These changes were famously satirized in the British press as creating a year of "Slippy, Nippy, Drippy, Wheezy, Sneezy, Showery, Flowery, Bowery, Heaty, Wheaty, Sweety." See William Doyle, *The Oxford History of the French Revolution* (Oxford: Oxford University Press, 1989), appendix 2, for conversion of dates and the British satire.

11. Joseph Fouché, *Ecrits révolutionnaires* (Paris: Paris-Zanzibar, 1998), p. 96.

12. Keith Michael Baker, *Inventing the French Revolution* (Cambridge: Cambridge University Press, 1990), p. 4.

13. Ibid., p. 24.

14. Ibid., p. 223.

15. Sophia Rosenfeld, *A Revolution in Language: The Problem of Signs in Late Eighteenth-Century France* (Stanford, Calif.: Stanford University Press, 2001); and Lynn Hunt, *Politics, Culture, and Class in the French Revolution* (Berkeley: University of California Press, 1984). On metaphor in the revolutionary period, see Antoine de Baecque, *The Body Politic: Corporeal Metaphor in Revolutionary France, 1770–1800,* trans. Charlotte Mandell (Stanford, Calif.: Stanford University Press, 1997). On representation during the French Revolution, see also de Baecque, *Glory and Terror: Seven Deaths under the French Revolution,* trans. Charlotte Mandell (New York: Routledge, 2001); Emmet Kennedy, *A Cultural History of the French Revolution* (New Haven, Conn.: Yale University Press, 1989); and Ronald Paulson, *Representations of Revolution, 1789–1820* (New Haven, Conn.: Yale University Press, 1983).

16. On nature and natural history in the eighteenth century, see Louise Lyle and David McCallan, eds., *Histoires de la terre: Earth Sciences and French Culture, 1740–1940* (Amsterdam: Éditions Rodopi, 2008); D. G. Charlton, *New Images of the Natural in France* (Cambridge: Cambridge University Press, 1984); Lorraine Daston, "The Nature of Nature in Early Modern Europe," *Configurations: A Journal of Literature, Science, and Technology* 6 (1998): 149–172; Lorraine Daston and Fernando Vidal, eds., *The Moral Authority of Nature* (Chicago: University of Chicago Press, 2004), E. C. Spary, *Utopia's Garden: French Natural History from Old Regime to Revolution* (Chicago: University of Chicago Press, 2000); Daniel Mornet, *Les Sciences de la nature en France au XVIIIe siècle* (Paris: A. Colin, 1911); Jean Ehrard, *L'Idée de nature en France dans la première moitié du XVIIIe siècle* (Paris: Albin Michel, 1994).

17. "Histoire naturelle," in *Encyclopédie, ou dictionnaire raisonné des sciences, des arts et des métiers,* ed. Denis Diderot and Jean Le Rond d'Alembert, 35 vols. (1751–); Robert Morrissey, ed., ARTFL Encyclopédie Projet, University of Chicago (winter 2008), available at http://encyclopedie.uchicago.edu/ (henceforth *Encyclopédie*), 8:228.

18. Spary, *Utopia's Garden,* p. 5.

19. The *Encyclopédie* counted physics, metaphysics, and mathematics as "sciences de la nature," while describing histories of the earth, minerals, plants, and animals as "histoire naturelle." "Explication Détaillée du Système des Connaissances Humaines," *Encyclopédie* 1:xlvii.

20. The narrative aspect of natural history is perhaps the most important and the most overlooked. Wilda Anderson has described Buffon's definition of natural history as follows: "Natural history is produced when the scientist has to turn the science into a story: the system goes from being a discovery to being a work of genius to be transmitted to a...reader" (Anderson, "Error in Buffon," *Modern Language Notes* 114.4 (1999): 699.

21. On science and popular science in the Enlightenment, see Michael Lynn, *Popular Science and Public Opinion in Old Regime France* (Manchester: Manchester University Press, 2006); Robert Darnton, *Mesmerism and the End of the Enlightenment in France* (Cambridge, Mass.: Harvard University Press, 1968); Charles Coulston Gillespie, *Science and Polity in France at the End of the Old Regime* (Princeton, N.J.: Princeton University Press, 1980); Jessica Riskin, *Science in the Age of Sensibility: The Sentimental Empiricists of the French Enlightenment*

(Chicago: University of Chicago Press, 2002); James Delbourgo, *A Most Amazing Scene of Wonders: Electricity and Enlightenment in Early America* (Cambridge, Mass.: Harvard University Press, 2006).

22. On natural collections, see L. W. B. Brockliss, *Calvet's Web* (Oxford: Oxford University Press, 2002); and Paula Findlen, *Possessing Nature: Museums, Collecting, and Scientific Culture in Early Modern Europe* (Berkeley: University of California Press, 1994). On public lectures, see Michael Lynn, "Enlightenment and the Public Sphere: The Musée de Monsieur and Scientific Culture in Late Eighteenth-Century Paris," *Eighteenth-Century Studies* 32.4 (1999).

23. *Nouvelles de la république des lettres*, 12 October 1785. Quoted in Darnton, *Mesmerism*, p. 26.

24. Daniel Mornet placed Buffon and Pluche atop his lists of best sellers, based on private libraries. "Les enseignements des bibliothèques privées, 1750–1780," *Revue d'histoire littéraire de la France* 17 (1910): 449–496. Robert Darnton critiques Mornet's methods, and places d'Holbach atop his calculations. *Forbidden Best-Sellers of Pre-Revolutionary France* (New York: Norton, 1995), esp. 63–65 and xviii for critique of Mornet.

25. See Malcolm Cook, *Bernardin de Saint-Pierre: A Life of Culture* (London: Legenda, 2006), letters quoted on pp. 91–94. Cook also estimates that Saint-Pierre sold ten copies of his very large text each *week* in early 1786, and notes the significant number of pirated copies of the text; see pp. 95–97. Bernardin himself would complain about losing money from these counterfeit editions during the Revolution: "Adresse de Jacques-Bernardin-Henry de St Pierre, à la Convention nationale," *Archives parlementaires de 1787 à 1860: recueil complet des débats législatifs et politiques des Chambres Françaises*, Vol. 72, 11–24 August 1793 (Paris: Librairie administrative P. Dupont, 1907), pp. 655–656 (henceforth, *AP*).

26. Baker, "Science and Politics at the End of the Old Regime," in Baker, *Inventing the French Revolution*, pp. 153–166.

27. On academies, see Daniel Roche, *Le siècle des lumières en province: académies et académiciens provinciaux, 1680–1789* (Paris: Mouton, 1978); Jeremy Caradonna, *The Enlightenment in Question: Prize Contests and the Francophone Republic of Letters, 1670–1794*, Ph.D. diss, Johns Hopkins University, 2007.

28. A 1777 chemistry course taught by Antoine-Louis Brogniart was attended by *abbés*, surgeons, a former musketeer, and several doctors (including Antoine François de Fourcroy, then only twenty-two years old), as well as a painter. Archives Nationales (henceforth, AN), AJ/15/509, document 274. The Jardin du Roi became the foundation of the Muséum d'Histoire Naturelle, which held a privileged position in the revolutionary period. See Spary, *Utopia's Garden*.

29. Lynn, "Enlightenment in the Public Sphere," p. 468.

30. The phrase "Republic of Science" is drawn from ibid., p. 467.

31. Darnton, *Mesmerism*, p. 40.

32. Nicolas Bergasse, *Lettre d'un médecin de la faculté de Paris* (The Hague, 1781), p. 54. Quoted in Darnton, *Mesmerism*, p. 120.

33. Georges-Louis Leclerc, Comte de Buffon. *Histoire Naturelle générale et particulière*, Vol. 2 (Paris: de l'impr. Royale, 1749), p. 2.

34. Baron d'Holbach, *Système de la Nature ou des loix du monde physique et du monde moral* (London, 1771), p. 1.

35. Anne-Robert-Jacques Turgot, "A Philosophical Review of the Successive Advances of the Human Mind," in *Turgot on Progress, Sociology, and Economics*, ed. Ronald L. Meek (Cambridge: Cambridge University Press, 1973), p. 46.

36. Rhoda Rappaport, *When Geologists Were Historians, 1665–1750* (Ithaca, N.Y.: Cornell University Press, 1997). See p. 94 in particular.

37. See Mercier's harsh commentary in *Tableau de Paris*, which also mocked—and distinguished between—the recent spate of books with "nature" in the title. Louis-Sébastien Mercier, "De l'Auteur du *Système de la nature*," in *Tableau de Paris*, ed. Jean-Claude Bonnet, Vol. 1 (Paris: Mercure de France, 1994), p. 1376.

38. Lorraine Daston, "Enlightenment Fears, Fears of Enlightenment," in *What's Left of Enlightenment: A Postmodern Question,* ed. Keith Baker and Peter Reill (Stanford, Calif.: Stanford University Press, 2001), p. 127. See also Daston, "The Nature of Nature in Early Modern Europe"; and E. C. Spary, "The Nature of Enlightenment," in *The Sciences in Enlightened Europe,* ed. William Clark, Jan Golinski, and Simon Schaffer, pp. 272–306 (Chicago: University of Chicago Press, 1999).

39. Hérault de Sechelles, *Voyage à Montbard, contenant des détails très-intéressans sur le caractère de la personne et les écrits de Buffon* (Paris: Chez Terrelonge et Chez Solvet, Year IX [1800/1801]); Jean-Antoine-Nicolas de Caritat, Marquis de Condorcet, *Eloge de M. le comte de Buffon* (Paris: Buisson, 1790).

40. See Caradonna, *The Enlightenment in Question,* appendix; Darnton, *Mesmerism,* p. 79 for Girondin involvement.

41. Several scholars have noted the impact that the political world of the Revolution had on the careers of scientists in France. See Spary, *Utopia's Garden;* Charles C. Gillespie, "The Encyclopédie and the Jacobin Philosophy of Science: A Study of Ideas and Consequences," in *Critical Problems in the History of Science,* ed. Marshall Clagett, pp. 255–289 (Madison: University of Wisconsin Press, 1959); Dorinda Outram, "The Ordeal of Vocation: The Paris Academy of Sciences and the Terror, 1793–1795," *History of Science* 21 (1983): 251–273.

42. Ken Alder makes this point in his *Engineering the Revolution: Arms and Enlightenment in France, 1763–1815* (Princeton, N.J.: Princeton University Press, 1997), p. 293.

43. *AP,* 74:181, 182, 182, 185 (15 September 1793). This is only a *selection* of the natural images used on that day.

44. Jacques-Henri Bernardin de Saint-Pierre, *Études de la Nature,* Vol. 1 (Paris: de l'impr. de Monsieur, chez Pierre-François Didot, 1784), p. 442.

45. De Baecque, *Glory and Terror,* p. 66.

46. Alexis de Tocqueville, *Old Regime and Revolution,* trans. Stuart Gilbert (New York: Doubleday, 1983), p. 192; David Andress, *The Terror: The Merciless War for Freedom in Revolutionary France* (New York: Farrar, Straus and Giroux, 2005), p. 102.

47. See David Bell, *The First Total War: Napoleon's Europe and the Birth of Warfare as We Know It* (Boston: Houghton Mifflin, 2007), pp. 67–68. The article "Paix" in *Encyclopédie* quoted on p. 68.

48. Patrice Higonnet, "Terror, Trauma, and the 'Young Marx' Explanation of Jacobin Politics," *Past & Present* 191.1 (2006): 121–164. See also Barry Shapiro, *Traumatic Politics: The Deputies and the King in the Early French Republic* (University Park: Pennsylvania State University Press, 2009).

49. Louis-Marie Prudhomme, *Révolutions de Paris,* no. 175, 10–17 November 1792.

50. Daniel Arasse, *The Guillotine and the Terror,* trans. Christopher Miller (London: Penguin, 1989).

51. Sophie Wahnich, *La Liberté ou la mort: essai sur la Terreur et le terrorisme* (Paris: La Fabrique éditions, 2003), p. 35 in particular. See also *La Longue patience du peuple: 1792, Naissance de la République* (Paris: Éditions Payot, 2008).

52. Colin Lucas, "Revolutionary Violence, the People, and the Terror," in *The French Revolution and the Creation of Modern Political Culture,* ed. Keith Baker, Vol. 4, *The Terror,* pp. 57–79 (Oxford: Pergamon, 1994).

53. Ibid., 73. See also Regina Janes, "Beheadings," *Representations,* no. 35 (summer 1991): 21–51, in which she argues that beheadings were a visible mark of popular sovereignty.

54. AN, W 112, document 23; see also documents 26 and 45.

55. AN, W 174.

56. Jean-Paul Marat, "Marat, l'ami du peuple, à ses concitoyens les electeurs," 10 September 1792, in *Oeuvres Politiques,* ed. Jacques de Cock and Charlotte Goëtz. Vol. 8 (Brussels: Pole Nord, 1995), p. 4721.

57. Maximilien Robespierre, *Oeuvres Complètes,* ed. Marc Bouloiseau and Albert Soboul, Vol. 10, *Discours 27 juillet 1793–27 juillet 1794* (Paris: Presses Universitaires de France, 1967)

p. 263 (henceforth, *OC*). He went on to suggest a decree creating a commission "to look into the means of freeing any patriots who may be incarcerated" (p. 264). He also suggested, however, that the manner in which the women presented their grievance to the Convention hinted at a counterrevolutionary plot.

58. Hannah Arendt, *On Violence* (New York: Harcourt, Brace, Jovanovich, 1969), p. 52.

59. Quoted in Patrice Gueniffey, *La Politique de la Terreur: Essai sur la violence révolutionnaire, 1789–1794* (Paris: Fayard, 2000), p. 70. From *L'Ami du Peuple*, no. 8–9, 18–19 September 1789.

60. D. M. G. Sutherland, *Murder in Aubagne: Lynching, Law, and Justice during the French Revolution* (Cambridge: Cambridge University Press, 2009), p. 290.

61. Fouché, *Écrits révolutionnaires*, p. 46.

62. Recent studies in political science have sought to combine cognitive linguistics with analyses of contemporary political language. See, in particular, the work of Christ'l De Landtsheer and Francis Beer, including De Landtsheer and Beer, eds., *Metaphorical World Politics* (East Lansing: Michigan State University Press, 2004).

63. Raymond Gibbs, *The Poetics of Mind: Figurative Thought, Language, and Understanding* (Cambridge: Cambridge University Press, 1994), p. 131.

64. George Lakoff and Mark Johnson, *Metaphors We Live By* (Chicago: University of Chicago Press, 1980), p. 156.

65. Bertrand Barère, *Rapport sur les crimes de l'Angleterre envers le Peuple Français, et sur ses attentats contre la liberté des nations, fait au nom du Comité de Salut Public* (Paris: de l'impr. Nationale, Year II [1794]), pp. 35–36.

66. Maximilien Robespierre, *Discours de M. Robespierre, prononcé dans la séance du septidi, 7 prairial, an 2e de la république une et indivisible* (Paris: de l'impr. Nationale, Year II [1794]), pp. 1–2.

67. AN, AF II 66, Dossier 484, Document 53.

68. Joachim Vilate, *Continuation des causes secrètes de la Révolution du 9 au 10 thermidor* (Paris: Year III [1794/95]), p. 22.

69. See Darrin McMahon, *Enemies of the Enlightenment: The French Counter-Enlightenment and the Making of Modernity* (Oxford: Oxford University Press, 2001); and Donald Sutherland, *France, 1789–1815: Revolution and Counterrevolution* (Oxford: Oxford University Press, 1986).

70. Tackett, "Interpreting the Terror," *French Historical Studies* 24.4 (2001): 577.

71. François Furet, *Interpreting the French Revolution*, trans. Elborg Forster (Cambridge: Cambridge University Press, 1981), p. 62.

72. Ibid., p. 51.

73. Edelstein, *The Terror of Natural Right*, pp. 206–214.

74. Louis-Maris Prudhomme, *Révolutions de Paris*, no. 213, 7–14 Brumaire, Year II [1793]). Despite Jean-Clément Martin's recent compelling argument that terror was never actually declared to be the "order of the day," Prudhomme certainly believed that it was. Indeed, he opened this article with the statement, "Terror is the order of the day: We have made it so too late." For Martin's argument, see *Violence et Révolution: essai sur la naissance d'un mythe national* (Paris: Seuil, 2006), 186–193. See also chapter five, note 44, below.

75. Prudhomme, *Révolutions de Paris*, no. 213.

Chapter 1

1. *Feuille du Salut Public*, no. 78, 16 September 1793.

2. Charlton, *New Images of the Natural*, p. 57.

3. Ponce Denis Échouchard Le Brun, *Oeuvres choisies de Le Brun: précédées d'une notice sur sa vie et ses ouvrages* (Paris: Janet et Cotelle, 1829), p. 55. Also quoted in Elie Fréron, *L'Année Littéraire*, Vol. 8 (Amsterdam and Paris, 1755), p. 211.

4. "Explication détaillée du système des connaissances humaines," *Encyclopédie*, 1:xlvii.

5. Jaucourt, "Prodige physique," *Encyclopédie,* 13:422.

6. Jaucourt, "Pluie prodigeuse," *Encyclopédie,* 12:796.

7. Diderot, "Imparfait," *Encyclopédie,* 8:584. See also Andrew Curran and Patrick Graille, "The Faces of Eighteenth-Century Monstrosity," *Eighteenth-Century Life* 21 (1997): 7.

8. See Curran and Graille, "The Faces of Eighteenth-Century Monstrosity"; Lorraine Daston and Katharine Park, eds., *Wonders and the Order of Nature, 1150–1750* (Cambridge, Mass.: MIT Press, 1998); Michael Hagner, "Enlightened Monsters," in Clark, Golinski, and Schaffer, *The Sciences in Enlightened Europe,* pp. 175–217.

9. Rappaport, *When Geologists Were Historians,* p. 240: "His predecessors...had mistaken 'local causes' and 'accidents' for 'general' ones: they had used unusual events...or local phenomena..., thus producing debatable 'systems.'" See Buffon, "Histoire et Théorie de la Terre," in *Histoire naturelle générale et particulière: avec la description du Cabinet du Roy,* Vol. 1 (Paris: de l'impr. Royale, 1749), pp. 95–96. By removing "abnormalities" from his study, he had no need to really deal with the Flood—a miraculous event that therefore has no place in any system or theory. Likewise, the *Encyclopédie* article on observation noted that medical studies that dealt specifically with monstrosities were of little use, as they could not reveal more general truths. See "Observation," *Encyclopédie,* 11:320.

10. Quoted in Spary, "The Nature of Enlightenment," p. 295.

11. Cf. Jeff Loveland, *Rhetoric and Natural History: Buffon in Polemical and Literary Context* (Oxford: Voltaire Foundation, 2001), p. 74. From Bernardin de Saint-Pierre, *Etudes,* Vol. 3, p. 57.

12. Loveland, *Rhetoric,* p. 65.

13. Ibid., pp. 66–69; see also Thierry Hoquet, *Buffon: Histoire naturelle et philosophie* (Paris: Honoré Champion, 2005), chap. 14.

14. Dennis Trinkle, "Noel-Antoine Pluche's *Le Spectacle de la Nature,* an Encyclopaedic Best-Seller," *Studies of Voltaire and the Eighteenth Century* 357 (1997): 131.

15. D'Holbach, *Système de la Nature,* pp. 165, 166. Also quoted in Voltaire, "Causes finales," *Dictionnaire philosophique,* in *Oeuvres de Voltaire,* Vol. 27 (Paris: Werdet et Lequien fils, Firmin Didot frères, 1829), p. 522.

16. Lorraine Daston and Fernando Vidal, "Introduction: Doing What Comes Naturally," in Daston and Vidal, *The Moral Authority of Nature,* p. 5.

17. D'Holbach, "Tremblemens de Terre," *Encyclopédie,* 16:583. Note that d'Holbach believed that earthquakes were caused by an internal fire, hence his use of the term "blazes" (*embrasements*).

18. D'Holbach, "Volcans," *Encyclopédie,* 17:443.

19. D'Holbach, *Système,* p. 448.

20. Ibid., p. 454.

21. Riskin, *Science,* p. 70.

22. Ibid., pp. 70–71.

23. Daston, "Attention and the Values of Nature in the Enlightenment," in Daston and Vidal, *The Moral Authority of Nature,* p. 102.

24. Jean-Jacques Rousseau, *Emile, ou de l'education* (Paris: Flammarion, 1996), p. 401.

25. Bernardin, *Etudes,* 1:442.

26. *Mandement de Monseigneur l'Archevêque de Paris, pour le saint tems de Carême, qui permet l'usage des Oeufs depuis le Mercredi des cendres inclusivement, jusqu'au Dimanche des rameaux exclusivement* (Paris: Chez Cl. Simon, Imprimeur de Monseigneur l'Archevêque, 1789), p. 5.

27. On natural disasters in the early modern world, see Alessa Johns, ed., *Dreadful Visitations* (New York: Routledge, 1999).

28. Conseil d'Etat du Roi, *Arrêt du conseil d'état du roi, portant création d'une loterie de Douze millions, en faveur des provinces ravagées par la grêle, du 26 juillet 1788* (Lille: de l'impr. de C. M. Peterinck-Cramé, 1788).

29. *Remise à l'Assemblée Nationale d'une Adresse au Roi, tendante à obtenir aux cultivateurs, sur l'avis des représentans de la nation, la liberté d'assurer leurs récoltes contre les événemens de la grêle* (Paris: de l'impr. de P. R. C. Ballard, 1789).

30. AN, H/1414.

31. Serge Briffaud, "Le role des catastrophes naturelles: Cas des Pyrénées centrales," in *La Nature en Révolution 1750–1800,* ed. Andrée Corvol, pp. 134–144 (Paris: Éditions de l'Harmattan, 1993).

32. The 250th anniversary of the Lisbon earthquake brought a wealth of new sources on the event, most notably E. D. Braun and John B. Radner, eds., *The Lisbon Earthquake of 1755: Representations and Reactions* (Oxford: Voltaire Foundation, 2005); Jan T. Kozak, Victor S. Moreira, and David R. Aldroyd, *Iconography of the 1755 Lisbon Earthquake* (Prague: Geophysical Institute of the Academy of Sciences of the Czech Republic, 2005); Jean Mondot, ed., *Lumières,* no. 6: *Lisbonne 1755: Un tremblement de terre et de Ciel* (Bordeaux: Centre Interdisciplinaire bordelais d'étude des Lumières, 2005). T. D. Kendrick's classic *The Lisbon Earthquake* (London: Methuen, 1956) remains the most comprehensive English-language monograph on the subject.

33. Florence Boulerie, "Dire le désastre de Lisbonne dans la presse française, 1755–1757," in Mondot, *Lisbonne 1755,* p. 61.

34. Voltaire, "Poem on the Lisbon Disaster," in *The Enlightenment: A Sourcebook and Reader,* ed. Paul Hyland (New York: Routledge, 2003), p. 77. Orig., Voltaire, *Poèmes sur la religion naturelle, et sur la destruction de Lisbonne, par M. V**** (Paris, 1756), pp. 52–53. The original is all the more heartfelt:

> Philosophes trompés qui criez "Tout est bien";
> Accourez, contemplez ces ruines affreuses,
> Ces débris, ces lambeaux, ces cendres malheureuses,
> Ces femmes ces enfants l'un sur l'autre entassés,
> Sous ces marbres rompus ces membres dispersés;
> Cent mille infortunés que la terre dévore,
> Qui, sanglants, déchirés, et palpitants encore,
> Enterrés sous leurs toits, terminent sans secours,
> Dans l'horreur des tourments leurs lamentables jours!
> Aux cris demi-formés de leurs voix expirantes,
> Au spectacle effrayant de leurs cendres fumantes,
> Direz-vous, "C'est l'effet des éternelles lois
> Qui d'un Dieu libre et bon nécessitent le choix"?
> Direz-vous, en voyant cet amas de victimes:
> "Dieu s'est vengé, leur mort est le prix de leurs crimes"?

35. Kendrick, *The Lisbon Earthquake,* pp. 135–141. The priest, Padre Gabriel Malagrida, went on to be found guilty of heresy by the Inquisition and was executed in 1761. See Malcolm Jack, "Destruction and Regeneration: Lisbon, 1755," in Braun and Radner, *Representations and Reactions,* p. 19.

36. Voltaire, *Candide,* trans. John Butt (London: Penguin, 1947), p. 33.

37. I owe the idea of throwing up hands in metaphysical frustration to Susan Neiman, who says nicely in her introduction that the problem of evil is, "the point at which ethics and metaphysics, epistemology and aesthetics, meet, collide, and throw up their hands." Neiman, *Evil in Modern Thought: An Alternative History of Philosophy* (Princeton, N.J.: Princeton University Press, 2002), p. 5.

38. Ibid., pp. 268, 277.

39. As Monika Gisler has pointed out, "The reactions [particularly in Protestant Switzerland] to Voltaire's *Poème* rather refer to a strong concern to maintain optimism." Gisler, "Optimism and Theodicy: Perceptions of the Lisbon Earthquake in Protestant Switzerland," in Braun and Radner, *Representations and Reactions,* p. 248.

40. Quoted in Neiman, *Evil,* p. 26. From Gottfried Wilhelm Leibniz, *Theodicy,* ed. Austin Farrar (La Salle, Ill.: Open Court, 1985), p. 248.

41. On universal and particular providence, see Alexandra Walsham, *Providence in Early Modern England* (Oxford: Oxford University Press, 1999), esp. pp. 229–230. Rhoda Rappaport has suggested that the predominance of a general providence over the idea of God punishing a particular people for its sins via natural disaster can be found in Thomas Burnet's *Sacred Theory of the Earth,* published in 1681. See Rappaport, *When Geologists were Historians,* p. 141. The 1752 translation of Johann Gottlob Kruger's *Histoire des anciennes révolutions du globe terrestre* noted that some recent theories, and primarily that of Père de Lamy, suggested that the Flood has not been a punishment at all but, rather, that it was God's means of lifting the curse on mankind inherited from the Edenic sin. Kruger, *Histoire des anciennes révolutions du globe terrestre, avec une relation chronologique et historique des tremblemens de terre, arrivés sur notre globe depuis le commencement de l'ere chrétienne jusqu'à présent,* trans. F. A. Deslandes (Amsterdam, et se vend à Paris chez Damonneville, 1752), p. 115.

42. Rousseau, "Lettre à Voltaire, 18 août 1756," in *Correspondance complète de Jean-Jacques Rousseau,* ed. R. A. Leigh, Vol. 4 (Geneva: Institut et musée Voltaire, 1965), p. 39.

43. Ibid., 4:45.

44. See Rousseau, *Emile,* esp. pp. 350–366.

45. Ana Cristina Araùjo, "The Lisbon Earthquake of 1755—Public Distress and Political Propaganda," *e-Journal of Portuguese History* 4.1 (summer 2006), p. 3. She also notes that the text became an important propaganda piece against England, just before the outbreak of the Seven-Years War. Most of the editions were published anonymously. On Goudar's political service, see Edmond Dziembowski, *Un nouveau patriotisme français, 1750–70* (Oxford: Voltaire Foundation, 1998), especially pp. 65–67 and 76–78 for the *Discours politique.*

46. Ange Goudar, *Discours politique sur les avantages que les Portugais pourroient retirer de leur malheur* (Lisbon: chez Philanthrope, 1756), p. 16.

47. Cf. d'Holbach, "Tremblemens de terre," in *Encyclopédie,* 16:582.

48. Boulerie, "Dire le désastre de Lisbonne," p. 72.

49. Grégory Quenet, "Un séisme philosophique ou un catastrophe naturelle?" in Braun and Rader, *Representations and Reactions,* p. 134.

50. Isnard (de Grasse), *Mémoire sur les tremblemens de terre, qui a remporté le prix de physique au jugement de l'Académie des sciences, belles-lettres et arts de Rouen, le 3 août 1757* (Paris: Veuve David Jeune, 1758).

51. Grégory Quenet, *Les Tremblements de Terre aux XVIIe et XVIIIe Siècles: La Naissance d'un risque* (Paris: Champ Vallon, 2005), p. 365.

52. Quoted in *L'Année Littéraire,* 8:210–211.

53. Elie Bertand, *Mémoires historiques et physiques sur les tremblemens de terre* (The Hague: chez Pierre Gosse junior, 1757), pp. 5–6. Note that Bertrand wrote to Voltaire after the publication of his *Poème sur le désastre,* demonstrating the connectedness between *savants* in the wake of the disaster.

54. *Journal des Savants* (June 1757): 379.

55. Bertrand, *Mémoires,* pp. 19, 20.

56. *Journal des Savants* (March 1756): 166.

57. William Hamilton, "An Account of the Earthquakes Which Happened in Italy, from February to May 1783. By Sir William Hamilton, Knight of the Bath, F. R. S.; in a Letter to Sir Joseph Banks, Bart. P. R. S.," *Philosophical Transactions of the Royal Society of London* 73 (1783): 172. On 4 April 1783 the *Gazette de France* gave an estimate of twenty-six thousand victims.

58. This account is a useful reminder of another reason why these tragedies were so powerful at this moment: the stronghold of sentimentalism and the important role of pity in morality. *Précis historique de la ville de Messine, de ses moeurs, de son commerce, et de ce qui s'y voyoit de plus remarquable avant sa destruction; avec une idée de la Calabre; suivi d'une description curieuse des Montagnes connues sous le nom d'Etna, ou Mont Gibel, et du Vésuve, fameuses par les*

fréquentes éruptions de flammes, de bitumes et de cailloux qu'elles vomissent (Paris: Chez Cailleau, 1783), p. 3.

59. Likely the 1752 *Histoire des anciennes révolutions du globe terrestre,* a work by the German geologist Johann Gottlob Kruger that suggested that the earth had been shaped by three primary "revolutions": two large earthquakes and a flood (Kruger, *Histoire des anciennes révolutions,* p. 230). It also included a lengthy list of previous earthquakes, as noted below.

60. *Journal de Paris,* no. 93, 3 April 1783.

61. *Le désastre de Messine, ou Les Volcans, ode philosophique* (Paris: Chez les Marchands de Nouveautés, de l'impr. de Pruault, 1783), p. 4. Its publication was noted in the *Journal des Savants* (December 1783): 819.

62. *Le désastre,* pp. 8, 13 n. 1.

63. Ibid., p. 15. The work, at least with any title resembling the proposed one, seems never to have been published.

64. *Description historique et géographique de la ville de Messine, etc. etc., et détails historiques et météorologiques du désastre que cette ville vient d'éprouver (le 5 fevrier 1783) par le tremblement de terre...* (Paris: Desnos, 1783), p. 1. The original can be found in Patrick Brydone, *A Tour through Sicily and Malta, in a Series of Letters to William Beckford, Esq.,* Vol. 1 (London, 1773), p. 23. The translation by the French author chose to replace Brydone's word "conflagrations" with the French *révolutions,* a decision of some importance, as I discuss in chapter 2.

65. *Lettre de M. à Mme la Maréchale de ***, sur le désastre de Messine et de la Calabre* (9 mai 1783), pp. 8–9. The *Catalogue des livres imprimés de la Bibliothèque des avocats à la Cour d'Appel de Paris,* Vol. 1 (Paris, 1880) suggests that this letter was written by Bernard Lambert, a Catholic priest from Angers (*Catalogue,* p. 15).

66. Matthias Georgi has found evidence that such interpretations could be found in several post-Lisbon sermons in England. Paraphrasing, and modernizing, Job, a London cleric announced to his parish in February 1756, "Hast thou entered into the treasures of the nitre, or hast thou seen the beds of sulphur; which God has reserved against the time of trouble, against the day of perplexity and distress?" John Cradock, *A Sermon preached in the parish church of St. Paul, Covent Garden, on Friday February 6, 1756, being appointed by authority for a general fast* (London, 1756), p. 14. Quoted in Matthias Georgi, "The Lisbon Earthquake and Scientific Knowledge in the British Public Sphere," in Braun and Rader, *Representations and Reactions,* p. 95.

67. Quenet, *Tremblements,* p. 266.

68. Kruger, *Histoire,* pp. 243ff.

69. Jeff Loveland, "*Collection académique* and the great Lisbon earthquake," in Braun and Rader, *Representations and Reactions,* p. 199.

70. Loveland, "Collection," p. 201.

71. Michel Perronet notes a similar trajectory in the eighteenth century, from the notion of a "scourge of God" to a "natural catastrophe" with clear and scientifically discernible causes. See his "Chatiments Divins et catastrophes naturelles," in *Météorologie et catastrophes naturelles dans la France méridionale à l'époque moderne,* ed. Anne Blanchard, Henri Michel, and Elie Pélaquier, pp. 259–282 (Montpelier: Université Paul-Valery III, 1993).

72. Matthew Mulcahy, *Hurricanes and Society in the British Greater Caribbean* (Baltimore, Md.: Johns Hopkins University Press, 2006), p. 47.

73. Pierre de Charlevoix, *Voyage to North America,* 2:335. Quoted in Mulcahy, *Hurricanes and Society,* p. 57. Likewise, Annie Le Brun has noted the lack of religious responses to the eruption of Vesuvius in the 1770s. Annie Le Brun, *Le perspective dépravée: Entre catastrophe réele et catastrophe imaginaire* (Paris: La Lettre Volée, 1991), p. 31.

74. Charles Bonnet, *Contemplation de la Nature,* in *Oeuvres,* Vol. 4 (Neuchâtel: S. Fauche, 1781 [1764]), p. 181. Spary notes its popularity in her "Nature of Enlightenment," p. 282.

75. Denis Diderot, *Diderot on Art II,* trans. John Goodman (New Haven, Conn.: Yale University Press, 1995), pp. 198–199: "The ideas ruins evoke in me are grand. Everything

comes to nothing, everything perishes, everything passes, only the world remains, only time endures. How old is this world! I walk between two eternities....A torrent drags each and every nation into the depths of a common abyss."

76. Bernardin, *Etudes,* 3:128.

77. Ibid., 3:191.

78. Note that eyewitness accounts did not substantiate this account of human harmony; rather, in the words of one pamphleteer, "in a public disaster, pity for one another is silenced." *Nouveaux détails historiques et météorologiques du tremblement de terre de Messine et la Calabre ultérieure, etc., arrivé le 5 février 1783: avec une idée générale de cette ville, de son administration, des curiosités qui s'y trouvent, du commerce et des moeurs de ses habitants, etc, auxquels on a joint quelques observations nouvelles sur les causes et les effets de ces désastres, etc.* (Paris: Chez Cailleau, rue Galande, 1783), p. 9.

79. Ibid., p. 18.

80. Louis-Sébastien Mercier, "Que deviendra Paris?" *Tableau de Paris,* Vol. 1 (Amsterdam, 1782), pp. 307–308.

81. Jeff Loveland makes this point in his *Rhetoric and Natural History,* p. 74. See Bernardin de Saint-Pierre, *Etudes,* 1:56–57.

82. Jacques-Henri Bernardin de Saint-Pierre, *Paul et Virginie,* Vol. 2 (Paris: de l'impr. de Monsieur, 1789), pp. 227–228.

83. B. E. Manuel, *L'Etude de la nature en général et de l'homme en particulier considérée dans ses rapports avec l'instruction publique* (Paris: Chez les directeurs du Cercle Social, 1793), pp. 6–7.

Chapter 2

1. As Jack Censer noted in *Prelude to Power,* Prudhomme was quite active in the editorial gatekeeping of his journal. Despite the numerous collaborators on the journal, the prose remained markedly similar across its history, suggesting that, "no matter who wrote, Prudhomme determined the parameters in opinion, content, and diction." Censer, *Prelude to Power: The Parisian Radical Press, 1789–1791* (Baltimore, Md.: Johns Hopkins University Press, 1976), p. 25. What is more, Prudhomme himself employed the Lisbon metaphor later, in his *General and Impartial History of the Errors, Offenses, and Crimes Committed during the French Revolution* published after the Terror, this time to describe the Revolution as a whole. Cf. Joseph Zizek, "'Plume de fer': Louis-Marie Prudhomme Writes the French Revolution," *French Historical Studies* 26.4 (2003): 641.

2. Louis-Marie Prudhomme, *Révolutions de Paris, dédiées à la nation,* no. 177 (24 November–1 December 1792).

3. Ibid.

4. Jules Michelet, *Oeuvres de Jules Michelet: Histoire de la Révolution,* Vol. 4 (Paris: A. Lemarre, 1888), p. 103. The most recent definitive account of the massacres is René Moulinas, *Les massacres de la Glacière: enquête sur un crime impuni, Avignon 16–17 octobre 1791* (Aix-en-Provence: Edisud, 2003).

5. "Copie de l'affiche trouvée dans différens endroits de cette ville d'Avignon aujourd'hui Dimanche 16 du mois octobre 1791," in AN, D/XXIV/3.

6. *Relation des événemens arrivés à Avignon, le 16 octobre 1791, et les jours suivans, publiée par les Notables, administrateurs provisoires de la commune de cette ville* (n.p., 20 October 1791), p. 24.

7. AN, BB/16/85, témoignage de Anne Michelon.

8. Eric Johnson, in a 2007 article detailing the political and religious conflict in revolutionary Avignon, notes that Jourdan likely was not in Paris in the summer of 1789. Eric F. Johnson, "The Sacred, Secular Regime: Catholic Ritual and Revolutionary Politics in Avignon, 1789–1791," *French Historical Studies* 30.1 (winter 2007): 71.

9. On the oath, see AN, BB/16/85, témoignage de Dame Marie Bondon.

10. *AP,* 35:114 (17 November 1791). On the Tour de la Glacière, see Gabriel Colombe, *Le Palais des Papes d'Avignon* (Paris: H. Laurens, 1939), p. 48.

11. L.S. Boisdesir, *Dénonciation à tous les françois, à tous les amis de l'humanité, du massacre commis à Avignon les 16,17, et 18 octobre 1791* (Paris: de l'impr. du Journal général de politique, etc., 1791), p. 4. Although this pamphlet was printed in Paris, it was signed and received by a Cizot Duplessis, who collaborated on the *Courrier d'Avignon*. I presume that Boisdesir was himself an Avignonnais—though clearly on the side of the papists.

12. Boisdesir, *Dénonciation,* p. 4.

13. Michelet, *Oeuvres,* 4:116.

14. *AP,* 35:114 (17 November 1791).

15. *AP,* 30:636 (14 September 1791).

16. *AP,* 30:583 (12 September 1791). Menou was himself a radical; see Timothy Tackett, *Becoming a Revolutionary: The Deputies of the French National Assembly and the Emergence of a Revolutionary Culture (1789–1790)* (Princeton, N.J.: Princeton University Press, 1996), p. 174 n. 268.

17. *AP,* 30:579 (12 September 1791); emphasis mine.

18. It is worth noting that in Jean-François Féraud's 1787–88 dictionary, the word "principe" was used often in physics to describe the "natural cause of action and of movement."

19. *AP,* 30:621 (13 September 1791). Lafayette then offered an even less opaque decree: he requested that "all those who have been arrested or accused based on the departure of the king" should "immediately [be] returned to liberty."

20. *AP,* 30:632 (14 September 1791).

21. *AP,* 31:444 (28 September 1791).

22. Boucher d'Argis, "Lettres d'Amnistie," *Encyclopédie,* 9:414

23. Jean-Baptiste Robinet, *Dictionnaire Universel des sciences morale, économique, politique, et diplomatique, ou Bibliothèque de l'homme-d'état et du citoyen,* Vol. 4 (London: Chez les libraires associés, 1777–83), p. 115.

24. Couturier, a Montagnard, would later be a representative on mission in Strasbourg, where he installed Jacobins in public office. See Hugh Gough, "Politics and Power: The Triumph of Jacobinism in Strasbourg, 1791–1793," *Historical Journal* 23.2 (June 1980): 348–349.

25. *AP,* 40:43 (16 March 1792).

26. *AP,* 40:43–44 (16 March 1792).

27. The other central debate revolved around timing: If the amnesty was promulgated prior to the massacres, then how could events that came after still be included in the amnesty? Again, however, this debate related to the question of "revolution" and precisely when the revolution in Avignon was definitively concluded, with Lasource, in particular, explaining that the amnesty could not be applied until the revolution ended there.

28. Although the Assembly had voted to accept Avignon into the nation on 14 September 1791, the treaty with Avignon was not promulgated until 8 November. Thus, according to the legislators, the revolution was not over in the region of Avignon until that date.

29. See below, *Rapport et conclusions de l'accusateur public, près le Tribunal criminel provisoire d'Avignon, sur l'application de l'Amnistie, aux crimes et délits commis dans cette Ville, le 16 et 17 octobre 1791* (Paris: Chez les Libraires Associés, 1792).

30. The "Girondins" were at this point more often called the "Brissotins," named for their spokesman, Jacques-Pierre Brissot, and they were participants in the Jacobin Club before it split in the summer and autumn of 1792. Though there had already been some conflicts between Brissotins and other members of the Jacobin Club, particularly over the issue of war in late 1791 and early 1792, the two groups remained hesitant allies; Gary Kates notes that Louvet's newspaper, *Sentinelle,* for example, supported Brissotins like Pétion as well as Montagnards including Robespierre, Collot d'Herbois, and Danton as candidates during elections to the Convention in August 1792. The real divide between the two factions would

come after the September Massacres (Brissot was expelled from the Jacobin Club in October 1792) and then, increasingly, with the trial against the king in December 1792 and January 1793. See Gary Kates, *The Cercle Social, the Girondins and the French Revolution* (Princeton, N.J.: Princeton University Press, 1985); and Michael Sydenham, *The Girondins* (London, 1961). On the Brissotin "circle," see also Marisa Linton, "Fatal Friendships: The Politics of Jacobin Friendship," *French Historical Studies* 31.1 (2008): 51–76.

31. *AP,* 40:144 (19 March 1792).

32. *AP,* 40:147–148 (19 March 1792). On the opposite side of the chamber was Claude André Fressenel, who also noted that the legislature was looking at issues "after the beneficial term of a long revolution." *AP,* 40:44 (16 March 1792).

33. Emerich de Vattel, *Le Droit des gens ou Principes de la loi naturelle appliqués à la conduite et aux affaires des nations et des souverains,* Vol. 2 (London: n.p., 1758), p. 266.

34. Mailhe, *AP,* 40:54 (16 March 1792).

35. *Rapport et conclusions de l'accusateur public,* pp. 87–88. This was the document produced by the tribunal noted above, which ultimately freed the prisoners in August 1792. Signed by "Randon, juge du district de Saint-Hippolyte."

36. Vergniaud, *AP,* 40:153 (19 March 1792).

37. Basire, *AP,* 40:51–52 (16 March 1792).

38. *Rapport,* p. 76. This precise argument was also used to argue *against* the amnesty; for example, Michel Gentil stated that amnesty could sometimes be granted for "crimes committed in the heat of popular riots" but that the Avignon massacres, as acts of *private vengeance,* did not apply to this definition. Gentil, *AP,* 40:147 (19 March 1792). See also Vienot-Vaublanc, *AP,* 40:151; and Charles de Paule Baert-Duholant, *A mes collègues, sur la prétendue amnisitie en faveur de Jourdan et ses complices* (Paris: de l'impr. du Pont, 1792), p. 2. Other arguments against the amnesty focused on the atrocity of the crimes, saying that to forgive them would be a scar on the French name (see Laureau, *AP,* 40:53) or on the constitutionality of discussing amnesty in the first place (see Dumas, *AP,* 40:52). Only Fressenel explicitly stated that "public" crimes were not in themselves forgivable (*AP,* 40:47).

39. *Rapport,* p. 104.

40. Ibid., p. 76.

41. The *Encyclopédie* defines "*secousse*" simply as, "a sudden oscillatory movement that shakes a body in its entirety; *les secousses* of an earthquake." ("Secousse," *Encyclopédie,* 14:862). Elsewhere in the *Encyclopédie* the term is used to describe medical crises, sensations, floods, apoplexy, and a host of other physical occurrences. A search in the ARTFL database between 1750 and 1789 suggests that the term also had political and economic meanings prior to the revolution, i.e., Barthélemy describing "a throne that has never felt the least convulsion [secousse]," in his *Voyages du jeune Anacharsis* (Paris: de Bure, 1788), p. 338. It was also a common term in sensationalism to describe the movement of bodies and nerves. Cf. d'Holbach's *Système de la Nature,* pp. 117, 119.

42. *AP,* 35:102 (16 November 1791).

43. On Duport and mesmerism, see Timothy Tackett, *Becoming a Revolutionary,* p. 53.

44. *AP,* 40:153 (19 March 1792).

45. *Relation des événemens,* pp. 22–23.

46. Brissot, *Le Patriote François,* no. 950 (17 March 1792).

47. G. Boisguyon, in *Le Patriote François,* no. 907 (3 February 1792). Boisguyon was a sporadic contributor to the *Patriote François.*

48. Baker, *Inventing the French Revolution,* p. 223.

49. Ibid., p. 206.

50. There is a rich historiography on the word "revolution" in the eighteenth century, including Hans Jurgen Lusebrink and Rolf Reichardt, "Révolution à la fin du XVIIIe siècle: Pour une relecture d'un concept clé du Siècle des Lumières," *Mots* 16 (March 1988): 35–68; Alain Rey, *Révolution: Histoire d'un Mot* (Paris: Gallimard, 1989); Jean Marie Goulemot, "Le

mot *révolution* et la formation du concept de révolution politique (fin XVIIe siècle)," *Annales historiques de la révolution française* 39 (1967): 417–444; I. Bernard Cohen, "The Eighteenth-Century Origins of the Concept of Scientific Revolution," *Journal of the History of Ideas* 37.2 (April–June 1976): 257–288; Rhoda Rappaport, "Borrowed Words: Problems of Vocabulary in Eighteenth-Century Geology," *British Journal for the History of Science* 15.1 (March 1982): 27–44; François Ellenberger, "Etude du terme Révolution," *Documents pour l'histoire du vocabulaire scientifique*, Vol. 9 (Paris: French National Centre for Scientific Research, 1989), pp. 69–90. These accounts reveal the elasticity of the word "revolution" in the eighteenth century, as applied to scientific, political, philosophical, and literary texts; I do not mean to refute their findings, only to bring to the fore this geological understanding that seems to underpin the particular meaning of the term "revolution" enunciated in the 1792 debates.

51. Baker notes that Vertot, the most widely read of this genre's authors, produced several texts that went through more than a dozen editions in the eighteenth century, including *Histoire des révolutions de Suède, Histoire des révolutions arrivées dans le gouvernement de la république romaine*, and *Histoire des révolutions de Portugal*. Baker, *Inventing the French Revolution*, p. 208.

52. Condorcet's *De l'influence de la Révolution d'Amérique en Europe* is particularly apt here: he almost entirely evacuated violence from the story of this "happy revolution" (p. 3). Jean-Antoine-Nicolas de Caritat Condorcet, *De l'influence de la Révolution d'Amérique en Europe*, in *Oeuvres de Condorcet*, Vol. 8 (Paris: Firmin Didot frères, 1847 [1786]).

53. One of the few exceptions that Baker notes is in Mably's call to attempt to make revolutions—often the products of "convulsive moments"—"useful to the *patrie*." Quoted in Baker, *Inventing the French Revolution*, p. 210.

54. The *Encyclopédie* included "revolution" as a political term, a historical term (referring specifically to England), a geometric term, an astronomical term, a natural term, and a term in watch making.

55. "Révolutions de la terre," *Encyclopédie*, 14:237–238.

56. *Description historique…de la ville de Messine*, p. 1; Brydone, *A Tour through Sicily and Malta*, p. 23. The complete quotation is given in chapter 1; see note 64.

57. D'Holbach, "Terre, révolutions de," *Encyclopédie*, 16:171. Alain Rey also sees the natural meanings of the term "revolution" acquired in the eighteenth century as formative: "It is…there, in this relationship between natural time and a reality that bears the traces of its past…that a new notion of *révolution*, preceding that of *evolution*, would influence the interpretation of history." Rey, *Révolution*, p. 55.

58. Buffon, "Histoire et théorie de la terre," in *Histoire naturelle générale et particulière: avec la description du Cabinet du Roy*, Vol. 1 (Paris: de l'impr. Royale, 1749), cf. pp. 94–95: "Il suffit pour notre objet d'avoir démontré que les montagnes n'ont point été placées au hazard, et qu'elles n'ont point été produites par des tremblemens de terre ou par d'autres causes accidentelles, mais qu'elles sont un effet résultant de l'ordre général de la nature" as well as p. 100, "[La Mer Méditerranée] a été formée par une irruption des eaux, produite par quelques causes accidentelles, comme seroit un tremblement de terre."

59. Ibid., p. 99.

60. Charles Bonnet, *La Palingénésie philosophique, ou Idées sur l'état passé et sur l'état futur des êtres vivants* (Geneva: C. Philibert and B. Chirol, 1769), p. 247.

61. Déodat Gratet de Dolomieu, *Mémoire sur les tremblemens de terre de la Calabre pendant l'année 1783* (Rome: A. Fulgoni, 1784), p. 16.

62. Rappaport, "Borrowed Words," p. 31. See also Ellenberger, "Etude du terme Révolution."

63. Rappaport, "Borrowed Words," p. 36.

64. Rey, *Révolution*, p. 78.

65. Reinhart Koselleck noted that when Robespierre promised to hasten the end of the Revolution, "it [was] possible to detect an unconscious secularization of eschatological expectation." Yet the history of the term, taken in its naturalistic meanings, in fact suggests

that the idea of revolution itself could convey a secular eschatology. Koselleck, "The Modern Concept of Revolution," in *Futures Past: On the Semantics of Historical Time,* trans. Keith Tribe (New York: Columbia University Press, 2004 [1979]), p. 50.

66. Bernard Germain Étienne de La Cépède, *Vues sur l'Enseignement Public* (Paris: Chez Desenne, 1790), p. 25

67. Quoted in Martin, *Violence et Révolution,* p. 143.

68. Hugh Gough, using numbers from Donald Greer, cites the total casualties as "over 1,000." David Andress gives the numbers, based on Philippe Caron, of 1,200–1,500. Gough, *The Terror in the French Revolution* (New York: St. Martin's, 1998), p. 2; Andress, *The Terror,* p. 104. See also Donald Greer, *The Incidence of the Terror in the French Revolution: A Statistical Interpretation* (Cambridge, Mass.: Harvard University Press, 1935). The definitive account of the massacres remains Philippe Caron, *Les Massacres de septembre* (Paris: La Maison du Livre Français, 1935).

69. Andress, *The Terror,* p. 102.

70. Quoted in *Révolutions de Paris,* no. 175 (10–17 November 1792).

71. Ibid.

72. Andress, *The Terror,* p. 104.

73. Marcel Dorigny, "Violence et Révolution: les Girondins et les Massacres de Septembre," in *Actes du colloque: Girondins et Montagnards,* ed. Albert Soboul, pp. 108–109 (Paris: Société des Études Robespierristes, 1980).

74. In fact, most historiography of the events has likewise accepted this rationale. See, in particular, the definitive work on the massacres, Caron's *Les Massacres de septembre.*

75. Marat, *Oeuvres Politiques, 1789–1793,* 8:4713: "Circulaire du Comité de Surveillance de la Commune de Paris," 3 September 1792.

76. Quoted in Dorigny, "Violence et Revolution," p. 108, from *Chronique de Paris,* 4 September 1792, p. 990.

77. Michel Azéma, *Rapport et décret présenté au nom du comité de législation, par Michel Azéma, député du Département de l'Aude, sur le sort des prisonniers élargis, à la suite des événements des premiers jours de Septembre dernier* (Paris: de l'impr. Nationale, 1792), p. 4.

78. Quoted in *Mercure Universel,* Vol. 19 (Paris: de l'impr. de Cussac, 1792), 6 September 1792, p. 86. The letter is also reprinted in *AP,* 49:265–267 (3 September 1792).

79. Quoted in Dorigny, "Violence et Revolution," p. 107.

80. Quoted in *Mercure Universel,* 19:85.

81. *Mercure Universel,* 19:85.

82. Ibid., 19:87.

83. Jean-Marie Roland, *Rapport du ministre de l'intérieur à la Convention Nationale, sur l'état de Paris, du 29 octobre 1792* (Paris: de l'impr. Nationale, 1792), p. 3.

84. Roland, *Rapport,* p. 3.

85. Jacques-Pierre Brissot, *A tous les républicains de France; sur la société des Jacobins de Paris* (Paris: chez les directeurs de l'impr. du Cercle Social, 1792), p. 38.

86. *AP,* 50:93 (17 September 1792).

87. *Révolutions de Paris,* no. 165 (1–8 September 1792).

88. Antoine De Baecque, *Glory and Terror,* p. 66.

89. Roland, quoted in *AP,* 49:265 (3 September 1792).

90. Michel Azéma, *Rapport et décret,* p. 6.

91. Jean-Lambert Tallien, *La Verité sur les événemens du 2 septembre* (Paris: de l'impr. Nationale, n.d. [1792]), p. 5.

92. Azéma, *Rapport et décret,* p. 7.

93. Ibid., p. 6; emphasis mine.

94. Ibid., p. 11.

95. Ibid., p. 17.

96. Ibid., p. 9.

97. Ibid., p. 15.

98. François-Alphonse Aulard, *La Société des Jacobins: Recueil de documents pour l'histoire du Club des Jacobins de Paris*, Vol. 4 (Paris: Maison Quantin, 1892), p. 461.

99. Claude Basire, *Discours de Claude Basire, vice-président du comité de surveillance à la Convention Nationale, sur l'état actuel de notre situation politique, au centre des affaires. Lue à la Société le 4 novembre 1792* (Paris: de l'impr. de L. Potier de Lille, 1792), p. 10. Emphasis mine. Aulard, in his records of the Jacobin Club, gives a slightly different text of the speech, in which Basire says that a revolution should be considered for its consequences "for the generation," not "regeneration." Aulard, *La Société des Jacobins*, 4:453.

100. Basire, *AP*, 40:51–52 (16 March 1792).

101. Aulard, *Jacobins*, 4:461.

102. Tallien, *La Verité*, p. 5.

103. Caron, *Les Massacres de septembre*, p. 436. See also Lucas, "Revolutionary Violence."

104. Azéma, *Rapport et décret*, p. 27. This same logic of punishment was set forth by Prudhomme and Garat in their assessments of the horrors of the September Massacres, and by Vergniaud in his speech about the Avignon killings.

105. Aulard, *Jacobins*, 4:539.

106. Madame Nicole-Mathieu Villiers, *Barra, ou la mère républicaine* (Dijon: impr. de P. Causse, Year II [1794]), pp. 24–25. Note, too, the use of the verb *s'opérer*, again a means of removing human action.

107. Ibid., p. 26.

Chapter 3

1. Robespierre, *OC*, 10:357.

2. Ibid., 10:444.

3. Ibid., 10:462.

4. This summary is based on an ARTFL search between the years 1770 and 1789. The terms "foudre" or "foudres" appeared in 71 out of 161 documents, used a total of 281 times.

5. L'Abbé Raynal, *Histoire philosophique et politique des établissements et du commerce des Européens dans les deux Indes*, Vol. 6 (The Hague, 1776), p. 426.

6. Jean Baptiste Claude Delisle de Sales, *De la Philosophie de la Nature* (Amsterdam: Arkstee et Merkus, 1770), p. 323; l'Abbé Augustin Barruel, *Les Helviennes* (Paris: Poilleux, 1830 [1781]), p. 45.

7. Louis-Sébastien Mercier, *Tableau de Paris*, Vol. 5 (Amsterdam, 1783), p. 251. Jouars-Pont-Chartrain's *cahier* can be found in *AP*, 4:621.

8. Antoine Furetière, "Foudre," in *Le Dictionnaire Universel d'Antoine Furetière*, Vol. 2 (Paris: Le Robert, 1978 [1690]). Although these figurative uses were common, there is little evidence to suggest that they had shed the connotation of "lightning" proper; that is, I see no evidence that an eighteenth-century French writer would translate "la foudre" as cannon fire rather than lightning. Instead, throughout the Revolution, that this was a metaphor rather than a synonym was made clear by depicting saltpeter as lightning bolts during festivals or making allusions linking the lightning of cannons with a stormy atmosphere. One sees, for instance, Pierre Rousselet in his description of the Bastille's cannon fire: "La foudre changée en féraille, / Du canon sort de toutes pars," a description that would be redundant if the figurative meaning had been lost. Pierre-Alexandre Rousselet, *Détail intéressant et jusqu'à présent ignoré sur la prise de la Bastille, et la suite des révolutions, fait par un assaillant de la Bastille, à un de ses amis, blessé au même siège* (Paris: n.p., 1789), p. 30.

9. Père Paulian, *Dictionnaire de physique, dédié à Monseigneur le Duc de Berry* (Avignon: Chez Louis Chambeau, 1761), 312.

10. *AP,* 4:605. The villagers of Jagny mentioned in *their* cahier that they believed the bells *caused* lightning strikes and hailstorms.

11. Jaucourt, "Foudre," *Encyclopédie,* 7:216.

12. Jean Lanteires, *Essai sur le tonnerre considéré dans ses effets moraux sur les hommes; et sur un coup de foudre remarquable* (Lausanne: Chez J.P. Heubach, Durand et Comp., 1789).

13. Ibid., p. 22.

14. Ibid., p. 26.

15. Jean-Paul Marat, *Recherches physiques sur l'électricité* (Paris: de l'impr. de Clousier; Chez Nyon l'Aîné, Nyon le cadet, et Belin, et au Bureau du Journal de la Physique, 1782), p. 1.

16. Marat, *Recherches physiques,* p. 358.

17. Georges-Louis Leclerc, Comte de Buffon, *Des Époques de la Nature* (Paris: de l'impr. Royale, 1778), p. 137.

18. Cf. Marat, *Mémoire sur l'electricité médicale, couronné le 6 août 1783, par l'Académie Royale des Sciences, Belles-Lettres et Arts de Rouen* (Paris: de l'impr. de L. Jorry; Chez N-T. Méquignon, 1783). See also Pierre-Jean-Claude Mauduyt de La Varenne, *Avis sur l'électricité médicale* (Paris: de l'impr. de P.-D. Pierres, 1781); *Avis et questions proposés par la Société Royale de Médecine, sur l'Electricité médicale, sur la Nyctalopie, ou Aveuglement de nuit, & sur les propriétés des Lézards dans le traitement de diverses maladies* (Paris: de l'impr. Royale, 1786); Masars de Cazeles, *Mémoire sur l'électricité médicale, et histoire… de vingt malades traités et la plupart guéris par l'électricité* (Paris: Méquignon l'aîné, 1780); Sigaud de la Fond, *Lettre de M. Sigaud de La Fond,… à M. de Causan,… sur l'électricité médicale; dans laquelle on expose les effets que la vertu électrique produit sur le corps humain, les maladies contre lesquelles l'auteur l'a employée avantageusement et les moyens qui paraissent les plus exacts pour administrer ce remède* (Amsterdam and Paris: Des Ventes de La Doué, 1771).

19. Bernardin de Saint-Pierre, *Etudes,* 1:56.

20. D'Alembert, "Foudre (grammaire et physique)," *Encyclopédie,* 7:214.

21. Maximilien Robespierre, *Plaidoyer pour le Sieur de Vissery de Bois-Vallé, appellant d'un jugement des echevins de Saint-Omer, qui avoit ordonné la destruction d'un Par-à-Tonnerre élevé sur sa maison* (Arras: de l'impr. de Guy Delasablonniere, 1783), p. 19. See Marie-Hélène Huet's analysis of this text in her *Mourning Glory: The Will of the French Revolution* (Philadelphia: University of Pennsylvania Press, 1997), pp. 9–25.

22. Robespierre, *Plaidoyer,* p. 4.

23. Robespierre's brief was published and, according to Jessica Riskin, broadly publicized. It was reviewed in *Mercure de France* and excerpted extensively in *Causes Célèbres.* See Riskin, "The Lawyer and the Lightning Rod," *Science in Context* 12.1 (1999): 93.

24. Marat, *Recherches physiques,* p. 415.

25. Even de Vissery's lightning rod was not spared; it was torn down after his death in 1784. Riskin, "Lawyer," p. 94.

26. Maximilien Robespierre, *Discours couronné par la Société Royale des arts et des sciences de Metz, sur les questions suivantes, proposées pour sujet du prix de l'année 1784. 1e. Quelle est l'origine de l'opinion, qui étend sur tous les individus d'une même famille, une partie de la honte attachée aux peines infamantes que subit un coupable? 2e. Cette opinion est-elle plus nuisible qu'utile? 3e. Dans le cas où l'on se décideroit pour l'affirmative, quels seroient les moyens de parer aux inconvéniens qui en résultent?* (Amsterdam [et se trouve à Paris, chez J.G. Merigot], 1785), p. 7.

27. D'Holbach, *Système de la Nature,* p. 441.

28. See Delbourgo, as well as Mary D. Sheriff, "Au Génie de Franklin": An Allegory by J.-H. Fragonard," *Proceedings of the American Philosophical Society* 127.3 (1983): 180–193.

29. *AP,* 54:178 (3 December 1792).

30. *AP,* 54:214, 298, 171 (3 December 1792).

31. *La foudre n'est pas toujours dans les mains de Jupiter,* an anonymous pamphlet dated only "11 July." The original has "1789" written in pencil on the cover.

32. Emmanuel Brosselard, "Stances pour l'anniversaire de la prise de la Bastille," in *Recueil de pièces intéressantes sur la Bastille* (Paris: de l'impr. de J. B. Hérault, 1790), p. vii; *Détail*

intéressant et jusqu'à présent ignoré, et la suite des révolutions, fait par un assaillant de la Bastille, à un de ses amis, blessés au meme siège (Chez l'auteur, n.d.); Jean Dusaulx, *De l'insurrection parisienne et de la prise de la Bastille; Discours historique, prononcé par extrait dans l'assemblée nationale, par M. Dusaulx, de l'académie des belles-letters, l'un des électeurs réunis le 14 juillet 1789, représentant de la Commune de Paris, et l'un des commissaires actuels du comité de la Bastille* (Paris: Chez Debure l'ainé, 1790), p. 95.

33. Anonymous, "Réflexions sur la présente Révolution," in *Recueil de pièces intéressantes sur la Bastille* (Paris: de l'impr. de J.B. Hérault, 1790), p. 38.

34. It is no doubt impossible to say that *no text* written after the event used such metaphorical language; however, I did not find any instances of the revolutionaries holding the power of *foudre* in any of the forty-plus documents I looked at that were written to report on, or commemorate, the event. See, among others, P. David, *La Prise de la Bastille, ou la Liberté Conquise, pièce nationale, en quatre actes, en prose* (n.p., 1790); Pierre Paul Raboteau, *La Prise de la Bastille, ode* (Paris: Chez Belin, 1790); François-Guillaume Ducray-Duminil, *La Semaine Memorable ou Récit exact de ce qui s'est passé à Paris depuis le 12 jusqu'au 17 juillet* (n.p., n.d.); *Les Lauriers du Fauxbourg Saint-Antoine, ou le Prix de la Bastille Renversé* (Paris: Gueffier jeune, 1789); [Etienne de Lacépède], *L'Achille Français, Le Héros de la Bastille, ou le Brave Élie recompensé* (Paris: de l'impr. de Momoro, 1789); *Journée de Jean-Baptiste Humbert, Horloger, qui le premier, a monté sur les Tours de la Bastille* (Paris: Chez Volland, 1789); *Epitre d'un prisonnier délivré de la Bastille* (n.p., 1789); Cousin Jacques, *Supplément nécessaire au précis exact de la prise de la Bastille* (n.p., 1789); J. Rouel ("cultivateur"), *Relation Véritable de la Prise de la Bastille le quatorze Juillet 1789* (Paris: de l'impr. de J. B. Hérault, 1790); *Les Nouvelles Philippiques, ou Le Te Deum des Français, après la destruction de la Bastille* (Paris: dans un coin de la Bastille, et aux dépens des Proscrits, L'an de la régéneration du Royaume, 1789); *Observations patriotiques sur la prise de la Bastille, du 14 juillet 1789, et sur les suites de cet événement* (Paris: Chez Debray, 1789).

35. Fauchet, *Discours sur la liberté française, prononcé le mercredi 5 août 1789, dans l'église paroissiale de St-Jacques et des Ss Innocens, durant une Solemnité consacrée à la mémoire des citoyens qui sont morts à la prise de la Bastille, pour la défense de la Patrie* (Paris: Chez Bailly, de Senne, Lottin, Cussac, 1789), pp. 11, 9.

36. Pierre-Jean-Baptiste Chaussard, *Eloge funèbre de nos frères d'armes, morts à la glorieuse journée du 10 août. Prononcé par Publicola-Chaussard, Homme de Lettres, en présence d'une deputation des fédérés des quatre-vingt-trois départemens, et des citoyens de la Section du Louvre assemblés dans l'enceinte de leurs séances, le vendredi 17 août, l'an 4e de la liberté, et le 1er de l'égalité* (Paris: de l'impr. de Martin, 1792), p. 13; Marie-Joseph Chénier, *Eloge funèbre des citoyens morts pour la défense de la liberté et de l'égalité... prononcé le 26 du même mois [août] en présence de l'Assemblée nationale... par M. Chénier* (Paris: de l'impr. Nationale, n.d.), p. 6.

37. Gabriel Bouquier, *La réunion du dix août ou L'inauguration de la république française; sanculotide dramatique; en cinq actes et en vers, mêlés de déclamations, chants, danses, et évolutions militaires au peuple souverain* (Paris: de l'impr. du journal des hommes libres, chez R. Vatar et ass., Year II [1793/1794]), p. 31.

38. Significantly the image does not seem to have been invoked during the debates in 1790 over who had the power to declare war, the king or the legislature.

39. Maximilien Robespierre, *Discours de Maximilien Robespierre, sur le parti que l'Assemblée nationale doit prendre relativement à la proposition de guerre annoncée par le pouvoir exécutif, prononcé à la Société [des amis de la Constitution] le 18 décembre 1791* (Paris: de l'impr. du Patriote Français, 1791).

40. Quoted in *Le Patriote François*, no. 878, 5 January 1792. Notably this journal was edited by Brissot, and not itself featured primarily pro-war speeches.

41. Jérôme Pétion de Villeneuve, séance du 11 mars 1792. Quoted in *Le Moniteur, ou la Gazette Universel*, no. 74; 14 March 1792.

42. It is important to read this flood of letters with some skepticism, as it was politically wise to express support for the government. Nevertheless, the preponderance of lightning images in these letters suggests that it was politically significant, although it does not seem to have been part of any formal effort to standardize language in praise of the Convention.

43. *AP,* 74:182, 184 (15 September 1793); *AP,* 76:617 (16 October 1793).

44. On sovereignty in the absence of a constitution, see Dan Edelstein, *The Terror of Natural Right,* chap. 4: "The Case of the Missing Constitution."

45. "Adresse des républicains de la commune de Vaugirard," *AP,* 76:91 (5 October 1793).

46. The imagery of the swamp is addressed in chapter 4.

47. Michael Walzer, *Regicide and Revolution: Speeches at the Trial of Louis XVI,* trans. Marian Rothstein (Cambridge: Cambridge University Press, 1974), p. 133.

48. Ibid., p. 123.

49. On the Vendée and the rhetoric of destruction, see Alain Gérard, *Par principe d'humanité: La Terreur et la Vendée* (Paris: Fayard, 1999); Jean-Clément Martin, *La Vendée et la France* (Paris: Seuil, 1987); Reynald Secher, *A French Genocide: The Vendée,* trans. George Holoch (Notre Dame, Ind.: University of Notre Dame Press, 2003).

50. On Toulon, see Malcolm Crook, *Toulon in War and Revolution* (Manchester: Manchester University Press, 1991), esp. pp. 126–157.

51. Crook, *Toulon,* p. 150.

52. Quoted in Bertrand Barère, *Convention Nationale: Rapport du Citoyen Barère, sur la reprise de Toulon par l'armée de la République* (Paris: de l'impr. Nationale, Year II [1793]), p. 7.

53. Barère, *Toulon,* p. 3.

54. Aristide Passot, *Discours prononcé dans le Temple de la Raison et à la Société des Sans-culottes de Nevers, le 1er décadi de Nivôse, à la fête civique donnée au sujet de la réduction de Toulon, livré par les traitres de cette cité, aux tyrans de l'Europe coalisés contre la République Française* (Nevers: de l'impr. de Lefebvre le jeune, Year II [1793]), p. 5. Passot apparently found this line important enough to reprint it as the epigraph to his discourse, p. 1.

55. In J. B. Gay, *Recueil de chansons patriotiques* (Strasbourg: J. B. Gay, Year II [1793/94]), pp. 7, 8.

56. William Doyle, *The Oxford History of the French Revolution,* p. 254.

57. Collot d'Herbois, *Convention Nationale: Rapport fait au nom du Comité de Salut Public, sur la situation de Commune-Affranchie,* 1 nivôse (Paris: de l'impr. Nationale, Year II [1793]), p. 10.

58. Collot d'Herbois, *Au nom du peuple français: proclamation des représentans du peuple, envoyés dans la Commune-Affranchie, pour y assurer le bonheur du peuple avec le triomphe de la République, dans tous les Départemens environnans, et près l'Armée des Alpes* (Commune-Affranchie: de l'impr. Républicaine, 15 Frimaire, Year II [1793]). Also signed Fouché, Albitte, Laporte.

59. Ibid.

60. Mona Ozouf, *L'homme régénéré: Essais sur la Révolution française* (Paris: Gallimard,1989), p. 125.

61. James Delbourgo, *A Most Amazing Scene of Wonders,* esp. chap. 4, "Electrical Politics and Political Electricity."

62. *AP,* 72:27 (11 August 1793). On the rich meanings of the "mountaintop" and the "swamps" here, see chapter 4.

63. Pierre Trassart, *Discours prononcé dans le temple de la morale de la section de Guillaume Tell, le décadi 30 fructidor, à l'occasion d'un concert donné par des artistes et des amateurs, pour concourir au soulagement des familles infortunées de ceux qui ont péri le 14 fructidor, par l'explosion de la poudrerie de la place de la Grenelle* (Paris: de l'impr. de Massot, 1794); also at AN, D/XXXVIII/2.

64. *Instruction pour tous les citoyens qui voudront exploiter eux-mêmes du salpêtre, envoyée dans toutes les municipalités par le comité de salut public de la Convention nationale, conformément au décret du 14 frimaire de l'an 2e de la République* (Paris: de l'impr. Nationale, Year II [1793/94]), p. 1.

65. On the history of this process, see Robert P. Multhauf, "The French Crash Program for Saltpeter Production, 1776–94," *Technology and Culture* 12.2 (April 1971): 163–181.

66. Claude-Antoine Prieur, *Rapport sur le salpêtre, fait à la Convention Nationale, au nom du comité de salut public* (Paris: de l'impr. Nationale, Year II [1793]), p. 3.

67. Ibid. Nor was Prieur the only individual to mention the malevolent plan; in an 1803 retrospective on science, in a section on the saltpeter educational program, J. B. Biot stated, "We looked for saltpeter even in the ruins of Lyon, and were supposed to collect soda [la soude] in the burnt forests of the Vendée." Biot, *Essai sur l'histoire générale des sciences pendant la Révolution Française* (Paris: Chez Duprat, Chez Fuchs, 1803), p. 53.

68. Louis-Pierre Dufourny, *Département de Paris: Salpêtres, Adresse aux citoyens pour l'extraction de tout le Salpêtre* (Paris: de l'impr. de Ballard, n.d. [18 frimaire, Year II (8 December 1793)]), pp. 2–3.

69. Bertrand Barère, *Convention Nationale: Rapport fait au nom du Comité du salut public, sur l'état de la fabrication révolutionnaire du salpêtre et de la poudre, et sur la nécessité de supprimer l'agence nationale, ci-devant Régie des poudres et salpêtres; par Barère, Séance du 17 messidor, l'an deuxième de la République française, une et indivisible* (Paris; de l'impr. Nationale, Year II [1794]), p. 3. Mercier, in his *Nouveau Paris*, suggested that this effort had, in fact, saved France from enemy forces: "This operation, which could never have been imagined, let alone executed, in any time other than the revolutionary moment we found ourselves in, prevented France from falling to a foreign power." In Louis-Sébastien Mercier, *Le Nouveau Paris*, ed. Jean-Claude Bonnet, pp. 588–589 (Paris: Mercure de France, 1995). Multhauf notes that in the year after the 14 Frimaire decree, nearly seventeen million pounds of saltpeter were produced. Multhauf, "The French Crash Program for Saltpeter Production," p. 175.

70. AN, W 112, Dossier 1, Document 20, "Rapport du citoyen Hanriot."

71. Reported in *Mercure Universel*, Vol. 41 (Paris: de l'impr. de Cussac, Year II [1794]), 1 Messidor, Year II [19 June 1794], p. 5.

72. Jean-Pierre Boudet, *Circulaire de J.-P. Boudet, inspecteur des poudres et salpêtres, nommé par le Comité de salut public* (n.p., Year II [1793/94]).

73. "Le Salpêtre," in Gay, *Recueil de Chansons Patriotiques*, pp. 90, 91.

74. Barère, *Rapport... sur salpêtre*, p. 5.

75. Ibid.

76. On the success of this educational program, see also Biot, *Essai sur l'histoire générale des sciences*, pp. 56–57.

77. Les commissaires nommés par l'académie par le jugement du Prix du salpêtre, *Recueil des Mémoires et d'Observations sur la formation et la fabrication du salpêtre* (Paris: Chez Lacombe; de l'impr. de Demonville, 1776). The Academy soon learned that Besançon had already held a *concours* on the same issue a few years prior.

78. "Le Salpêtre," in Gay, *Recueil de Chansons Patriotiques*, p. 89.

79. The Fete de l'Etre Suprême in Strasbourg featured salpêtriers in the procession, who carried with them "emblems that announce that the heavens protect people who facilitate the fall of kings." *Procès-Verbal et description de la fête de l'Etre Suprême, célébrée le 20 prairial, l'an second de la République française une et indivisible* (Strasbourg: de l'impr. de Ph. J. Dannbach, 1794), pp. 7–8.

80. Jean-Baptiste Avril, *Commune de Paris, séance eu 27 ventôse de l'an II de la République. Arrêté, portant que le Conseil général de la Commune accompagnera les Élèves de la République, pour la fabrication des Poudres et de Salpêtres et la fonte des Canons, qui doivent porter Décadi prochain, leurs premiers travaux à la Convention nationale* (n.p., 1794).

81. "Stances chantées dans le Jardin National, avant l'épreuve du canon, à la fête des la Réunion des élèves de la République, pour la fabrication des canons et salpêtres, le décadi 30 ventôse," *La Lyre de la Raison, ou Hymnes, cantiques, odes et stances à l'Etre Suprême pour la célébration des fêtes décadaires* (Paris: Chez Dufart, Year II [1794]), p. 46.

82. Charles-Louis Tissot, *Les Salpêtriers républicains, comédie en un acte et en prose, mêlée de vaudevilles et d'airs nouveaux. Représentée, pour la première fois, sur le théâtre de la Cité Variétés, le octodi 8 messidor, l'an 2 de la République* (Paris: Chez la Citoyenne Toubon; de l'impr. de Cordier, 1794).

83. Ibid., p. 3.

84. Ibid., p. 44.

85. Ibid., p. 28.

86. Ibid., p. 41.

87. Barère, *Rapport . . . sur salpêtre*, p. 7.

88. "Rapport de l'agence des Salpêtres et Poudres sur l'explosion de la poudrerie de Grenelle, aux représentants du peuple composant le Comité de salut public." [14 Fructidor, Year II (31 August 1794)], AN, AF II/57, Dossier 421, Document 54.

89. "Arrêts pris le 14 fructidor, à sept heures et demi du matin." AN, AF II/57, Dossier 420, Document 4.

90. Dated Year II, but that would be impossible, and therefore it was probably Year III. "Cn Dumas aux citoyens représentans du peuple composant le comité de secours de la Convention Nationale," AN, F/15/3293.

91. *Journal de la Montagne*, no. 124 (15 Fructidor, Year II [1794]). See also Treilhard, *Rapport fait au nom des Comités de Salut Public et de Sureté Générale, sur l'explosion de la poudrerie de Grenelle, par Treilhard, dans la séance du 15 fructidor, an IIe de la République Française, une et indivisible* (Paris: de l'impr. Nationale, 1794). Note, too, that there were also more political reasons for this decree—the Convention needed to reestablish popular support in the wake of Thermidor. Treilhard himself had only recently been released from prison. Yet the means by which they chose to compensate the victims—in honoring them as *défenseurs de la patrie*—is significant.

92. A handwritten note indicates that this request was responded to verbally, so Citoyen Dobigny's fate is unrecorded. "Citoyen Chenot Dobigny, Pétition au Comité de Salut Public." Thermidor, Year III (1795). AN, F/15/3293.

93. Trassart, *Discours . . . pour concourir au soulagement des familles infortunées de ceux qui ont péri le 14 fructidor.*

94. Ibid.

95. Barère, *Rapport . . . sur salpêtre*, p. 18.

Chapter 4

1. Aristide Valcour, *Les Petits Montagnards: Opéra-Bouffon en trois actes en prose, mêlé d'ariettes* (Paris: de l'impr. de Cailleau, Year II [1794]), p. 3. Valcour was an editor of the *Journal de la Montagne* in addition to his literary pursuits; he was the author of several plays during the revolutionary period as well as a small number of allegorical texts and speeches.

2. Valcour, *Les Petits Montagnards*, pp. 63–64. Plays and operas based on William Tell were particularly popular during the period of the Terror, perhaps in part because of its setting in the mountains of Switzerland (and the frequent image of Tell atop, or descending, a mountain), in addition to the obvious thematic appeal of the overthrow of tyranny. For more on its popularity, see Beatrice Hyslop, "The Theater during a Crisis: The Parisian Theater during the Reign of Terror," *Journal of Modern History* 17.4 (December 1945), p. 342.

3. Valcour, *Les Petits Montagnards*, p. 63.

4. AN, W 112, Document 11.

5. *Journal de Paris National* no. 386, 2 pluviôse, Year II (21 January 1794).

6. See "Vaudeville des Petits Montagnards," in *Hymnes adoptés par la Section du Panthéon Français, pour être chantées au Temple de la Raison* (Paris: de l'impr. de Lion et Compagnie, n.d.), pp. 20–22; Aristide Valcour, *Hymne en l'honneur de la Montagne, air nouveau* (Paris: de l'impr. des 86 départemens et de la Société aux Jacobins, n.d.); *Journal de Paris National*, no. 386, 2 pluviôse, Year II (1794).

7. Ferdinand Brunot, *Histoire de la Langue Française des origines à 1900*, Vol. 9, *La Révolution et l'Empire* (Paris: Librairie Armand Colin, 1937), p. 631.

8. James Leith, in his *Space and Revolution* (p. 133), has gestured toward these textual antecedents.

9. I have chosen to translate Marais, sometimes translated as "marsh," as "swamp," based largely on the connotations that the term seemed to be intended to evoke, and following Arthur Goldhammer's translation in François Furet and Mona Ozouf's *Critical Dictionary of the French Revolution*. See "Montagnards," *Critical Dictionary of the French Revolution* (Cambridge, Mass.: Harvard University Press, 1989).

10. Cf. Joseph Eschassériaux, *Rapport et projet de décret, présentés au nom du comité d'agriculture, sur les desséchemens des marais* (Paris: de l'impr. Nationale, n.d. [12 prairial, Year II handwritten on title page]), p. 4.

11. Ozouf, *Festivals,* p. 114.

12. "La Montagne," attributed to Cit. C. Gassicourt, in *Le Chansonnier de la Montagne ou recueil de chansons, vaudevilles, pots-pourris et hymnes patriotiques* (Paris: Chez Favre, Year II [1793/94]), p. 5. Also printed in Léonard Bourdon, *Recueil des actions héroïques et civiques des républicains français,* no. 3 (Paris: de l'impr. Nationale, Year II [1793/94]).

13. "Les officiers, sous-officiers, et volontaires du 1er bataillon du Calvados, à la Convention nationale," *AP,* 70:41 (31 July 1793).

14. "Ceux qui ont vu le Champ de Mars il y a peu de jours et qui le revoyent aujourd'hui sont surpris…" (Anonymous etching, Paris: Chez J. Cherau, 1790). BNF Estampes, De Vinck 3729. See also De Vinck 3740 for another image of the "mountain" at this festival.

15. *AP,* 34:441 (27 October 1791).

16. Lequinio also prided himself on his ability to speak to "the people" in his newspaper, *Le Journal des Laboureurs.*

17. *AP,* 34:441 (27 October 1791).

18. Quoted in Albert Soboul, *Dictionnaire historique de la Révolution Française* (Paris: Presses Universitaires de France, 1989), p. 758.

19. Charlton, *New Images of the Natural;* Philippe Joutard, *L'invention du Mont Blanc* (Paris: Gallimard, 1986). On mountain imagery in the eighteenth century, see also Numa Broc, *Les Montagnes vues par les Géographes et les Naturalistes de langue française au XVIIIème siècle* (Paris: Bibliothèque Nationale, 1969); and Marjorie Hope Nicolson, *Mountain Gloom and Mountain Glory: The Development of the Aesthetics of the Infinite* (New York: Norton, 1963).

20. Joutard, *Invention,* p. 197.

21. Horace-Benedict de Saussure, *Voyages dans les Alpes, précédés d'un essai sur l'histoire naturelle des environs de Génève,* Vol. 1 (Neufchatel: Chez Samuel Fauche, 1779), p. iii.

22. Ibid., 1:iv.

23. Saussure, *Relation abrégée d'un voyage à la cîme du Mont-Blanc, en août 1787* (Geneva: Barde, 1787), p. 15.

24. Fouché, *Ecrits révolutionnaires,* p. 80.

25. See, for example, James Guillaume, ed., *Procès-verbaux du Comité d'instruction publique de la Convention nationale,* Vol. 4 (1 Germinal—11 Fructidor, Year II [21 March–28 August 1794]) (Paris: de l'impr. Nationale, 1901), pp. 75, 266, 267, 304, 382, 436, 468, 546, 615, 653, 823. After years of requests for the geologist Desmarest to complete his work on the Auvergne, the Committee apparently lost interest in the project after the end of Messidor (July 1794).

26. Pierre-Jean-Baptiste Legrand d'Aussy, *Voyage d'Auvergne* (Paris: E. Onfroy, 1788), p. 11.

27. Briffaud, "Le role des catastrophes naturelles," p. 138.

28. Ibid., p. 221 n. 15.

29. Buffon, *Epoques,* p. 132.

30. Bernardin de Saint-Pierre, *Etudes,* "Explication des Figures," 3:521. The image itself was the frontispiece to volume 1.

31. D'Holbach, "Montagnes," *Encyclopédie,* 10:672.

32. Joutard, *Invention,* pp. 84–85.
33. Rousseau, *Emile,* p. 345.
34. Rousseau, *Lettres écrites de la montagne,* in *Oeuvres Complètes de J.-J. Rousseau,* ed. P. R. Auguis, Vol. 7 (Paris: Chez Dalibon, 1824), p. 180. Although this text was not particularly popular or widely read, especially compared to *La Nouvelle Héloise,* Rousseau was often pictured holding it in Revolution-era images; see, for example, "J. J. Rousseau, en Suisse, persécuté et sans asile" (Dessiné par Bouchot, Gravé par Charon; Impr. par Vayron; A Paris, chez Charon), BNF Estampes, De Vinck 6331.
35. Jean-Jacques Rousseau, *Julie ou La Nouvelle Héloise* (Paris: Flammarion, 1967), p. 44. Also noted in Joutard, *Invention,* p. 85.
36. Brissot, *Le Patriote Français,* 3 April 1792.
37. Aulard, *Société,* 4:433, 458.
38. Ibid., 4:601.
39. Quoted in Joutard, *Invention,* pp. 126–127. From Saussure, *Voyages dans les Alpes,* 1:ix.
40. Mercier, "Vue des Alpes," *Tableau de Paris,* Vol. 5 (Amsterdam, 1783), pp. 348–349.
41. Excerpted in Eugène Hatin, *Histoire politique et littéraire de la presse en France,* Vol. 6 (Paris: Poulet-Malassis et de Broise, 1860), p. 374; emphasis in original.
42. In fact, it was the festival of désintéressement that distinguished Robespierre's plan from others' proposals.
43. Rousseau, *Nouvelle Héloise,* p. 46.
44. *OC,* 10:445.
45. Valcour, *Petits Montagnards,* p. 9.
46. This decision met with some opposition; Chaumette, the president of the Commune, disapproved, saying that it would be evidence of a schism among the representatives of the nation. Chaumette asked them instead to name themselves after a "virtue of the republic," but the section refused. *Réimpression du Moniteur,* Vol. 17, no. 233, p. 437 (21 August 1793).
47. *Réimpression du Moniteur* 16, no. 157: 557–558 (6 June 1793).
48. The *sans-culottes*—literally, "without knee-breeches"—were distinguished sartorially from the elite classes, but more importantly distinguished themselves politically through direct involvement in local sections and their support for the radical revolution. While the *sans-culottes* were typically associated with the laboring classes of Paris, this group from Montmirail chose to adopt the term in their correspondence with the Convention. On the *sans-culottes,* see Michael Sonenscher, *Sans-Culottes: An Eighteenth-Century Emblem in the French Revolution* (Princeton, N.J.: Princeton University Press, 2008) and Albert Soboul, *The Sans-Culottes,* trans. Rémy Inglis Hall (Princeton, N.J.: Princeton University Press, 1980).
49. "Adresse à la Convention Nationale, par la Société Républicaine de *sans-culottes* de la municipalité au comité de surveillance de la commune de Montmirail, district de la Ferté-Bernard," AN, D/XXXVIII/3. Although it may have been mere typographic inconsistency, this letter seemed to make a distinction between *Montagnards,* which referred specifically to the political entity seated in the Convention, and the noncapitalized *montagnards,* which was how they referred to themselves.
50. Robespierre, *OC,* 10:492.
51. Rousseau, *La Nouvelle Héloise,* p. 46.
52. Edmund Burke, *A Philosophical Enquiry into the Origin of Our Ideas of the Sublime and the Beautiful* (London: R. and J. Dodsley, 1757), p. 13. Burke's text was translated (with some editorial deletions and additions) into French in 1775, as *Recherches philosophiques sur l'origine des idées que nous avons du Beau et du Sublime, précedées d'une dissertation sur le goût, traduites de l'Anglais de M. Burke par l'Abbé des François* (London and Paris, 1775).
53. Burke, *Philosophical Enquiry,* pp. 43, 60.
54. In 1955 Frederick Staver suggested that the "sublime" was only used to describe the natural world in English beginning in the early eighteenth century. See Frederick Staver, "'Sublime' as Applied to Nature," *Modern Language Notes* 70.7 (November 1955): 484–487.

55. Diderot, *Diderot on Art*, Vol. 2 (Salon of 1767), p. 126. Diderot wrote, "Everything that astonishes the soul, everything that impresses a feeling of terror on it, leads to the sublime."

56. Mercier, *Tableau de Paris*, 1:175–176.

57. Lacépède, *Discours de clôture du cours d'histoire naturelle de l'an VIII, sur les avantages que les naturalistes peuvent procurer au corps social, dans l'état actuel de la civilisation et des connoissances humaines* (Paris: de l'impr. de Plassan, Year VIII [1799/1800]), p. 15.

58. Saussure, *Voyages dans les Alpes*, 1:ii.

59. Ibid., 1:iii.

60. Burke, *Philosophical Enquiry*, p. 42.

61. Jaucourt, "Sublime," *Encyclopédie*, 15:566.

62. Arasse, *Guillotine*, esp. pp. 98–103; Marie-Hélène Huet, *Mourning Glory*.

63. Huet, *Mourning Glory*, pp. 76–77.

64. Pithou de Loinville, *Description Générale*, p. 21.

65. John Baillie, *Essay on the Sublime* (London: R. Dodsley, 1747), p. 5.

66. Alexander Gerard, *An Essay on Taste, with three dissertations on the same subject, by M. de Voltaire, Mr. d'Alembert, F.R.S. Mr. de Montesquieu* (London: A. Millar, 1759), p. 19.

67. Burke, *Philosophical Enquiry*, p. 42.

68. Commission d'Instruction Publique, *Fêtes à l'Etre Suprême: Pièces Dramatiques, Rapport et Arrêté* (Paris: de l'impr. de la Commission d'Instruction Publique, 11 messidor Year II [29 June 1794]), p. 3.

69. Valcour, *Les Petits Montagnards*, p. 64.

70. Robespierre, *OC*, 10:492.

71. Ibid., 10:493.

72. Baillie, *Essay*, p. 23.

73. Commission d'Instruction Publique, *Fêtes à l'Etre Suprême: Pièces Dramatiques*, p. 5.

74. On the mountain at this festival as an icon of the sublime, see Monique Mosser, "Le temple et la montagne: généalogie d'un décor de fête révolutionnaire," *Revue de l'Art* 1 (1989): 21–35, esp. p. 29.

75. *Décalogue Républicain* (Puy: de l'impr. de P. B. F. Clet, [1793]), p. 1. The *décalogue* seems to have been reproduced throughout France and integrated into several Jacobin Club meetings. Versions were printed in Paris and Marseilles as well as Puy.

76. "La Montagne," in *Le Chansonnier de la Montagne*, pp. 6–7.

77. *AP*, 70:154 (3 August 1793).

78. *Collection des meilleures prières, hymnes et hommage à l'Eternel, suivie d'un détail sur les cérémonies de la fête à l'Etre Suprême et autres fêtes décadaires. Utile aux écoles primaires. Présentée à la Convention Nationale* (Paris: Chez Prévost, Year II [1794]), p. 9.

79. "Les amis de l'Unité et de l'Indivisibilité de la République à Sainte-Mère-Eglise, district de Carenton, dept de la Manche," *AP*, 76:98 (5 October 1793).

80. "Discours prononcé à la société populaire de Perpignan par Rousillon cordelier, jacobin de Paris le 6e pluviôse l'an deuxieme de la République." AN, D XXXVIII/5.

81. Chabot referred to the "marais de la législature" as early as 14 October 1792. Aulard, *Société des Jacobins*, 4:385. Unlike most of the other metaphors studied in this text, "marais" seems to have had limited metaphorical uses prior to the Revolution, based on an ARTFL search. It was, however, already a term for the neighborhood in the fourth arrondissement.

82. Gassicourt, "La Montagne," in *Le Chansonnier de la Montagne*, pp. 5–6.

83. Alain Corbin, *The Foul and the Fragrant*, trans. Miriam Kochan (Cambridge, Mass.: Harvard University Press, 1986), p. 92.

84. Ibid., p. 78.

85. Reynald Abad, in his *Conjuration contre les carpes*, has detailed the debates surrounding the ultimately un-enforced decree against *étangs*. For a nice overview of the various attempts to wipe out *étangs* during the eighteenth century, which also provides insight into

contemporary debates about swamplands, see Abad, *La conjuration contre les carpes: Enquête sur les origines du décret du dessèchement des étangs du 14 frimaire an II* (Paris: Fayard, 2006), pp. 53–111.

86. Louis-Etienne Beffroy, *Avantages du dessèchement des marais, et manière de profiter des terreins desséchés* (Paris: Chez Froullé, 1793 [1786]; written for the Société d'agriculture de Laon), p. 11.

87. Beffroy betrayed a physiocratic faith in the power of agriculture to improve a nation's overall wealth, explaining that maximizing the agricultural output of land would benefit every aspect of commerce.

88. Duchosal, *Discours sur la nécessité de dessécher les marais, de supprimer les étangs, et de replanter les forêts; prononcé le 12 mai, dans la société patriotique de la section de la Bibliothèque* (Paris: de l'impr. de L. Potier de Lille, 1791), p. 7. The BNF attributes the text to Marie-Emile-Guillaume Duchosal, who also authored a denunciation of the Comédie Française in 1790; an individual bearing the same name edited *L'Ami des Sans-Culottes*, a radical journal published briefly in 1793.

89. Duchosal, *Discours*, p. 13.

90. For criticism of the deputies on the right, see ibid., p. 7.

91. Jacques-Antoine Boudin, *Convention Nationale: Du dessèchement des marais et terreins submergés* (Paris: de l'impr. Nationale, n.d.), p. 8.

92. Ibid., pp. 8–9.

93. Ibid., p. 12.

94. Ibid., p. 14.

95. Eschassériaux, *Rapport et project*, p. 4. Eschassériaux saw more of a topographical cause to *marais* than did Boudin, admitting that certain areas were susceptible to flooding and stagnation. He also insisted, however, that these natural phenomena were greatly exacerbated by feudalism; see pp. 2–3.

96. Ibid., p. 3.

97. Lyon actually erupted in violence two days prior to the *journées* of 31 May 31–2 June, but the purges certainly seem to have been the "catalyst" for the more widespread rebellion that took place in Caen, Bordeaux, and Marseille, as well as Lyon. See Paul Hanson, *The Jacobin Republic under Fire: The Federalist Revolt in the French Revolution* (University Park: Pennsylvania State University Press, 2003), esp. p. 97.

98. *Procès-Verbal des monuments*, p. 17.

99. Aristide Valcour, *Discours prononcé à l'Assemblée générale des citoyens de la commune de Nogent-sur-Marne, le 12 prairial de la second année de la République Française. . . . jour de l'anniversaire du 31 mai 1793* (Nogent-sur-Marne: l'impr. de Rauderie jeune, Year II [1794]), p. 9.

100. Aristide Valcour, *Les Trois Evangiles, de la Veille, du Jour, et du Lendemain: Instruction allégorique à l'usage des jeunes républicains* (Paris: de l'impr. de Cailleau, Year II [1793/94]), p. 14.

101. Jean-Joseph Pithou de Loinville and Jacques-Louis David, *Description générale*, p. 23.

102. *AP*, 76:98 (5 October 1793).

103. "Adresse du conseil général du Département des Alpes-Maritimes," *AP*, 76:80 (5 October 1793).

104. "La société populaire de Guéret, chef-lieu du département de la Creuse," *AP*, 76:83 (5 October 1793).

105. *Collection des meilleures prières*, p. 46.

106. Boudin, *Dessèchement*, p. 33.

107. Cf. ibid.; Etienne Légier, *Observations sur le projet de dessécher les marais d'Arles et de Fontvielle* (Aix: de l'impr. de la Veuve d'André Adibert, 1792); Eschassériaux, *Rapport et projet*, p. 3.

108. Eschassériaux, *Rapport et projet*, p. 8.

109. Briois, *La Mort du jeune Barra, ou une Journée de la Vendée, Drame historique en un acte. Représenté, pour la première fois, à Paris, sur le Théâtre Républicain, le 15 Floréal, l'an second de la République* (Paris: Chez Barba, Libraire, rue Gît-le-Coeur, Year II [1794]), p. 21.

110. C. Thiébaut, *La Guerre de la Vendée, pièce révolutionnaire en trois actes et en prose, pour être représentée par de jeunes citoyens et citoyennes, les jours de Décade et autres Fêtes nationales* (Nancy: Chez la veuve Bachot, Year II [1793/94]), p. 30.

111. François Cizos-Duplessis, *Les Peuples et les Rois, ou le tribunal de la Raison: Allégorie Dramatique en cinq actes et en prose* (Paris: Chez Barba, Year II [1794]), p. 51.

112. Cizos-Duplessis, *Les Peuples et les rois*, pp. 54, 55.

113. Cf. *Le Père Duchesne* no. 272, 306, 312, 326. The idea of monarchist frogs was indeed an old one; La Fontaine's *Fables* had included the tale of "Les Grenouilles qui demandent un roi," in which a group of frogs, "weary of democracy," asked Jupiter to send them a king.

114. Jacques-Nicolas Billaud-Varenne, *Décret du 14 frimaire précédé du Rapport fait au nom du Comité de Salut Public, sur un mode de Gouvernement provisoire et révolutionnaire* (Paris: de l'impr. des Régies Nationales, Year II [1793]), pp. 5–6.

115. Billaud-Varenne, *Décret du 14 frimaire*, p. 20 (Section 2, Article 1).

116. Prieur, *Rapport sur le salpêtre*, esp. p. 2.

117. Abad, *Conjuration*, esp. pp. 149–165. For the text of the decree, see Abad, Appendix III, pp. 178–179.

118. R. R. Palmer, *Twelve Who Ruled: The Year of the Terror in the French Revolution* (Princeton, N.J.: Princeton University Press, 1989 [1941]), p. 330.

119. Ozouf, *Festivals*, p. 116.

120. AN, D/XXXVIII/5, "Fête décadaire célébrée à Bellevue pour l'inauguration des bustes de Lepeletier, de Brutus, de Marat, Chalier, Voltaire, et Rousseau, les uns restaurateurs, les autres martyres de la liberté française," 20 Floréal, Year II [9 May 1794].

121. Robespierre, *OC*, 10:457.

122. Ibid., 10:451.

123. Robespierre, *Discours de Maximilien Robespierre, Président de la Convention Nationale, au peuple réuni pour la fête de l'Être Suprême, décadi 20 prairial, an second de la République française, une et indivisible* (Paris: de l'impr. de Testu, n.d. [1794]). This was a large broadsheet reproduction of his speech on a single page, suggesting the desired diffusion of his remarks. Also quoted in *OC*, 10:482.

124. *OC*, 10:473–474.

125. Ibid., 10:481.

126. Ozouf, *Festivals*, pp. 111–118.

127. *Procès-verbal et description de la fête de l'Etre Suprême, célébrée le 20 prairial, l'an second de la République française une et indivisible* (Strasbourg: de l'imprimerie de Ph. J. Dannbach, 1794), pp. 7–8.

128. *Rituel Républicain: Fête à l'Être-Suprême, Exécutée à Paris, le 20 Prairial, l'an 2e de la République. Avec la musique des Hymnes* (Paris: Chez Aubry, Year II [1794]), p. 12; armed adolescents are noted on p. 2.

129. *OC*, 10:482.

130. *Rituel Républicain*, p. 25.

131. *Collection des meilleures prières*, p. 11. Outside Paris the same rhetoric rang out at sister festivals around the nation: "You want us to be free, you want to make the arms of the Republic triumph.... Be always among our defenders, protect our armies, they are preparing the world's happiness," proclaimed a citizen Beuzelin in Caen. *Discours prononcé par le citoyen Beuzelin, agent national de la commune de Caen, le décadi 20 prairial, l'an 2 de la République française, une & indivisible, pour la fête de l'Eternel* (Caen, Year II [1794]), p. 7.

132. Deschamps, "Hymne à la Divinité, chantée par les aveugles," *Rituel Républicain*, p. 17.

133. "Hymne a l'Etre Supreme," *Ordre et marche de la fête à l'Etre Suprême, qui aura lieu le décadi prochain, 20 prairial, conformément au décret de la Convention nationale* (n.p., Year II [1794]), p. 2; *Rituel Républicain*, p. 30. Chénier's hymn was not, at the last minute, sung.

134. Jean-Baptiste Radet, *Le Canonier Convalescent, fait historique en un acte et en vaudevilles* (Paris: Chez la Librairie au Théâtre du Vaudeville, et à l'imprimerie, rue des Droits de l'Homme, Year II [1794]), p. 17.

135. *Collection des meilleures prières,* p. 7.

136. The circular included advice on farming, current events, and a "moral education."

137. [Sylvain Maréchal], *Décades des Cultivateurs, contenant Précis historique des événemens révolutionnaires de l'an II de la Révolution; cours de morale naturelle et républicaine; l'Agriculture pratique, tant de jardins potagers et à fruits, que de la campagne en général, avec les planches nécessaires à l'intelligence de l'agriculture,* Vols. 1 and 2 (Paris: Chez Duffart; Chez Basset, Langlois, Caillot, et Louis, Year III [1794/95]), p. 66.

138. [Maréchal], *Décades,* p. 72.

139. Ozouf, *Festivals,* p. 118.

Chapter 5

1. Louis-Marie Prudhomme, *Révolutions de Paris,* no. 212 (3 August—28 October 1793).

2. Quoted in Marvin A. Carlson, *The Theatre of the French Revolution* (Ithaca, N.Y.: Cornell University Press, 1966), p. 177.

3. Pierre Sylvain Maréchal, *Le Jugement dernier des rois, prophétie en un acte, en prose* (Paris: de l'impr. de C-F. Patris, Year II [1793]), p. 36. For the Committee of Public Safety bequest, see AN, AF/II/67, Dossier 493, "Arrête du 19 brumaire 2e année." See also Jean-Marie Apostolidès, "Theater and Terror: *Le Jugement dernier des rois,*" in *Terror and Consensus: Vicissitudes of French Thought,* ed. Jean-Joseph Goux and Philip R. Wood (Stanford, Calif.: Stanford University Press, 1998), p. 139.

4. Prudhomme, *Révolutions de Paris,* no. 212.

5. Apostolidès, "Theater and Terror," p. 137.

6. Maréchal, *Le Jugement dernier des rois,* p. 36.

7. Although a small number of articles have been written on the symbol of the volcano during the Revolution, no one has yet linked the use of the symbol to broader trends in both natural histories and popular literature, and in the political sphere. See, in particular, Apostolidès, "Theater and Terror"; and Ebe Nannoni, "Le peuple-volcan: analyse d'une métaphore," in *Révolution Française, Peuples et Littératures,* ed. André Peyronie (Paris: Klincksieck, 1991). For an insightful look at the role of geology in conceptualizing political change in the German context, see Maiken Umbach, "Visual Culture, Scientific Images and German Small-State Politics in the Late Enlightenment," *Past and Present* 158 (February 1998): 110–145.

8. Sylvain Maréchal, *Antiquités d'Herculanum avec leurs explications en françois* (Paris: Chez David, graveur, 1780).

9. On the *Encyclopédie* images, see Rebecca Ford, "Images of the Earth, Images of Man: The Mineralogical Plates of the *Encyclopedie,*" in Lyle and McCallan, *Histoires de la terre,* pp. 57–74.

10. On the French interest in artifacts of volcanic eruption in the eighteenth and nineteenth centuries, see Göran Blix, *From Paris to Pompeii: French Romanticism and the Cultural Politics of Archaeology* (Philadelphia: University of Pennsylvania Press, 2009).

11. See Aubin-Louis Millin, *Elémens d'histoire naturelle,* 3rd ed. (Paris: Léger, 1802), p. 77. The terms seem to have taken root by the 1790s; see Kenneth Taylor, "Nicolas Desmarest and Geology in the Eighteenth Century," in *Towards a History of Geology,* ed. Cecil J. Schneer (Cambridge, Mass.: MIT Press, 1969), p. 354; and Rhoda Rappaport, "Dangerous Words: Diluvialism, Neptunism, Catastrophism," in *Advancements of Learning: Essays in Honor of Paolo Rossi* (Florence: L. S. Olschki, 2007), p. 111. Both Taylor's and Rappaport's essays have convinced me to be cautious in applying the terms to naturalists before the turn of the century.

12. Bernardin de Saint-Pierre, *Études de la Nature,* 1:306–307.

13. On the frequent overlap between "neptunists" and "vulcanists," see Taylor, "Nicolas Desmarest," pp. 339–356. On Buffon's changing ideas about the role of fire, see Rappaport, "Dangerous Words," p. 114.

14. Quoted in Haraldur Sigurdsson, *Melting the Earth: The History of Ideas on Volcanic Eruptions* (Oxford: Oxford University Press, 1999), p. 126.

15. On Dolomieu's journeys in the Messina and Calabria region, see Simone Messina, "Le naturaliste et la catastrophe: Dolomieu en Calabre, 1784," in *L'invention de la catastrophe au XVIIIe siècle*, ed. Anne-Marie Mercier-Faivre and Chantal Thomas, pp. 285–302 (Paris: Librairie Droz, 2008).

16. Déodat Gratet de Dolomieu, *Mémoire sur les îles Ponces et catalogue raisonné des produits de l'Etna, pour servir à l'histoire des volcans, suivis de la description de l'éruption de l'Etna, du mois de Juillet 1787* (Paris: Chez Cuchet, 1788), pp. 10–11.

17. Martin J. S. Rudwick, *Bursting the Limits of Time: The Reconstruction of Geohistory in the Age of Revolution* (Chicago: University of Chicago Press, 2005), p. 206.

18. Buffon, *Epoques de la Nature*, p. 136.

19. Marat, *Recherches physiques sur l'électricité*, pp. 427–452.

20. Ibid., pp. 450–451.

21. Kenneth Taylor, "Volcanoes as Accidents: How 'Natural' Were Volcanoes to 18th-Century Naturalists?" in *Volcanoes and History*, ed. Nicoletta Morello (Genoa: Brigati, 1998), p. 597; emphasis in original.

22. D'Holbach, "Volcans," *Encyclopédie*, 17:443.

23. Bernardin de Saint-Pierre, *Études*, 1:306.

24. Pluche, *Spectacle de la Nature*, 3:219.

25. William Hamilton, "Letter to Mathew Maty, M.D., Secretary to the Royal Society: An Account of a Journey to Mount Etna" and "Remarks upon the Nature of the Soil of Naples" both in Hamilton, *Observations on Mount Vesuvius, Mount Etna, and other volcanos: in a series of letters, addressed to the Royal Society, from the Honourable Sir W. Hamilton* (London: T. Cadell, 1772). See, esp., pp. 57, 161, for his discussion of fertility.

26. Hamilton, *Observations*, p. 161.

27. Jaucourt, "Vésuve," *Encyclopédie*, 17:219.

28. Quoted in *Description historique et géographique de la ville de Messine*, p. 1.

29. This is inspired in part by Hannah Arendt's statement that "in the household of nature, destruction and creation are but two sides of the natural process." Arendt, *On Violence*, p. 75.

30. Jean-Jacques Rousseau, *Essai sur l'origine des langues* (Paris: Gallimard, 1990), p. 101.

31. Jean-Jacques Rousseau, *Discours sur l'origine et les fondements de l'inégalité parmi les hommes* (Paris: Flammarion, 1992), p. 223.

32. Ibid., p. 232.

33. See, for example, Gabriel Sénac de Meilhan, *L'Emigré*, in which he said of the wealthy residents of Paris, "The fleeting abundance produced by the assignats, luxury, and pleasures lulled them to sleep near the volcano whose eruption was imminent." Sénac de Meilhan, *L'Emigré*, in *Romanciers du 18e siècle*, ed. René Etiemble, Vol. 2 (Paris: Gallimard, 1965), p. 1692. Jean-Gabriel Peltier, an émigré, wrote in 1793, "France declared war on Leopold, like a volcano that erupts and that spreads its destruction everywhere without being stopped by any obstacle." *Dernier tableau de Paris, ou récit historique de la révolution du 10 août 1792*, Vol. 2 (London, 1793), p. 138. Charles Alexandre de Calonne wrote, in 1790, that *not* to engage in counterrevolution would be "to maintain and augment a volcano whose flames cannot be stopped from spreading into our sorrowful country, and reducing it to ashes." *De l'Etat de la France tel qu'il peut et qu'il doit être* (London, 1790), p. 20.

34. *Le Gazette Nationale ou le Moniteur Universel*, no. 6 (6 January 1792). Isnard, of course, was the kinsman of the winner of the 1757 Rouen essay contest about the causes of earthquakes.

35. *La Juste vengeance du peuple: détail exact de tout ce qui s'est passé dans les prisons de l'abbaye, Bicêtre, les Carmes* (Paris: de l'impr. de Tremblay, n.d. [1792]), p. 6.

36. Chaussard, *Eloge funèbre de nos frères d'armes*, p. 10.

37. For example, Delisle de Sales's *Philosophie de la Nature,* written in 1770, used the metaphor repeatedly to warn of the dangers of religious intolerance and overzealousness. Delisle de Sales, *Philosophie,* pp. 2, 36, 57.

38. *Rapport et conclusions de l'accusateur public, près le Tribunal criminel provisoire d'Avignon,* p. 23.

39. Isnard, *Le Gazette Nationale ou le Moniteur Universel,* 6 January 1792.

40. Prudhomme, *Révolutions de Paris,* no. 194 (23–30 March 1793).

41. "Hymne à l'Etre Suprême," in *Rituel Républicain,* pp. 30–31.

42. Louis-Antoine Saint-Just, *Oeuvres Complètes,* ed. Michèle Duval (Paris: G. Lebovici, 1984), pp. 763, 910.

43. Bertrand Barère, *Rapport... sur la reprise de Toulon,* 4 nivôse, Year II (1793), p. 7.

44. Jean-Clément Martin has argued that Terror was never officially made the "order of the day" in his *Violence et Révolution,* pp. 186–193. It is true that, in his discourse in the National Convention on behalf of the Committee of Public Safety on 5 September, Bertrand Barère simply cited the sections' request to make terror the order of the day, without stating, definitively, that it *was.* Yet his words suggested that terror would be made the order of the day by the revolutionary army; moreover, the widespread perception seems to have been that terror was, in fact, "à l'ordre du jour," a point Martin himself notes on page 189. Thus, for example, *Révolutions de Paris* reported, in early November, that "terror is the order of the day: we made it so too late" (no. 213, 7—14 brumaire, Year II [28 October–4 November 1793]), and in his speech of 28 brumaire (18 November 1793), Billaud-Varenne spoke of the circumstance "when the march of the revolution forces the legislator to make terror the order of the day" (*AP,* 79:456). Likewise, in several towns, representatives on mission made terror the "order of the day"; see, for example, Prieur de la Marne, 10e jour du 2e mois an II (31 October 1793), quoted in Pierre Bliard, *Le Conventionnel Prieur de la Marne en mission dans l'ouest (1793–1794)* (Paris: Emile Paul, 1906). Even if Martin is correct that the revolutionary government never definitively put terror on the agenda, the idea that "terror" was deployed as a positive, constructive, revolutionary concept during this period cannot be denied.

45. F. Braesch, ed., *Papiers de Chaumette* (Paris: Société de l'Histoire de la Révolution française, 1908), p. 80.

46. *Feuille du Salut Public,* no. 70 (8 September 1793). See also *AP,* 73:412.

47. Jean-Marie Apostolidès, "Theater and Terror," p. 139; Annie Le Brun, *Perspective dépravée,* esp. p. 30.

48. On sentimentalism, see David Denby, *Sentimental Narrative and Social Order in France, 1760–1820* (Cambridge: Cambridge University Press, 1994); G. J. Barker-Benfield, *The Culture of Sensibility: Sex and Society in Eighteenth Century Britain* (Chicago: University of Chicago Press, 1992); Anne C. Vila, *Enlightenment and Pathology: Sensibility in the Literature and Medicine of Eighteenth-Century France* (Baltimore, Md.: Johns Hopkins University Press, 1998), Anne Vincent-Buffault, *A History of Tears,* trans. Teresa Bridgeman (New York: St. Martin's, 1991).

49. Cf. Ozouf, *Festivals,* p. 9.

50. William Reddy, *The Navigation of Feeling* (Cambridge: Cambridge University Press, 2001), p. 193.

51. Quoted in Andress, *The Terror,* p. 212.

52. Saint-Just, *OC,* p. 527.

53. For more on the passionate army of pikesmen, see also Bell, *The First Total War,* pp. 138–139.

54. Robespierre, *OC,* 10:276.

55. Ibid.

56. Marat, *Recherches,* pp. 451–452.

57. Joseph-Pierre Buch'oz, *Recueil et représentation des phénomènes de la nature et des monuments de l'art, qu'on a remarqué anciennement, et qu'on remarque encore dans differens endroits de la terre* (Paris: Chez l'auteur rue des Grands Augustins, 1794).

58. *Journal de la Montagne,* no. 56 (4 Messidor, Year II [22 June 1794]); *Feuille de la République,* no. 376 (28 Messidor, Year II [16 July 1794]).

59. Saint-Just, *Organt,* in *OC,* p. 199.

60. Jacques Guilhaumou, "La formation d'un mot d'ordre: 'Plaçons la terreur à l'ordre du jour' (13 juillet 1793–5 septembre 1793)"; *Bulletin du Centre d'analyse du discours,* no. 5: "La rhétorique du discours, objet d'histoire (XVIIe–XXe siècles)" (Lille: Presses Universitaires de Lille, 1981), pp. 149–196.

61. George Armstrong Kelly, "Conceptual Sources of the Terror," *Eighteenth-Century Studies* 14.1 (fall 1980): 21.

62. Jaucourt, "Peur, Frayeur, Terreur (*Synon.*)," *Encyclopédie,* 12:480.

63. Robespierre, *OC,* 10:357.

64. Robespierre, *Discours couronné par la Société Royale des arts et des sciences de Metz,* pp. 26–27.

65. *AP,* 74:183, 187 (15 September 1793).

66. This image has alternately been called "Le triomphe de la Montagne" and "Le triomphe de la République." Here I use the title that was given by the département des estampes of the BNF.

67. Tissot, *Les Salpêtriers Républicains,* p. 8.

68. Charles-Louis Lesur, *La veuve du républicain ou le Calomniateur: comédie en trois actes* (Paris: de l'impr. de Crapelet, Chez Maradan, Year II [1793]), p. 50. The play was highly praised, and a petition was sent to the Comité d'Instruction Publique to request that it be presented in "all the theaters of the Republic." *Procès-verbaux du Comité d'Instruction Publique,* Vol. 3 (Paris: de l'impr. Nationale, 1897), p. 134 n. 1.

69. Valcour, *Les Petits Montagnards,* p. 64.

70. Buffon, *Epoques,* p. 145.

71. *AP,* 76:405 (21 vendémiaire [12 October 1793]).

72. Quoted in Jacques Guilhaumou, *"La terreur à l'ordre du jour: un parcours en révolution (1793–1794),"* *Révolution Française.net, Mots* (6 January 2007), revolution-francaise. net/2007/01/06/94-la-terreur-a-lordre-du-jour-un-parcours-en-revolution-juillet-1793-mars-1794.

73. "Adresse du conseil général du Département des Alpes-Maritimes," *AP,* 76:80 (5 October 1793).

74. *AP,* 76:85 (5 October 5 1793); *AP,* 76:97 (5 October 1793); *AP,* 74:185 (15 September 1793). See also the account of the festival of 10 August in Ernée, which noted that "the Mountain has vomited all that was impure from its depths." *AP,* 74:189 (15 September 1793).

75. Aulard, *Recueil des actes du comité de salut public,* Vol. 11 (9 February 1794–15 March 1794), pp. 252–253.

76. Maréchal, *Le Jugement dernier des rois,* p. 1.

77. Ibid., p. vi.

78. *Le Journal des Spectacles,* no. 112 (22 October 1793).

79. Quoted in ibid.

80. Maréchal, *Le Jugement dernier des rois,* pp. 26–27.

81. Ibid., p. 3.

82. Apostolidès, "Terror and Theater," pp. 138–140.

83. Maréchal, *Le Jugement dernier des rois,* p. 13.

84. For more on the justifications of the humanity of the guillotine, see Arasse, *The Guillotine and the Terror.*

85. de Baecque, *Glory and Terror,* p. 91.

86. Dan Edelstein, "War and Terror: The Law of Nations from Grotius to the French Revolution," *French Historical Studies* 31.2 (spring 2008): 229–262.

87. Maréchal, *Le Jugement dernier des rois,* pp. 24–25. The kings' "impotent rage" contrasts with the *productive* anger of the *sans-culottes,* as well as with the hatred aroused by the play itself, which was seen as a service to the Republic.

88. Citoyen Desbarreaux, *Les Potentats foudroyés par la Montagne et la Raison, ou La Déportation des rois de l'Europe, pièce prophétique et révolutionnaire* (Toulouse: Chez le Citoyen P. Frances, Year II [1793]), p. 30.

89. Citoyen Gamas, *Les Émigrés aux terres australes, ou le dernier chapitre d'une grande révolution, comédie en un acte et en prose* (Paris: de l'impr. de Cordier, 1794). The show premiered on 16 July 1792, according to Henri Quentin in *Le Théâtre sous la Terreur (Théâtre de la peur), 1793–1794* (Paris: Emile Paul Frères, 1913), p. 217.

90. Gamas, *Émigrés*, p. 5.

91. Maréchal, *Le Jugement dernier des rois*, p. 3.

92. While *Le Journal des Spectacles* allows for the possibility of escape, saying "the savages [les *sauvages*] also leave *la place;* the kings remain alone," Maréchal's text certainly did not provide dialogue or stage directions that would indicate that they were no longer on the island. No other account of the play suggested likewise, and even the *Journal des Spectacles* leaves ambiguity as to whether the islanders left *the island,* or simply left the stage. See *Le Journal des Spectacles,* no. 103 (11 October 1793). One key difference between Maréchal's play and Desbarreaux's is that the "savages" and *sans-culottes* in the *Potentats foudroyés* explicitly— and dubiously—escape the volcanic eruption by climbing to the top of a hill where the lava cannot reach them.

93. Desbarreaux, *Potentats foudroyés*, p. 16.

94. I have found only four uses of the volcano in his public discourses: during the king's trial; in an article in his journal, *La Défenseur de la Constitution;* in a speech of 7 Prairial, and on 8 Thermidor. The two earlier uses operate in a way that was akin to the pre-Terror discourse about volcanoes, used primarily to urge watchfulness. See Robespierre, Speech of 3 December 1792, in Walzer, *Regicide and Revolution*, p. 132. On 7 Prairial he used the image in an ambiguous way, suggesting that the Convention sat atop a dangerous volcano, but also insinuating that they had managed to harness the powers of nature: "It will be a lovely subject of discussion for posterity; it is already a spectacle worthy of heaven and earth to see the assembly of representatives of the French people, placed atop an inextinguishable volcano of conspiracies, with one hand bringing the respects of a great people to the feet of the eternal author of all things and, with the other, throwing thunderbolts at the tyrants conspiring against him; [to see them] founding the first republic in the world, and returning liberty, justice, and exiled nature to humanity" (*OC*, 10:473).

95. Robespierre, *OC,* 10:560–561.

96. I have identified a small number of outliers to this chronology. The first two were prior to the period of the Terror, and both referred to the possibilities of universal revolution; the first was Brissot's speech on war in February 1792, when he asked, "What mortal has been given the power to read the future and to determine for the revolution the time and country where it should stop?" He continued: "Volcanoes are ready everywhere; once again, we need only a spark for a universal explosion." And yet Brissot immediately recognized the volatility of this metaphor by adding, "It is not patriotism that should fear the consequences, it only threatens thrones." Brissot's revolutionary volcano could, miraculously, be directed only at royalty and oppressive governments. Quoted in Brissot, *Le Patriote François,* no. 906 (2 February 1792), p. 3. At the Jacobin Society on 26 November 1792 Édouard Jean-Baptiste Milhaud, a deputy from Cantal, speaking in favor of integrating Savoy into France (and perhaps eventually creating a "universal republic"), said, "If only it were true that the reveille of the people had sounded; if only it were true that the overthrow of all thrones should be the immediate consequence of the success of our armies and of the revolutionary volcano." Although he did not appeal to the purgative or regenerative powers of the revolutionary volcano, he certainly used the term as a positive metaphor. Aulard, *Société des Jacobins,* 4:525. The third was in a song written for a "festival for victories," which makes it difficult to date; the festival probably took place either in the winter of 1793 (10 Nivôse, Year II [30 December 1793]), which would place it within the time line suggested here, or on 30

Vendémiaire, Year III (21 October 1794), on the same date as Chénier's Fête des Victoires, which would place it slightly outside this chronology. See Charles-Francois-Gregoire-Michel-Etienne Desgrouas, "Chanson pour la fête des victoires," (Mortagne: de l'impr. de Marre, n.d.), pp. 2–3: "Bring, to all kings, / The inevitable catastrophe…/ Driven by this boiling ardor, / That directs your vengeful arms,…/ May Spain, who abhors us / Succumb under your volcano; / Purge the earth of aristocracy, / Everywhere you go."

97. *Mercure Universel,* 26 and 27 Messidor, Year II (14 and 15 July 1794).

98. *Feuille de la République,* 29 Messidor, Year II (17 July 1794).

99. Barère, *Rapport…sur salpêtre,* 17 Messidor, p. 18.

100. Dominique Joseph Garat, *Mémoires sur la Révolution, ou Exposé de ma conduite dans les Affaires et dans les fonctions publiques* (Paris: de l'impr. de J. J. Smits, Year III [1795]), p. 72.

101. Aulard, *Paris pendant la réaction thermidorienne et sous le Directoire,* Vol. 1 (Paris: L. Cerf, 1898), p. 245 (citing from *Le Messager du soir,* 26 brumaire, Year III [16 November 1794]).

102. Quoted in Aulard, *Paris pendant,* 1:637 (citing from *Le Messager du soir,* 16 germinal, Year III [5 April 1795]).

103. P. T., *Les synonymes jacobites: du pain.[=] Insurrection. Constitution de 1793. [=]Prétexte. Jacobins.[=] Massacre de la Convention. Succès. [=] Pillage, Anarchie, Horreurs* ([Paris]: de l'impr. des Femmes, n.d.). The text is dated 1793 in the BNF catalog, but it refers to both Thermidor and to the fall of Carrier, so I presume it is from 1795. "Volcaniser" as a revolutionary neologism is noted in Nannoni, "Le peuple-volcan," p. 45.

104. *Discours prononcé par le Président de l'Administration centrale du Département de l'Orne, à la Fête du 2 pluviôse, l'an sept de la République Française* (Alençon: Malassis, Year VII [1799]), p. 6.

105. *OC,* 10:567.

106. Emmanuel de las Cases, *Le Mémorial de Sainte Hélène* (Paris: Gallimard, 1956–57), p. 39.

Conclusion

1. *Réimpression De l'Ancien Moniteur,* Vol. 21 (Paris: au Bureau central, 1841), p. 759. 30 fructidor, Year II (16 September 1794).

2. Mountain dismantlement cited in Leith, *Space and Revolution,* p. 262; end of saltpeter program on 4 March 1795 noted in Multhauf, "The French Crash Program for Saltpeter Production," p. 175.

3. Lynn, *Popular Science,* p. 2.

4. Jean-François Féraud, "Métaphore," *Dictionnaire critique de la langue française* (Marseille: Mossy, 1787–88). Ironically he made this assertion to argue *against* many metaphors drawing on the sciences, as he believed that the analogies would not be comprehensible to the average man. The revolutionary generation clearly disagreed.

5. The development of a natural "particular providence" suggests that, in making use of new notions about the natural world inherited from a century of naturalized study, and in manipulating the authority and order of the natural world that had been produced by natural histories, revolutionaries also reshaped understandings of the natural world. In the wake of Thermidor, as noted in chapter 5, the volcano's purgative and constructive connotations were diminished; Maiken Umbach suggests that Goethe abandoned vulcanism as a result of the fiery destruction of the French Revolution (Umbach, "Visual Culture," p. 129). The geologist Cuvier's catastrophism, in which he envisioned the world as having endured many destructions only to start again, may well have been informed by his experiences in the Revolution. Roy Porter has demonstrated that, in the wake of the Revolution, the British naturalist G. H. Toulmin—who had previously held that destruction was a necessary part of terrestrial change—abandoned his geological pursuits in favor of prose and theology

(Porter, "Philosophy and Politics of a Geologist: G. H. Toulmin (1754–1817)," *Journal of the History of Ideas* 39.3 (1978): 435–450).

6. Robespierre, *OC,* 10:357.

7. Edelstein, *Terror of Natural Right,* p. 220.

8. Ibid., p. 11.

9. Bell, *The First Total War.*

10. See Mona Ozouf, "The Terror after the Terror: An Immediate History" in Baker, *The French Revolution and the Creation of Modern Political Culture,* Vol. 4, *The Terror,* pp. 3–18, in which she traces the roots of this debate to the Thermidorean period.

11. Sergio Cotta, *Why Violence? A Philosophical Interpretation,* trans. Giovanni Gullace (Gainesville: University Press of Florida, 1985); Howard G. Brown, *Ending the French Revolution: Violence, Justice, and Repression from the Terror to Napoleon* (Charlottesville: University of Virginia Press, 2007). See also Brown's lucid article "Domestic State Violence: Repression from the Croquants to the Commune," *Historical Journal* 42.3 (1999): 597–622, which applies Cotta's theories to various French cases.

12. Brown, *Ending the French Revolution,* p. 50.

13. See also Anton Blok, who suggests that even "senseless" violence is not entirely irrational. Blok, "The Enigma of Senseless Violence," in *Meanings of Violence: A Cross-Cultural Perspective,* ed. Göran Aijmer and Jon Abbink (Oxford: Berg, 2000), pp. 23–38.

14. Brian Singer, "Violence in the French Revolution: Forms of Ingestion/Forms of Expulsion," in *The French Revolution and the Birth of Modernity,* ed. Ferenc Féher (Berkeley: University of California Press, 1990), pp. 150–168.

15. Arendt, *On Violence,* p. 75.

16. *Le docteur Pangloss et le docteur Martin, ou tout est au mieux dans le meilleur royaume du meilleur des mondes possibles* ("Constantinople": n.p., 1790), p. 9.

17. Louis-Marie Prudhomme, *Histoire générale et impartiale des erreurs, des fautes, et des crimes commis pendant la Révolution française,* Vol. 1 (Paris: rue des Marais, Year V [1797]), p. ii.

BIBLIOGRAPHY

Archival Sources

Archives Nationales, Paris:

AF II/57
AF II/66
AF II/67
AJ 15/509
BB 16/85
D XXIV/3
D XXXVIII/2
D XXXVIII/3
D XXXVIII/5
F 15/3293
H 1414
W 112
W 174

Newspapers

L'Année Littéraire
Feuille de la République
Feuille du Salut Public
Gazette de France
Journal de la Montagne
Journal de Paris
Journal des Spectacles
Journal des Savants
Mercure Universel
Le Moniteur, ou la Gazette Universel
Le Patriote François
Réimpression de l'Ancien Moniteur
Révolutions de Paris

Primary Sources

Archives parlementaires: de 1787 à 1860, recueil complet des débats législatifs et politiques des Chambres françaises. Ed. Jérome Mavidal and Émile Laurent; continué par l'Institut d'histoire de la Révolution française, Université de Paris I. Paris: Librairie admin- istrative P. Dupont, puis Éditions du Centre national de la recherche scientifique, 1867–1972.

Aulard, François-Alphonse, ed. *Recueil des actes du Comité de salut public avec la correspon- dance officielle des représentants en mission et le registre du Conseil exécutif provisoire.* 19 vols. Paris: de l'impr. Nationale, 1889–1910.

———. *La Société des Jacobins: Recueil de documents pour l'histoire du Club des Jacobins de Paris.* 6 vols. Paris: Maison Quantin, 1889–97.

Avril, Jean-Baptiste. *Arrêté, portant que le Conseil général de la Commune accompagnera les Élèves de la République, pour la fabrication des Poudres et de Salpêtres et la fonte des Canons, qui doivent porter Décadi prochain, leurs premiers travails à la Convention nationale.* N.p., 1794.

Azéma, Michel. *Rapport et décret présenté au nom du comité de législation, par Michel Azéma, député du Département de l'Aude, sur le sort des prisonniers élargis, à la suite des événements des premiers jours de septembre dernier.* Paris: de l'impr. Nationale, 1792.

Baert-Duholant, Charles-Alexandre-Balthazar-François de Paule, Bon de. *A mes collègues, sur la prétendue amnisitie en faveur de Jourdan et ses complices.* Paris: de l'impr. du Pont, 1792.

Baillie, John. *An Essay on the Sublime.* London: Printed for R. Dodsley, 1747.

Barère, Bertrand. *Convention Nationale: Rapport du Citoyen Barère, sur la reprise de Toulon par l'armée de la République.* Paris: de l'impr. Nationale, Year II [1793].

———. *Convention Nationale: Rapport fait au nom du Comité du salut public, sur l'état de la fabrication révolutionnaire du salpêtre et de la poudre, et sur la nécessité de supprimer l'agence nationale, ci-devant Régie des poudres et salpêtres; par Barère, Séance du 17 messidor, l'an deuxième de la République française, une et indivisible.* Paris: de l'impr. Nationale, Year II [1794].

———. *Rapport sur les crimes de l'Angleterre envers le Peuple Français, et sur ses attentats contre la liberté des nations, fait au nom du Comité de Salut Public.* Paris: de l'impr. Nationale, Year II [1794].

Barthélemy, Jean-Jacques. *Voyages du jeune Anacharsis.* Paris: de Bure, 1788.

Basire, Claude. *Discours de Claude Basire, vice-président du comité de surveillance à la Convention Nationale, sur l'état actuel de notre situation politique, au centre des affaires. Lue à la Société le 4 novembre 1792.* Paris: de l'impr. de L. Potier de Lille, 1792.

Beffroy, Louis-Etienne. *Avantages du desséchement des marais, et manière de profiter des terreins desséchés.* Paris: Chez Froullé, 1793.

Bernardin de Saint Pierre, Jacques-Henri. *Etudes de la nature.* 3 vols. Paris: de l'impr. de Monsieur, chez Pierre-François Didot, 1784.

———. *Paul et Virginie.* Paris: de l'impr. de Monsieur, 1789.

Bertand, Elie. *Mémoires historiques et physiques sur les tremblemens de terre.* The Hague: Chez Pierre Gosse junior, 1757.

Beuzelin, Citoyen. *Discours prononcé par le citoyen Beuzelin, agent national de la commune de Caen, le décadi 20 prairial, l'an 2 de la République française, une & indivisible, pour la fête de l'Eternel.* Caen, [1794].

Billaud-Varenne, Jacques-Nicolas. *Décret du 14 frimaire précédé du Rapport fait au nom du Comité de Salut Public, sur un mode de Gouvernement provisoire et révolutionnaire.* Paris: de l'impr. des Régies Nationales, Year II [1793].

Biot, Jean-Baptiste. *Essai sur l'histoire générale des sciences pendant la Révolution Française.* Paris: Chez Duprat, Chez Fuchs, 1803.

Boisdesir, L. S. *Dénonciation à tous les françois, à tous les amis de l'humanité, du massacre commis à Avignon les 16,17, et 18 octobre 1791.* [Paris]: de l'impr. du Journal général de politique, etc., 1791.

Bonnet, Charles. *Contemplation de la Nature.* In *Oeuvres.* Vol. 4. Neuchâtel: S. Fauche, 1781 [1764].

———. *La palingénésie philosophique, ou Idées sur l'état passé et sur l'état futur des êtres vivants.* Geneva: C. Philibert and B. Chirol, 1769.

Boudet, Jean-Pierre. *Circulaire de J.-P. Boudet, inspecteur des poudres et salpêtres, nommé par le Comité de salut public.* N.p., Year II (1793/94).

Boudin, Jacques-Antoine. *Convention Nationale: Du desséchement des marais et terreins submergés.* Paris: de l'impr. Nationale, n.d.

Bouquier, Gabriel. *La Réunion du dix août ou L'inauguration de la république française; sanculotide dramatique; en cinq actes et en vers, mêlés de déclamations, chants, danses, et évolutions militaires au peuple souverain.* Paris: de l'impr. du journal des hommes libres, chez R. Vatar et ass., Year II (1793/94).

Bourdon, Léonard. *Recueil des actions héroiques et civiques des républicains français*, no. 3. Paris: de l'impr. Nationale, Year II (1793/94).

Braesch, Fritz, ed. *Papiers de Chaumette.* Paris: Société de l'Histoire de la Révolution française, 1908.

Briois, Citoyen. *La Mort du jeune Barra, ou une Journée de la Vendée, Drame historique en un acte.* Paris: Chez Barba, Year II (1794)].

Brissot, Jacques-Pierre. *A tous les républicains de France; sur la société des Jacobins de Paris.* Paris: chez les directeurs de l'impr. du Cercle Social, 1792.

Brosselard, Emmanuel. "Stances pour l'anniversaire de la prise de la Bastille." In *Recueil de pièces intéressantes sur la Bastille.* [Paris]: de l'impr. de J. B. Hérault, 1790.

Brydone, Patrick. *A Tour through Sicily and Malta, in a Series of Letters to William Beckford, Esq.* London, 1773.

Buch'oz, Joseph-Pierre. *Recueil et représentation des phénomènes de la nature et des monuments de l'art, qu'on a remarqué anciennement, et qu'on remarque encore dans differens endroits de la terre.* Paris: Chez l'auteur, rue des Grands Augustins, 1794.

Buffon, Georges-Louis Leclerc, Comte de. *Des Époques de la Nature.* Paris: de l'impr. Royale, 1778.

———. *Histoire naturelle, générale et particulière avec la description du Cabinet du Roy.* 15 vols. Paris: de l'impr. Royale, 1749–1767.

Buffon, Henri Nadault de, ed. *Correspondance inédite de Buffon, à laquelle ont été réunies toutes les lettres publiées jusqu'à ce jour.* 2 vols. Paris: Hachette, 1860.

Burke, Edmund. *A Philosophical Enquiry into the Origin of Our Ideas of the Sublime and the Beautiful.* London: R. and J. Dodsley, 1757.

Le Chansonnier de la Montagne ou recueil de chansons, vaudevilles, pots-pourris et hymnes patriotiques par différents auteurs. Paris: Chez Favre, Year II (1793/1794).

Chaussard, Pierre-Jean-Baptiste. *Eloge funèbre de nos frères d'armes, morts à la glorieuse journée du 10 août.* Paris: de l'impr. de Martin, 1792.

Chénier, Marie-Joseph. *Eloge funèbre des citoyens morts pour la défense de la liberté et de l'égalité...prononcé le 26 du même mois [août] en présence de l'Assemblée nationale...par M. Chenier.* Paris: de l'impr. Nationale, n.d. [1792].

———. "Hymne à l'Etre Suprême." In *Rituel Républicain: Fête à l'Être-Suprême, Exécutée à Paris, le 20 Prairial, l'an 2e de la République. Avec la musique des Hymnes.* Paris: Chez Aubry, Libraire, rue Baillet, Year II [1794].

Cizos-Duplessis, François. *Les Peuples et les Rois, ou le tribunal de la Raison: Allégorie Dramatique en cinq actes et en prose.* Paris: Chez Barba, Year II (1794).

Collection des meilleures prières, hymnes et hommage à l'Eternel, suivie d'un détail sur les cérémonies de la fête à l'Etre Suprême et autres fêtes décadaires. Utile aux écoles primaires. Présentée à la Convention Nationale. Paris: Chez Prévost, Year II (1794).

Collot d'Herbois, Jean-Marie. *Au nom du peuple français: proclamation des représentans du peuple, envoyés dans la Commune-Affranchie, pour y assurer le bonheur du peuple avec le triomphe de la République, dans tous les Départemens environnans, et près l'Armée des Alpes.* Commune-Affranchie: de l'impr. Républicaine, 15 Frimaire, Year II [1793].

———. *Convention Nationale: Rapport fait au nom du Comité de Salut Public, sur la situation de Commune-Affranchie, 1 Nivôse.* Paris: de l'impr. Nationale, Year II [1793].

Les commissaires nommés par l'académie par le jugement du Prix du salpêtre. *Recueil des memoires et d'observations sur la formation et la fabrication du salpêtre.* Paris: Chez Lacombe; de l'impr. de Demonville, 1776.

Commission d'Instruction Publique. *Fêtes à l'Etre Suprême: Pièces Dramatiques, Rapport et Arrêté.* Paris: de l'impr. de la Commission d'Instruction Publique, Year II [1794].

Condorcet, Marie-Jean-Antoine-Nicolas de Caritat, marquis de. *Eloge de M. le comte de Buffon.* Paris: Buisson, 1790.

———. *Oeuvres de Condorcet.* Paris: Firmin Didot frères, impr. de l'Institut, 1847.

Conseil d'Etat du Roi. *Arrêt du conseil d'état du roi, portant création d'une loterie de Douze millions, en faveur des provinces ravagées par la grêle, du 26 juillet 1788.* Lille: de l'impr. de C. M. Peterinck-Cramé, 1788.

Cousin Jacques. *Supplément nécessaire au précis exact de la prise de la Bastille.* N.p., 1789.

David, P. *La Prise de la Bastille, ou la Liberté Conquise, pièce nationale, en quatre actes, en prose.* N.p., 1790.

Décalogue Républicain. Puy: de l'impr. de P. B. F. Clet [1793].

Delisle de Sales, Jean-Baptiste Claude. *De la Philosophie de la Nature.* Amsterdam: Arkstee et Merkus, 1770.

Le désastre de Messine, ou Les Volcans, ode philosophique. Paris: Chez les Marchands de Nouveautés, de l'impr. de Pruault, 1783.

Desbarreaux, Citoyen. *Les Potentats foudroyés par la Montagne et la Raison, ou La Déportation des rois de l'Europe, pièce prophétique et révolutionnaire.* Toulouse: Chez le Citoyen P. Francès, Year II (1793).

Description historique et géographique de la ville de Messine, etc. etc., et détails historiques et météorologiques du désastre que cette ville vient d'éprouver (le 5 février 1783) par le tremblement de terre. Paris: Desnos, 1783.

Desgrouas, Charles-Francois-Gregoire-Michel-Etienne. "Chanson pour la fête des victoires." Mortagne: de l'impr. de Marre, n.d.

Desmarest, Nicolas. *Conjectures physico-méchaniques sur la propagation des secousses dans les tremblements de terre, et sur la disposition des lieux qui en ont ressenti les effets.* N.p., 1756.

Détail de la fête de l'Unité et de l'Indivisibilité de la République qui a eu lieu le 10 août. Paris: de l'impr. de Chaudrillié, n.d.

Diderot, Denis. *Diderot on Art II: The Salon of 1767.* Trans. John Goodman. New Haven, Conn.: Yale University Press, 1995.

Diderot, Denis, and Jean Le Rond d'Alembert, eds. *Encyclopédie, ou dictionnaire raisonné des sciences, des arts et des métiers.* 35 vols. (1751–). University of Chicago: ARTFL Encyclopédie Project (winter 2008 ed.), ed. Robert Morrissey. Available at http://encyclo pedie.uchicago.edu/.

Discours prononcé par le Président de l'Administration centrale du Département de l'Orne, à la Fête du 2 pluviôse, l'an sept de la République Française. Alençon: Malassis, Year VII [1799].

Le Docteur Pangloss et le docteur Martin, ou tout est au mieux dans le meilleur royaume du meilleur des mondes possibles. "Constantinople": n.p., 1790.

Dolomieu, Déodat Gratet de. *Mémoire sur les îles Ponces et catalogue raisonné des produits de l'Etna, pour servir à l'histoire des volcans, suivis de la description de l'éruption de l'Etna, du mois de Juillet 1787.* Paris: Chez Cuchet, 1788.

———. *Mémoire sur les tremblemens de terre de la Calabre pendant l'année 1783.* Rome: A. Fulgoni, 1784.

———. *Voyage aux îles de Lipari fait en 1781, ou Notices sur les îles Aeoliennes pour servir à l'histoire des volcans.* Paris: de l'impr. de J.-M. Boursy, 1783.

Duchosal, [Marie-Emile-Guillaume]. *Discours sur la nécessité de dessécher les marais, de supprimer les étangs, et de replanter les forêts; prononcé le 12 mai, dans la société patriotique de la section de la Bibliothèque.* Paris: de l'impr. de L. Potier de Lille, 1791.

Ducray-Duminil, François-Guillaume. *La Semaine memorable ou Récit exact de ce qui s'est passé à Paris depuis le 12 jusqu'au 17 juillet.* N.p., n.d. [1789].

Dufourny, Louis-Pierre. *Département de Paris: Salpêtres, Adresse aux citoyens pour l'extraction de tout le salpêtre.* Paris: de l'impr. de Ballard, n.d. [1793].

Dusaulx, Jean. *De l'Insurrection parisienne et de la prise de la Bastille; Discours historique, prononcé par extrait dans l'assemblée nationale, par M. Dusaulx.* Paris: Chez Debure l'ainé, 1790.

Epitre d'un prisonnier délivré de la Bastille. N.p., 1789.

Eschassériaux, Joseph. *Rapport et projet de décret, sur les dessèchemens des marais.* Paris: de l'impr. Nationale, n.d. [1794].

Fauchet, l'Abbé Claude. *Discours sur la liberté française, prononcé le mercredi 5 août 1789, dans l'église paroissiale de St-Jacques et des Ss Innocens, durant une solemnité consacrée à la mémoire des citoyens qui sont morts à la prise de la Bastille, pour la défense de la Patrie.* Paris: Chez Bailly, de Senne, Lottin, Cussac, etc., 1789.

Féraud, Jean-François. *Dictionnaire critique de la langue française.* Marseille: Mossy, 1787–88.

Fouché, Joseph. *Ecrits révolutionnaires.* Paris: Paris-Zanzibar, 1998.

La Foudre n'est pas toujours dans les mains de Jupiter. N.p., n.d. [1789].

Furetière, Antoine. *Le Dictionnaire Universel d'Antoine Furetière.* Paris: Le Robert, 1978 [1690].

Gamas, Citoyen. *Les Emigrés aux terres australes, ou le dernier chapitre d'une grande révolution, comédie en un acte et en prose.* Paris: de l'impr. de Cordier, 1794.

Garat, Dominique Joseph. *Mémoires sur la Révolution, ou Exposé de ma conduite dans les Affaires et dans les fonctions publiques.* Paris: de l'impr. de J. J. Smits, Year III [1795].

Gay, J. B. *Recueil de chansons patriotiques.* Strasbourg: J. B. Gay, Year II.

Gerard, Alexander. *An Essay on Taste, with three dissertations on the same subject, by M. de Voltaire, Mr. d'Alembert, F. R. S., Mr. de Montesquieu.* London: A. Millar, 1759.

Goudar, Ange. *Discours politique sur les avantages que les Portugais pourroient retirer de leur malheur.* Lisbon: Chez Philanthrope, 1756.

Guillaume, James, ed. *Procès-verbaux du Comité d'instruction publique de la Convention nationale.* Vol. 4 (1 Germinal—11 Fructidor, Year II [21 March-28 August 1794]). Paris: de l'impr. Nationale, 1901.

Hamilton, William. "An Account of the Earthquakes Which Happened in Italy, from February to May 1783. By Sir William Hamilton, Knight of the Bath, F. R. S.; in a Letter to Sir Joseph Banks, Bart. P. R. S." *Philosophical Transactions of the Royal Society of London* 73 (1783): 169–208.

——. *Détails historiques des tremblements de terre arrivés en Italie depuis le 5 février jusqu'en mai 1783.* Trans. Jean-Baptiste Lefebvre de Villebrune. Paris: T. Barrois, 1783.

——. *Observations on Mount Vesuvius, Mount Etna, and other volcanos: in a series of letters, addressed to the Royal Society, from the Honourable Sir W. Hamilton.* London: T. Cadell, 1772.

Hérault de Sechelles, Marie-Jean. *Recueil des six discours prononcés par le président de la Convention Nationale, le 10 août l'an 2me de la République aux six stations de la fête de l'unité et de l'indivisibilité de la République.* Paris: de l'impr. de Chaudrillié, n.d. [1793].

———. *Voyage à Montbard, contenant des détails très-intéressans sur le caractère de la personne et les écrits de Buffon.* Paris: Chez Terrelonge et Chez Solvet, Year IX (1800/01) [1785].

d'Holbach, Paul-Henri Thiry, Baron. *Système de la Nature, ou, Des loix du monde physique & du monde moral.* London, 1771.

Humbert, Jean-Baptiste. *Journée de Jean-Baptiste Humbert, Horloger, qui, le premier, a monté sur les Tours de la Bastille.* Paris: Chez Volland, 1789.

Hymnes adoptés par la Section du Panthéon Français, pour être chantées au Temple de la Raison. Paris: de l'impr. de Lion et Compagnie, n.d. [Year II (1793/4)].

Instruction pour tous les citoyens qui voudront exploiter eux-mêmes du salpêtre, envoyée dans toutes les municipalités par le comité de salut public de la Convention nationale, conformément au décret du 14 frimaire de l'an 2e de la République. Paris: de l'impr. Nationale, Year II (1793/94).

Isnard (de Grasse). *Mémoire sur les tremblemens de terre, qui a remporté le prix de physique au jugement de l'Académie des sciences, belles-lettres et arts de Rouen, le 3 août 1757.* Paris: Veuve David Jeune, 1758.

La Juste vengeance du peuple. Paris: de l'impr. de Tremblay, [1792].

Kruger, Johann Gottlob. *Histoire des anciennes révolutions du globe terrestre, avec une relation chronologique et historique des tremblemens de terre, arrivés sur notre globe depuis le commencement de l'ère chrétienne jusqu'à présent.* Trans. F. A. Deslandes. Amsterdam, et se vend à Paris chez Damonneville, 1752.

[Lacépède, Bernard Etienne de]. *L'Achille Français, Le Héros de la Bastille, ou le Brave Élie recompensé.* [Paris]: de l'impr. de Momors, 1789.

Lacépède, Bernard Germain Etienne de. *Discours de clôture du cours d'histoire naturelle de l'an VIII, sur les avantages que les naturalistes peuvent procurer au corps social, dans l'état actuel de la civilisation et des connoissances humaines.* Paris: de l'impr. de Plassan, Year VIII (1799/1800).

———. *Vues sur l'enseignement public.* Paris: Chez Desenne, 1790.

Lanteires, Jean. *Essai sur le tonnerre considéré dans ses effets moraux sur les hommes; et sur un coup de foudre remarquable.* Lausanne: Chez J. P. Heubach, Durand et Comp., 1789.

Las Cases, Emmanuel-Auguste-Dieudonné, Comte de. *Le Mémorial de Sainte Hélène.* Ed. G. Walter. Paris: Gallimard, 1956–57.

Les Lauriers du Fauxbourg Saint-Antoine, ou le Prix de la Bastille Renversé. Paris: Gueffier jeune, 1789.

Le Brun, Ponce Denis Échouchard. *Oeuvres choisies de Lebrun: précédées d'une notice sur sa vie et ses ouvrages.* Ed. Jean-Baptiste-Denis Desprès. Paris: Janet et Cotelle, 1829.

———. *Oeuvres de Ponce-Denis-Ecouchard Lebrun.* Ed. P-L Guinguené. Vol. 1. Paris: G. Warée, 1811.

Legier, [Etienne]. *Observations sur le projet de dessécher les marais d'Arles et de Fontvielle.* Aix: de l'impr. de la Veuve d'André Adibert, 1792.

Legrand d'Aussy, Pierre-Jean-Baptiste. *Voyage d'Auvergne.* Paris: E. Onfroy, 1788.

Lesur, Charles-Louis. *La Veuve du républicain ou le Calomniateur: comédie en trois actes.* Paris: de l'impr. de Crapelet, Chez Maradan, Year II [1793].

*Lettre de M. à Mme la Maréchale de ***, sur le désastre de Messine et de la Calabre, 9 mai 1783.* N.p., [1783].

Locke, John. *An Essay concerning Human Understanding.* 9th ed. London, 1726.

La Lyre de la Raison, ou Hymnes, cantiques, odes et stances à l'Etre Suprême pour la célébration des fêtes décadaires. Paris: Chez Dufart, Year II [1794].

Maistre, Joseph de. *Considerations on France.* Trans. Richard Lebrun. Cambridge: Cambridge University Press, 1994.

Mandement de Monseigneur l'Archevêque de Paris, pour le saint tems de Carême, qui permet l'usage des Oeufs depuis le Mercredi des cendres inclusivement, jusqu'au Dimanche des rameaux exclusivement. Paris: Chez Cl. Simon, de l'impr. de Monseigneur l'Archevêque, 1789.

Manuel, B. E. *L'Etude de la nature en général et de l'homme en particulier considérée dans ses rapports avec l'instruction publique.* Paris: Chez les directeurs du Cercle Social, 1793.

Marat, Jean-Paul. *Mémoire sur l'électricité médicale, couronné le 6 août 1783, par l'Académie Royale des Sciences, Belles-Lettres et Arts de Rouen.* Paris: de l'impr. de L. Jorry; Chez N-T. Méquignon, 1783.

——. *Oeuvres Politiques.* Ed. Jacques de Cock and Charlotte Goëtz. Vol. 8. Brussels: Pole Nord, 1995.

——. *Recherches physiques sur l'électricité.* Paris: de l'Impr. de Clousier; Chez Nyon l'Aîné, Nyon le cadet, et Belin, et au Bureau du Journal de la Physique, 1782.

Maréchal, Pierre-Sylvain. *Antiquités d'Herculanum avec leurs explications en françois.* Paris: Chez David, graveur, 1780.

——. *Le Jugement dernier des rois, prophétie en un acte, en prose.* Paris: de l'impr. de C-F. Patris, Year II [1793].

[Maréchal, Sylvain]. *Décades des Cultivateurs, contentant Précis historique des événemens révolutionnaires de l'an II de la Révolution; cours de morale naturelle et républicaine; l'Agriculture pratique, tant de jardins potagers et à fruits, que de la campagne en général, avec les planches nécessaires à l'intelligence de l'agriculture.* Vols. 1 and 2. Paris: Chez Duffart; Chez Basset, Langlois, Caillot, et Louis, Year III (1794/95).

Mercier, Louis-Sebastien. *Le Nouveau Paris.* Ed. Jean-Claude Bonnet. Paris: Mercure de France, 1995.

——. *Tableau de Paris.* Ed. Jean-Claude Bonnet. Vol. I. Paris: Mercure de France, 1994.

——. *Tableau de Paris.* Vol. 1. Amsterdam, 1782.

——. *Tableau de Paris.* Vol. 5. Amsterdam, 1783.

Millin, Aubin-Louis. *Elémens d'histoire naturelle.* 3rd ed. Paris: Léger, 1802.

Nouveaux détails historiques et météorologiques du tremblement de terre de Messine et la Calabre ultérieure, etc., arrivé le 5 février 1783: avec une idée générale de cette ville, de son administration, des curiosités qui s'y trouvent, du commerce et des moeurs de ses habitants, etc, auxquels on a joint quelques observations nouvelles sur les causes et les effets de ces désastres, etc. Paris: Chez Cailleau, rue Galande, 1783.

Les Nouvelles Philippiques, ou Le Te Deum des Français, après la destruction de la Bastille. Paris: dans un coin de la Bastille, et aux dépens des Proscrits, L'an de la régéneration du Royaume, 1789.

Observations patriotiques sur la prise de la Bastille, du 14 juillet 1789, et sur les suites de cet évenement. Paris: Chez Debray, 1789.

Ordre et marche de la fête de l'Unité et de l'Indivisibilité de la République. Paris: de l'impr. de Chaudrillié, n.d. [1793].

Ordre et marche de la fête à l'Etre Suprême, qui aura lieu le décadi prochain, 20 prairial, conformément au décret de la Convention nationale. N.p., n.d.[1794].

P. T. *Les Synonymes jacobites: du pain.[=] Insurrection. Constitution de 1793. [=]Prétexte. Jacobins. [=] Massacre de la Convention. Succès. [=] Pillage, Anarchie, Horreurs.* [Paris]: de l'impr. des Femmes, [1795].

Passot, Aristide. *Discours prononcé dans le Temple de la Raison et à la Société des Sans-culottes de Nevers, le 1er décadi de Nivôse, à la fête civique donnée au sujet de la réduction de Toulon, livré par les traitres de cette cité, aux tyrans de l'Europe coalisés contre la République Française.* Nevers: de l'impr. de Lefebvre, le jeune, Year II (1794).

Paulian, Père Aimé-Henri. *Dictionnaire de physique, dédié à Monseigneur le Duc de Berry.* Avignon: Chez Louis Chambeau, 1761.

Pithou de Loinville, Jean-Joseph, and Jacques-Louis David. *Description générale de la première fête républicaine de la réunion, cette fête a été célébrée en mémoire de la fameuse journée qui s'est passée au Tuileries, le 10 août 1792, et à l'occasion de l'acceptation de la constitution par le souverain.* Paris: n.p., n.d. [1793].

Pluche, Noel Antoine. *Spectacle de la Nature; or, Nature Display'd.* Trans. Samuel Humphreys. 2nd ed. London, 1737.

Précis historique de la ville de Messine, de ses moeurs, de son commerce, et de ce qui s'y voyoit de plus remarquable avant sa destruction; avec une idée de la Calabre; suivi d'une description curieuse des Montagnes connues sous le nom d'Etna, ou Mont Gibel, et du Vésuve, fameuses par les fréquentes éruptions de flammes, de bitumes et de cailloux qu'elles vomissent. Paris: Chez Cailleau, 1783.

Prieur, Claude-Antoine. *Rapport sur le salpêtre, fait à la Convention Nationale, au nom du comité de salut public.* Paris: de l'impr. Nationale, Year II [1793].

Procès-verbal des monumens, de la marche, et des discours de la fête consacrée de la Constitution de la République française, le 10 août 1793. Paris: de l'impr. Nationale, Year II [1793].

Procès-verbal et déscription de la fête de l'Etre Suprême, célébrée le 20 prairial, l'an second de la République française une et indivisible. Strasbourg: de l'impr. de Ph. J. Dannbach, 1794.

Prudhomme, Louis-Marie. *Histoire générale et impartiale des erreurs, des fautes, et des crimes commis pendant la Révolution française.* Paris: rue des Marais, Year V (1797).

Raboteau, Pierre Paul. *La Prise de la Bastille, ode.* Paris: Chez Belin, 1790.

Radet, Jean-Baptiste. *Le Canonier convalescent, fait historique en un acte et en vaudevilles.* Paris: Chez la Librairie au Théâtre du Vaudeville, et à l'imprimerie, rue des Droits de l'Homme, Year II (1794).

Rapport et conclusions de l'accusateur public, près le Tribunal criminel provisoire d'Avignon, sur l'application de l'Amnistie, aux crimes et délits commis dans cette Ville, le 16 et 17 octobre 1791. Paris: Chez les Libraires Associés, 1792.

Raynal, Guillaume-Thomas-François. *Histoire philosophique et politique des établissements et du commerce des Européens dans les deux Indes.* The Hague, 1776.

Recueil des Memoires et d'Observations sur la formation et la fabrication du salpêtre. Paris: Chez Lacombe; de l'impr. de Demonville, 1776.

Recueil de pièces intéressantes sur la Bastille. Paris: de l'impr. de J. B. Hérault, 1790.

Relation des événemens arrivés à Avignon, le 16 octobre 1791, et les jours suivans, publiée par les Notables, administrateurs provisoires de la commune de cette ville. N.p., 20 October 1791.

Remise à l'Assemblée Nationale d'une Adresse au Roi, tendante à obtenir aux cultivateurs, sur l'avis des représentans de la nation, la liberté d'assurer leurs récoltes contre les événemens de la grêle. Paris: de l'impr. de P. R. C. Ballard, imprimeur du roi, 1789.

Rituel Républicain: Fête à l'Être-Suprême, Exécutée à Paris, le 20 Prairial, l'an 2e de la République. Avec la musique des Hymnes. Paris: Chez Aubry, Libraire, rue Baillet, Year II (1794).

Robespierre, Maximilien. *Discours couronné par la Société Royale des arts et des sciences de Metz, sur les questions suivantes, proposées pour sujet du prix de l'année 1784. 1e. Quelle est l'origine de l'opinion, qui étend sur tous les Individus d'une même famille, une partie de la honte attachée aux peines infamantes que subit un coupable? 2e. Cette opinion est-elle plus nuisible qu'utile? 3e. Dans le cas où l'on se décideroit pour l'affirmative, quels seroient les moyens de parer aux inconvéniens qui en résultent?* Amsterdam [et se trouve à Paris, chez J.G. Merigot], 1785.

———. *Discours de M. Robespierre, prononcé dans la seance du septidi, 7 prairial, an 2e de la république une et indivisible.* Paris: de l'impr. nationale, Year II (1794).

———. *Discours de Maximilien Robespierre, sur le parti que l'Assemblée nationale doit prendre relativement à la proposition de guerre annoncée par le pouvoir exécutif, prononcé à la Société [des amis de la Constitution] le 18 décembre 1791.* Paris: de l'impr. du Patriote Français, 1791.

———. *Discours de Maximilien Robespierre, Président de la Convention Nationale, au peuple réuni pour la fête de l'Être Suprême, décadi 20 prairial, an second de la République française, une et indivisible.* Paris: de l'impr. de Testu, n.d. [1794].

———. *Oeuvres Complètes.* Ed. Marc Bouloiseau and Albert Soboul. Vol. 10. Paris: Presses Universitaires de France, 1967.

———. *Plaidoyer pour le Sieur de Vissery de Bois-Vallé, appellant d'un jugement des echevins de Saint-Omer, qui avoit ordonné la destruction d'un Par-à-Tonnerre élevé sur sa maison.* Arras: de l'impr. de Guy Delasablonniere, 1783.

Robinet, Jean-Baptiste. *Dictionnaire Universel des sciences morale, économique, politique, et diplomatique, ou Bibliotheque de l'homme-d'état et du citoyen.* Vol. 1. London [Likely Neufchatel]: Chez les libraires associés, 1777–83.

Roland, Jean-Marie. *Rapport du ministre de l'intérieur à la Convention Nationale, sur l'état de Paris, du 29 octobre 1792.* Paris: de l'impr. Nationale, 1792.

Rouel, J. ("cultivateur"). *Relation véritable de la prise de la Bastille le quatorze Juillet 1789.* Paris: de l'impr. de J. B. Hérault, 1790.

Rousseau, Jean-Jacques. *Correspondance complète de Jean-Jacques Rousseau.* Ed. R. A. Leigh. Geneva: Institut et musée Voltaire, 1965.

———. *Discours sur l'origine et les fondements de l'inégalité parmi les hommes.* Paris: Flammarion, 1992.

———. *Emile, ou de l'education.* Paris: Flammarion, 1996.

———. *Essai sur l'origine des langues.* Paris: Gallimard, 1990.

———. *Julie ou La Nouvelle Héloise.* Paris: Flammarion, 1967.

———. *Lettres écrites de la montagne.* In *Oeuvres Complètes de J.-J. Rousseau,* ed. P. R. Auguis. Vol. 7. Paris: Chez Dalibon, 1824.

Rousselet, Pierre-Alexandre. *Détail intéressant et jusqu'à présent ignoré, et la suite des révolutions, fait par un assaillant de la Bastille, à un de ses amis, blessés au meme siège.* Paris: Chez l'auteur, n.d. [1789].

Saint-Just, Louis-Antoine. *Oeuvres Complètes,* ed. Michèle Duval. Paris: G. Lebovici, 1984.

Saussure, Horace-Benedict de. *Relation abrégée d'un voyage à la cîme du Mont-Blanc, en août 1787.* Geneva: Barde, 1787.

———. *Voyages dans les Alpes, précédés d'un essai sur l'histoire naturelle des environs de Génève.* Neufchatel: Chez Samuel Fauche, 1779.

Tallien, Jean-Lambert. *La Verité sur les événemens du 2 septembre.* Paris: de l'impr. Nationale, n.d. [1792].

Thiébaut, C. *La Guerre de la Vendée, pièce révolutionnaire en trois actes et en prose, pour être représentée par de jeunes citoyens et citoyennes, les jours de décade et autres Fêtes nationales.* Nancy: Chez la veuve Bachot, Year II (1794).

Tissot, Charles-Louis. *Les Salpêtriers républicains, comédie en un acte et en prose, mêlée de vaudevilles et d'airs nouveaux. Représentée, pour la première fois, sur le théâtre de la Cité Variétés, le octodi 8 messidor, l'an 2 de la République.* Paris: Chez la Citoyenne Toubon; de l'impr. de Cordier, 1794.

Trassart, Pierre. *Discours prononcé dans le temple de la morale de la section de Guillaume Tell, le décadi 30 fructidor, à l'occasion d'un concert donné par des artistes et des amateurs, pour concourir au soulagement des familles infortunées de ceux qui ont péri le 14 fructidor, par l'explosion de la poudrerie de la place de la Grenelle.* Paris: de l'impr. de Massot, 1794.

Treilhard, Jean-Baptiste. *Rapport fait au nom des Comités du Salut Public et de Sureté Générale, sur l'explosion de la poudrerie de Grenelle, par Treilhard, dans la séance du 15 fructidor, an IIe de la République Française.* Paris: de l'impr. Nationale, 1794.

Turgot, Anne-Robert-Jacques. "A Philosophical Review of the Successive Advances of the Human Mind." In *Turgot on Progress, Sociology and Economics,* ed. Ronald L. Meek. Cambridge: Cambridge University Press, 1973.

Valcour, Aristide. *Discours prononcé à l'Assemblée générale des citoyens de la commune de Nogent-sur-Marne, le 12 prairial de la second année de la République Française. . . . jour de l'anniversaire du 31 mai 1793.* Commune de Nogent sur Marne: de l'impr. de Rauderie jeune, Year II (1794).

——. *Hymne en l'honneur de la Montagne, air nouveau.* Paris: de l'impr. des 86 départemens et de la Société aux Jacobins, n.d.

——. *Les Petits Montagnards: Opéra-Bouffon en trois actes en prose, mêlé d'ariettes.* Paris: de l'impr. de Cailleau, Year II (1793).

——. *Les Trois Evangiles, de la Veille, du Jour, et du Lendemain: Instruction allégorique à l'usage des jeunes Républicains.* Paris: de l'impr. de Cailleau, Year II (1793/94).

de Vattel, Emerich. *Le Droit des gens ou Principes de la loi naturelle appliqués à la conduite et aux affaires des nations et des souverains.* London: n.p., 1758.

Vilate, Joachim. *Continuation des causes secrètes de la Révolution du 9 au 10 thermidor.* Paris, Year III (1794/95).

Villiers, Madame Nicole-Mathieu. *Barra, ou la mère républicaine.* Dijon: de l'impr. de P. Causse, Year II (1794).

Voltaire. *Candide.* Trans. John Butt. London: Penguin, 1947.

——. *Dictionnaire philosophique.* In *Oeuvres de Voltaire,* ed. Adrien-Jean-Quentin Beuchot. Vol. 27. Paris: Werdet et Lequien fils, Firmin Didot frères, 1829.

——. *Poèmes sur la religion naturelle, et sur la destruction de Lisbonne, par M. V***.* Paris: 1756.

Winckelmann, Johann Joachim. *Recueil de lettres de M. Winckelmann, sur les découvertes faites à Herculanum, à Pompeii, à Stabia, à Caserte, et à Rome, traduit de l'allemand.* Trans. Henri Jansen. Paris: Chez Barrois l'aîné, 1784.

Wordsworth, William. *The Prelude: The Four Texts,* ed. Jonathan Wordsworth. London: Penguin, 1995.

Secondary Sources

Abad, Reynald. *La conjuration contre les carpes: Enquête sur les origines du décret du dessèchement des étangs du 14 frimaire an II.* Paris: Fayard, 2006.

Alder, Ken. *Engineering the Revolution: Arms and Enlightenment in France, 1763–1815.* Princeton, N.J.: Princeton University Press, 1997.

Anderson, Judith. *Translating Investments: Metaphor and the Dynamic of Cultural Change in Tudor-Stuart England.* New York: Fordham University Press, 2005.

Anderson, Wilda. "Error in Buffon." *Modern Language Notes* 114.4 (1999): 691–701.

——. "Scientific Nomenclature and Revolutionary Rhetoric." *Rhetorica* 7 (winter 1989): 45–54.

Andress, David. *The Terror: The Merciless War for Freedom in Revolutionary France.* New York: Farrar, Straus and Giroux, 2005.

Apostolides, Jean-Marie. "Theater and Terror: *Le Jugement dernier des rois.*" In *Terror and Consensus: Vicissitudes of French Thought,* ed. Jean-Joseph Goux and Philip R. Wood, pp. 135–145. Stanford, Calif.: Stanford University Press, 1998.

Arasse, Daniel. *The Guillotine and the Terror.* Trans. Christopher Miller. London: Penguin, 1989.

Araùjo, Ana Cristina. "The Lisbon Earthquake of 1755—Public Distress and Political Propaganda," *e-Journal of Portuguese History* 4.1 (summer 2006).

Arendt, Hannah. *On Violence.* New York: Harcourt, Brace, Jovanovich, 1969.

de Baecque, Antoine. *The Body Politic: Corporeal Metaphor in Revolutionary France, 1770–1800.* Trans. Charlotte Mandell. Stanford, Calif.: Stanford University Press, 1997.

———. *Glory and Terror: Seven Deaths under the French Revolution.* Trans. Charlotte Mandell. New York: Routledge, 2001.

de Baere, Benoit. "Pluche lecteur de la *Telluris theoria sacra* de Burnet." In *Ecrire la nature au XVIIIe siècle: Autour de l'Abbé Pluche,* ed. Françoise Gevrey, Julie Boch, and Jean-Louis Haquette, pp. 41–54. Paris: Presses de L'Université Paris-Sorbonne, 2006.

Baker, Keith Michael, ed. *The French Revolution and the Creation of Modern Political Culture.* Vol. 4, *The Terror.* Oxford: Pergamon, 1994.

———. *Inventing the French Revolution.* Cambridge: Cambridge University Press, 1990.

Banzhaf, H. Spencer. "Productive Nature and the Net Product: Quesnay's Economics Animal and Political." *History of Political Economy* 33.3 (2000): 517–551.

Barker-Benfield, G. J. *The Culture of Sensibility: Sex and Society in Eighteenth-Century Britain.* Chicago: University of Chicago Press, 1992.

Bastien, Pascal. "Fête populaire ou cérémonial d'Etat? Le rituel de l'exécution publique selon deux bourgeois de Paris (1718–1789)." *French Historical Studies* 24.3 (summer 2001): 501–526.

Bates, David. *Enlightenment Aberrations: Error and Revolution in France.* Ithaca, N.Y.: Cornell University Press, 2002.

Beck-Saiello, Emilie. *Le Chevalier Volaire: un peintre français à Naples au XVIII siècle.* Naples: Centre Jean Berard, 2004.

Bell, David A. *The Cult of the Nation in France: Inventing Nationalism, 1680–1800.* Cambridge, Mass.: Harvard University Press, 2001.

———. *The First Total War: Napoleon's Europe and the Birth of Warfare as We Know It.* Boston: Houghton Mifflin, 2007.

Bliard, Pierre. *Le Conventionnel Prieur de la Marne en mission dans l'ouest.* Paris: Émile-Paul, 1906.

Blix, Göran. *From Paris to Pompeii: French Romanticism and the Cultural Politics of Archaeology.* Philadelphia: University of Pennsylvania Press, 2009.

Blok, Anton. "The Enigma of Senseless Violence." In *Meanings of Violence: A Cross-Cultural Perspective,* ed. Göran Aijmer and Jon Abbink, pp. 23–38. Oxford: Berg, 2000.

Bonnet, Jean-Claude. *La Naissance du Panthéon: Essai sur le culte des grands hommes.* Paris: Fayard, 1998.

Boulerie, Florence. "Dire le désastre de Lisbonne dans la presse francaise, 1755–1757." In *Lumières,* no. 6, *Lisbonne 1755: Un tremblement de terre et de Ciel,* ed. Jean Mondot, pp. 59–76. Bordeaux: Centre Interdisciplinaire bordelais d'étude des Lumières, 2005.

Braun, E. D., and John B. Radner, eds., *The Lisbon Earthquake of 1755: Representations and Reactions.* Oxford: Voltaire Foundation, 2005.

Briffaud, Serge. "Le role des catastrophes naturelles: Cas des Pyrénées centrales." In *La Nature en Révolution 1750–1800,* ed. Andrée Corvol, pp. 134–144. Paris: Éditions de l'Harmattan, 1993.

Broc, Numa. *Les Montagnes vues par les Géographes et les Naturalistes de langue française au XVIIIème siècle.* Paris: Bibliothèque Nationale, 1969.

Brockliss, L. W. B. *Calvet's Web.* Oxford: Oxford University Press, 2002.

Brockliss, Lawrence, and Colin Jones, eds. *The Medical World of Early Modern France.* Oxford: Clarendon, 1997.

Brown, Howard G. "Domestic State Violence: Repression from the Croquants to the Commune." *Historical Journal* 42.3 (1999): 597–622.

——. *Ending the French Revolution: Violence, Justice, and Repression from the Terror to Napoleon.* Charlottesville: University of Virginia Press, 2007.

Brunot, Ferdinand. *Histoire de la Langue Française des origines à 1900.* Vol. 9, *La Révolution et l'Empire.* Paris: Librairie Armand Colin, 1937.

Caradonna, Jeremy. *The Enlightenment in Question: Prize Contests and the Francophone Republic of Letters, 1670–1794.* Ph.D. diss., Johns Hopkins University, 2007.

Carlson, Marvin. *The Theatre of the French Revolution.* Ithaca, N.Y.: Cornell University Press, 1966.

Caron, Philippe. *Les Massacres de septembre.* Paris: La Maison du Livre Français, 1935.

Castonguay-Bélanger, Joël. "Le Sort de Galilée: Paul et Virginie et la théorie des marées de Bernardin de Saint-Pierre." *Eighteenth Century Fiction* 20.2 (winter 2007–2008): 177–196.

Censer, Jack. *Prelude to Power: The Parisian Radical Press, 1789–1791.* Baltimore, Md.: Johns Hopkins University Press, 1976.

Charlton, Donald Geoffrey. *New Images of the Natural in France.* Cambridge: Cambridge University Press, 1984.

Cladis, Mark. "Tragedy and Theodicy: A Meditation on Rousseau and Moral Evil." *Journal of Religion* 75.2 (April 1995): 181–199.

Cohen, I. Bernard. "The Eighteenth-Century Origins of the Concept of Scientific Revolution." *Journal of the History of Ideas* 37.2 (April–June 1976): 257–288.

Colombe, Gabriel. *Le Palais des Papes d'Avignon.* Paris: H. Laurens, 1939.

Cook, Malcolm. *Bernardin de Saint-Pierre: A Life of Culture.* London: Legenda, 2006.

Corbin, Alain. *The Foul and the Fragrant.* Trans. Miriam Kochan. Cambridge, Mass.: Harvard University Press, 1986.

Corvol, Andrée, ed. *La Nature en Révolution 1750–1800.* Paris: Éditions de l'Harmattan, 1993.

Cotta, Sergio. *Why Violence? A Philosophical Interpretation.* Trans. Giovanni Gullace. Gainesville: University Press of Florida, 1985.

Crook, Malcolm. *Toulon in War and Revolution.* Manchester, England: Manchester University Press, 1991.

Curran, Andrew, and Patrick Graille. "The Faces of Eighteenth-century Monstrosity." *Eighteenth-Century Life* 21 (1997): 1–15.

Darnton, Robert. *Forbidden Best-Sellers of Pre-Revolutionary France.* New York: Norton, 1995.

——. *Mesmerism and the End of the Enlightenment in France.* Cambridge, Mass.: Harvard University Press, 1968.

Daston, Lorraine. "Attention and the Values of Nature in the Enlightenment." In *The Moral Authority of Nature,* ed. Lorraine Daston and Fernando Vidal, pp. 100–126. Chicago: University of Chicago Press, 2004.

——. "Enlightenment Fears, Fears of Enlightenment." In *What's Left of Enlightenment: A Postmodern Question,* ed. Keith Baker and Peter Reill, pp. 115–128. Stanford, Calif.: Stanford University Press, 2001.

——. "The Nature of Nature in Early Modern Europe." *Configurations: A Journal of Literature, Science, and Technology* 6 (1998): 149–172.

Daston, Lorraine, and Katharine Park, eds. *Wonders and the Order of Nature, 1150–1750.* Cambridge, Mass.: MIT Press, 1998.

Daston, Lorraine, and Fernando Vidal, eds. *The Moral Authority of Nature.* Chicago: University of Chicago Press, 2004.

Delbourgo, James. *Electricity, Experiment, and Enlightenment in Eighteenth-Century North America.* Ph.D. diss., Columbia University, 2003.

——. *A Most Amazing Scene of Wonders: Electricity and Enlightenment in Early America.* Cambridge, Mass.: Harvard University Press, 2006.

Denby, David. *Sentimental Narrative and Social Order in France, 1760–1820.* Cambridge: Cambridge University Press, 1994.

De Landtsheer, Christ'l, and Francis Beer, eds. *Metaphorical World Politics.* East Lansing: Michigan State University Press, 2004.

Dorigny, Marcel. "Violence et Revolution: les Girondins et les Massacres de Septembre." In *Actes du colloque: Girondins et Montagnards,* ed. Albert Soboul, pp. 103–120. Paris: Société des Études Robespierristes, 1980.

Douglas, Mary. *Natural Symbols: Explorations in Cosmology.* New York: Pantheon Books, 1982.

Doyle, William. *The Oxford History of the French Revolution.* Oxford: Oxford University Press, 1989.

Dziembowski, Edmond. *Un nouveau patriotisme français, 1750–1770: La France face à la puissance anglaise à l'époque de la guerre de Sept Ans.* Oxford: Voltaire Foundation, 1998.

Edelstein, Dan. *The Terror of Natural Right: Republicanism, the Cult of Nature, and the French Revolution.* Chicago: University of Chicago Press, 2009.

——. "War and Terror: The Law of Nations from Grotius to the French Revolution." *French Historical Studies* 31.2 (spring 2008): 229–262.

Ehrard, Jean. *L'Idée de nature en France dans la première moitié du XVIIIe siècle.* Paris: Albin Michel, 1994.

Ellenberger, François. "Etude du terme Révolution." In *Documents pour l'histoire du vocabulaire scientifique,* 9:69–90. Paris: French National Centre for Scientific Research, 1989.

Findlen, Paula. *Possessing Nature: Museums, Collecting, and Scientific Culture in Early Modern Europe.* Berkeley: University of California Press, 1994.

Foucault, Michel. *The Order of Things.* New York, Vintage Books, 1994 [1970].

Friedland, Paul. "Beyond Deterrence: Cadavers, Effigies, Animals, and the Logic of Executions in Premodern France." *Historical Reflections* 29.3 (2003): 295–317.

Furet, François. *Interpreting the French Revolution.* Trans. Elborg Forster. Cambridge: Cambridge University Press, 1981.

Furet, François, and Mona Ozouf. *A Critical Dictionary of the French Revolution.* Trans. Arthur Goldhammer. Cambridge, Mass.: Harvard University Press, 1989.

Gérard, Alain. *Par principe d'humanité: La Terreur et la Vendée.* Paris: Fayard, 1999.

Gibbs, Raymond. *The Poetics of Mind: Figurative Thought, Language, and Understanding.* Cambridge: Cambridge University Press, 1994.

Gillespie, Charles Coulston. "The *Encyclopédie* and the Jacobin Philosophy of Science: A Study of Ideas and Consequences." In *Critical Problems in the History of Science,* ed. Marshall Clagett, pp. 255–289. Madison: University of Wisconsin Press, 1959.

——. *Science and Polity in France at the End of the Old Regime.* Princeton, N.J.: Princeton University Press, 1980.

Gipper, Andreas. "La Nature entre Utilitarianisme et Ethétisation: L'Abbé Pluche et la physico- théologie européene." In *Ecrire la nature au XVIIIe siècle: Autour de l'Abbé Pluche,* ed.Françoise Gevrey, Julie Boch, and Jean-Louis Haquette, pp. 27–40. Paris: Presses de L'Université Paris—Sorbonne, 2006.

Gisler, Monika. "Optimism and Theodicy: Perceptions of the Lisbon Earthquake in Protestant Switzerland." In *The Lisbon Earthquake of 1755: Representations and Reactions,* ed. E. D. Braun and John B. Radner, pp. 247–264. Oxford: Voltaire Foundation, 2005.

Gough, Hugh. "Politics and Power: The Triumph of Jacobinism in Strasbourg, 1791–1793." *Historical Journal* 23.2 (June 1980): 327–352.

——. *The Terror in the French Revolution*. New York: St. Martin's, 1998.

Goulemot, Jean Marie. "Le mot *révolution* et la formation du concept de révolution politique (fin XVIIe siècle)." *Annales historiques de la révolution française* 39 (1967): 417–444.

Goux, Jean-Joseph, and Philip R. Wood, eds. *Terror and Consensus: Vicissitudes of French Thought*. Stanford, Calif.: Stanford University Press, 1998.

Greer, Donald. *The Incidence of the Terror in the French Revolution: A Statistical Interpretation*. Cambridge, Mass.: Harvard University Press, 1935.

Gueniffey, Patrice. *La Politique de la Terreur: Essai sur la violence révolutionnaire, 1789–1794*. Paris: Fayard, 2000.

Guilhaumou, Jacques. "La formation d'un mot d'ordre: 'Plaçons la terreur a l'ordre du jour' (13 juillet 1793–5 septembre 1793)." *Bulletin du Centre d'analyse du discours*, no. 5: "La rhétorique du discours, objet d'histoire (XVIIe–XXe siècles)," pp. 149–196. Lille: Presses Universitaires de Lille, 1981.

——, "La terreur à l'ordre du jour: un parcours en révolution (1793–1794)." *Révolution Française.net*. *Mots* (6 January 2007), revolution-francaise.net/2007/01/06/94-la-terreur-a-lordre-du-jour-un-parcours-en-revolution-juillet-1793-mars-1794.

Hanson, Paul R. *The Jacobin Republic under Fire: The Federalist Revolt in the French Revolution*. University Park: Pennsylvania State University, 2003.

Harrison, Peter. *The Bible, Protestantism, and the Rise of Natural Science*. Cambridge: Cambridge University Press, 1998.

Hatin, Eugène. *Histoire politique et littéraire de la presse en France*. Vol. 6. Paris: Poulet-Malassis et de Broise, 1860.

Hesse, Carla. "The Law of the Terror." *Modern Language Notes* 114 (1999): 702–718.

——. "La preuve par la lettre: pratiques juridiques au tribunal révolutionnaire de Paris (1793–1794)." *Annales: Histoire, Sciences Sociales* 3 (1996): 629–642.

Higonnet, Patrice. "Terror, Trauma, and the 'Young Marx' Explanation of Jacobin Politics." *Past and Present* 191.1 (2006): 121–164.

Hoquet, Thierry. *Buffon: Histoire naturelle et philosophie*. Paris: Honoré Champion, 2005.

Huet, Marie-Hélène. *Mourning Glory: The Will of the French Revolution*. Philadelphia: University of Pennsylvania Press, 1997.

Hunt, Lynn. *The Family Romance of the French Revolution*. Berkeley: University of California Press, 1992.

——. *Politics, Culture, and Class in the French Revolution*. Berkeley: University of California Press, 1984.

Hyland, Paul, ed. *The Enlightenment: A Sourcebook and Reader*. New York: Routledge, 2003.

Hyslop, Beatrice. "The Theater during a Crisis: The Parisian Theater during the Reign of Terror." *Journal of Modern History* 17.4 (December 1945): 332–355.

Janes, Regina. "Beheadings," *Representations* 35 (summer 1991): 21–51.

Johns, Alessa, ed. *Dreadful Visitations*. New York: Routledge, 1999.

Johnson, Eric F. "The Sacred, Secular Regime: Catholic Ritual and Revolutionary Politics in Avignon, 1789–1791," *French Historical Studies* 30.1 (winter 2007): 49–76.

Joutard, Philippe. *L'invention du Mont Blanc*. Paris: Gallimard, 1986.

Kates, Gary. *The Cercle Social, the Girondins and the French Revolution*. Princeton, N.J.: Princeton University Press, 1985.

Kelly, George Armstrong. "Conceptual Sources of the Terror." *Eighteenth-Century Studies* 14.1 (fall 1980): 18–36.

Kendrick, T. D. *The Lisbon Earthquake*. London: Methuen, 1956.

Kennedy, Emmet. *A Cultural History of the French Revolution*. New Haven, Conn.: Yale University Press, 1989.

Koselleck, Reinhart. *Futures Past: On the Semantics of Historical Time.* Trans. Keith Tribe. New York: Columbia University Press, 2004 [1979].

Kozak, Jan T., Victor S. Moreira, and David R. Aldroyd. *Iconography of the 1755 Lisbon Earthquake.* Prague: Geophysical Institute of the Academy of Sciences of the Czech Republic, 2005.

Laissus, Yves. "Les Cabinets d'Histoire Naturelle." In *L'Enseignement et diffusion des sciences au XVIIIe siècle,* ed. René Taton, pp. 619–645. Paris: Hermann, 1964.

Lakoff, George, and Mark Johnson. *Metaphors We Live By.* Chicago: University of Chicago Press, 1980.

Le Brun, Annie. *Le perspective dépravée: Entre catastrophe réele et catastrophe imaginaire.* Paris: La Lettre Volée, 1991.

Leith, James A. *Space and Revolution: Projects for Monuments, Squares, and Public Buildings in France, 1789–1799.* Montreal: McGill-Queen's University Press, 1991.

Linton, Marisa. "Fatal Friendships: The Politics of Jacobin Friendship." *French Historical Studies* 31.1 (winter 2008): 51–76.

Loveland, Jeff. "Pancoucke and the Circle Squarers." *Eighteenth-Century Studies* 37.2 (winter 2004): 215–236.

——. *Rhetoric and Natural History: Buffon in Polemical and Literary Context.* Oxford: Voltaire Foundation, 2001.

Lucas, Colin. "Revolutionary Violence, the People, and the Terror." In *The French Revolution and the Creation of Modern Political Culture,* ed. Keith Baker. Vol. 4, *The Terror,* pp. 57–79. Oxford: Pergamon, 1994.

Lusebrink, Hans Jurgen, and Rolf Reichardt. *The Bastille: History of a Symbol of Despotism and Freedom.* Durham: Duke University Press, 1997.

——. "Révolution à la fin du XVIIIe siècle: Pour une relecture d'un concept clé du Siècle des Lumières." *Mots* 16 (March 1988): 35–68.

Lyle, Louise and David McCallan, eds., *Histoires de la terre: Earth Sciences and French Culture, 1740–1940.* Amsterdam: Editions Rodopi, 2008.

Lynn, Michael. "Divining the Enlightenment: Public Opinion and Popular Science in Old Regime France." *Isis* 92.1 (March 2001): 34–54.

——. "Enlightenment in the Public Sphere: The Musée de Monsieur and Scientific Culture in Late Eighteenth-Century Paris." *Eighteenth-Century Studies* 32.4 (1999): 463–476.

——. *Popular Science and Public Opinion in Old Regime France.* Manchester, England: Manchester University Press, 2006.

Malandain, Pierre. *Delisle de Sales: philosophe de la nature, Studies on Voltaire & the Eighteenth Century.* Vols. 203–204. Oxford: Voltaire Foundation, 1982.

Martin, Jean-Clément. *La Vendée et la France.* Paris: Seuil, 1987.

——. *Violence et Révolution: essai sur la naissance d'un mythe national.* Paris: Seuil, 2006.

Martin, Xavier. *Human Nature and the French Revolution: From the Enlightenment to the Napoleonic Code.* Trans. Patrick Corcoran. New York: Berghahn Books, 2001.

Maza, Sarah. "Politics, Culture, and the Origins of the French Revolution." *Journal of Modern History* 61.4 (December 1989): 704–723.

McMahon, Darrin. *Enemies of the Enlightenment: The French Counter-Enlightenment and the Making of Modernity.* Oxford: Oxford University Press, 2001.

McPhee, Peter. *Revolution and Environment in Southern France: Peasants, Lords, and Murder in the Corbières, 1780–1830.* Oxford: Oxford University Press, 1999.

Mercier-Faivre, Anne-Marie, and Chantal Thomas, eds. *L'Invention de la catastrophe au XVIIIe siècle.* Paris: Librairie Droz, 2008.

Michelet, Jules. *Oeuvres de Jules Michelet: Histoire de la Révolution.* Paris: A. Lemarre, 1888.

Mondot, Jean, ed. *Lumières*, no. 6: *Lisbonne 1755: Un tremblement de terre et de Ciel.* Bordeaux: Centre Interdisciplinaire bordelais d'étude des Lumières, 2005.

Mornet, Daniel. "Les enseignements des bibliothèques privées, 1750–1780." *Revue d'histoire littéraire de la France* 17 (1910): 449–496.

———. *Les sciences de la nature en France au XVIIIe Siècle.* Paris, 1911.

Mosser, Monique. "Le temple et la montagne: généalogie d'un décor de fête révolutionnaire." *Revue de l'Art*, no. 1 (1989): 21–35.

Moulinas, René. *Les massacres de la Glacière: Enquête sur un crime impuni, Avignon 16–17 octobre 1791.* Aix-en-Provence: Edisud, 2003.

Mulcahy, Matthew. *Hurricanes and Society in the British Greater Caribbean.* Baltimore, Md.: Johns Hopkins University Press, 2006.

Multhauf, Robert P. "The French Crash Program for Saltpeter Production, 1776–94." *Technology and Culture* 12.2 (April 1971): 163–181.

Nannoni, Ebe. "Le peuple-volcan: analyse d'une métaphore." In *Révolution Française, Peuples et Littératures: Actes du XXIIe Congrès de la Société Française de la Littérature Générale et Comparée*, ed. André Peyronie. Paris: Klincksieck, 1991.

Neiman, Susan. *Evil in Modern Thought: An Alternative History of Philosophy.* Princeton, N.J.: Princeton University Press, 2002.

Nicolson, Marjorie Hope. *Mountain Gloom and Mountain Glory: The Development of the Aesthetics of the Infinite.* New York: Norton, 1963.

Ortony, Andrew, ed. *Metaphor and Thought.* 2nd ed. Cambridge: Cambridge University Press, 1993 [1979].

Outram, Dorinda. "The Ordeal of Vocation: The Paris Academy of Sciences and the Terror, 1793–1795." *History of Science* 21 (1983): 251–273.

Ozouf, Mona. *Festivals and the French Revolution.* Trans. Alan Sheridan. Cambridge, Mass.: Harvard University Press, 1988.

———. *L'homme régénéré: Essais sur la Révolution française.* Paris: Gallimard, 1989.

———. "The Terror after the Terror: An Immediate History." In *The French Revolution and the Creation of Modern Political Culture*, Vol. 4, *The Terror*, ed. Keith Baker, pp. 3–18. Oxford: Pergamon, 1994.

Palmer, R. R. *Twelve Who Ruled: The Year of the Terror in the French Revolution.* Princeton, N.J.: Princeton University Press, 1989 [1941].

Paulson, Ronald. *Representations of Revolution, 1789–1820.* New Haven, Conn.: Yale University Press, 1983.

Perronet, Michel. "Chatiments divins et catastrophes naturelles." In *Météorologie et catastrophes naturelles dans la France méridionale à l'époque moderne*, ed. Anne Blanchard, Henri Michel, and Elie Pélaquier, pp. 259–282. Montpelier: Université Paul-Valéry III, 1993.

Pinault-Sorensen, Madeleine. "Les planches du *Spectacle de la Nature*." In *Ecrire la nature au XVIIIe siècle: Autour de l'Abbé Pluche*, ed. Françoise Gevrey, Julie Boch, and Jean-Louis Haquette, pp. 141–161. Paris: Presses de L'Université Paris-Sorbonne, 2006.

Porter, Roy. *The Making of Geology: Earth Science in Britain, 1660–1815.* Cambridge: Cambridge University Press, 1977.

———. "Philosophy and Politics of a Geologist: G. H. Toulmin (1754–1817)." *Journal of the History of Ideas* 39.3 (1978): 435–450.

Quenet, Grégory. *Les tremblements de terre aux XVIIe et XVIIIe siècles: La Naissance d'un risque.* Paris: Champ Vallon, 2005.

Quentin, Henri. *Le théâtre sous la Terreur (Théâtre de la peur), 1793–1794.* Paris: Emile Paul Frères, 1913.

Rappaport, Rhoda. "Borrowed Words: Problems of Vocabulary in Eighteenth-Century Geology." *British Journal for the History of Science* 15.1 (March 1982): 27–44.

——. "Dangerous Words: Diluvialism, Neptunism, Catastrophism." In *Advancements of Learning: Essays in Honor of Paolo Rossi*, ed. J. L. Heilbron, pp. 101–131. Florence: L.S. Olschki, 2007.

——. *When Geologists Were Historians, 1665–1750.* Ithaca, N.Y.: Cornell University Press, 1997.

Reddy, William. *The Navigation of Feeling.* Cambridge: Cambridge University Press, 2001.

Rey, Alain. *Révolution: Histoire d'un Mot.* Paris: Gallimard, 1989.

Reynaud, Denis. "Journalisme d'Ancien Régime et vulgarisation scientifique." In *Le partage des savoirs, XVIIIe-XIXe siècles*, ed. Lise Andries, pp. 121–134. Lyon: Presses universitaires de Lyon, 2003.

Ricoeur, Paul. *The Rule of Metaphor: Multi-disciplinary Studies of the Creation of Meaning in Language.* Trans. Robert Czerny, with Kathleen McLaughlin and John Costello. Toronto: University of Toronto Press, 1981.

Riskin, Jessica. "The Lawyer and the Lightning Rod." *Science in Context* 12.1 (1999): 61–99.

——. "Rival Idioms for a Revolutionized Science and a Republican Citizenry." *Isis* 89 (1998): 203–232.

——. *Science in the Age of Sensibility: The Sentimental Empiricists of the French Enlightenment.* Chicago: University of Chicago Press, 2002.

Roche, Daniel. *Le siècle des lumières en province: académies et académiciens provinciaux, 1680–1789.* Paris: Mouton, 1978.

Rosenfeld, Sophia. *A Revolution in Language: The Problem of Signs in Late Eighteenth-Century France.* Stanford, Calif.: Stanford University Press, 2001.

Rudwick, Martin J. S. *Bursting the Limits of Time: The Reconstruction of Geohistory in the Age of Revolution.* Chicago: University of Chicago Press, 2005.

Secher, Reynald. *A French Genocide: The Vendée.* Trans. George Holoch. Notre Dame, Ind.: University of Notre Dame Press, 2003.

Shapiro, Barry. *Traumatic Politics: The Deputies and the King in the Early French Republic.* University Park: Pennsylvania State University Press, 2009.

Sheriff, Mary D. "'Au Génie de Franklin:' An Allegory by J.-H. Fragonard." *Proceedings of the American Philosophical Society* 127.3 (1983): 180–193.

Sigurdsson, Haraldur. *Melting the Earth: The History of Ideas on Volcanic Eruptions.* Oxford: Oxford University Press, 1999.

Singer, Brian. "Violence in the French Revolution: Forms of Ingestion/Forms of Expulsion." In *The French Revolution and the Birth of Modernity*, ed. Ferenc Fehér, pp. 150–168. Berkeley: University of California Press, 1990.

Soboul, Albert. *Dictionnaire historique de la Révolution Française.* Paris: Presses Universitaires de France, 1989.

Solé, Jacques. "Lecture et classes populaires à Grenoble au 18e siècle." In Centre Aixois d'Etudes et de Recherches sur le Dix-Huitieme Siecle, *Images du peuple au dix-huitième siècle, Colloque Aix-en- Provence, 25–26 Octobre 1969*, pp. 95–102. Paris: Colin, 1973.

Sonenscher, Michael. "Physiocracy as a Theodicy." *History of Political Thought* 23.2 (Summer 2002): 326–339.

——. *Sans Culottes: An Eighteenth-Century Emblem in the French Revolution.* Princeton, N.J.: Princeton University Press, 2008.

Spary, E. C. "The Nature of Enlightenment." In *The Sciences in Enlightened Europe*, ed. William Clark, Jan Golinski, and Simon Schaffer, pp. 272–306. Chicago: University of Chicago Press, 1999.

——. *Utopia's Garden: French Natural History from Old Regime to Revolution*. Chicago: University of Chicago Press, 2000.

Staver, Frederick. "'Sublime' as Applied to Nature." *Modern Language Notes* 70.7 (November 1955): 484–487.

Sutherland, Donald. *France, 1789–1815: Revolution and Counterrevolution*. Oxford: Oxford University Press, 1986.

——. *Murder in Aubagne: Lynching, Law, and Justice during the French Revolution*. Cambridge: Cambridge University Press, 2009.

Tackett, Timothy. *Becoming a Revolutionary: The Deputies of the French National Assembly and the Emergence of a Revolutionary Culture (1789–1790)*. Princeton, N.J.: Princeton University Press, 1996.

——. "Interpreting the Terror." *French Historical Studies* 24.4 (fall 2001): 569–578.

Taylor, Kenneth. "Nicolas Desmarest and Geology in the Eighteenth Century." In *Towards a History of Geology*, ed. Cecil J. Schneer, pp. 339–356. Cambridge, Mass.: MIT Press, 1969.

——. "Volcanoes as Accidents: How 'Natural' Were Volcanoes to 18th-Century Naturalists?" In *Volcanoes and History: Proceedings of the 20th INHIGEO Symposium*, ed. Nicoletta Morello, pp. 595–618. Genoa: Brigati, 1998.

de Tocqueville, Alexis. *Old Regime and Revolution*. Trans. Stuart Gilbert. New York: Doubleday, 1983.

Trinkle, Dennis. "Noel-Antoine Pluche's *Le Spectacle de la Nature*, an Encyclopaedic Best-Seller," *Studies of Voltaire and the Eighteenth Century* 357 (1997): 93–134.

Tuck, Richard. *The Rights of War and Peace: Political Thought and the International Order from Grotius to Kant*. Oxford: Oxford University Press, 1999.

Umbach, Maiken. "Visual Culture, Scientific Images, and German Small-State Politics in the Late Enlightenment." *Past & Present* 158 (February 1998): 110–145.

Viard, Jean. *Le tiers espace: essai sur la nature*. Paris: Klincksieck méridiens, 1990.

Vila, Anne C. *Enlightenment and Pathology: Sensibility in the Literature and Medicine of Eighteenth-Century France*. Baltimore, Md.: Johns Hopkins University Press, 1998.

Vincent-Buffault, Anne. *A History of Tears*. Trans. Teresa Bridgeman. New York: St. Martin's, 1991.

Wahnich, Sophie. *La Liberté ou la mort: essai sur la Terreur et le terrorisme*. Paris: La Fabrique éditions, 2003.

——. *La Longue patience du peuple: 1792, Naissance de la République*. Paris: Éditions Payot, 2008.

Walsham, Alexandra. *Providence in Early Modern England*. Oxford: Oxford Universty Press, 1999.

Walzer, Michael. *Regicide and Revolution: Speeches at the Trial of Louis XVI*. Trans. Marian Rothstein. Cambridge: Cambridge University Press, 1974.

Woloch, Isser. "War-Widows' Pensions: Social Policy in Revolutionary and Napoleonic France," *Societas* 6 (1976): 235–254.

Zizek, Joseph. "'Plume de fer': Louis-Marie Prudhomme Writes the French Revolution." *French Historical Studies* 26.4 (2003): 619–660.

INDEX